EVALUATING, DOING AND
WRITING RESEARCH
IN PSYCHOLOGY

Philip Bell is Foundation Chair of Media and Communications at the University of New South Wales. He has published widely on social and psychological aspects of the media and has a long-standing interest in research method and theory in the humanities and social sciences. While his PhD is in Psychology, he has worked in inter-disciplinary studies throughout most of his academic life.

Phillip Staines is Senior Lecturer in the School of Philosophy at the University of New South Wales. He teaches courses in Cognitive Science, Philosophy of Language and the foundations of Artificial Intelligence, as well as an introductory course in reasoning and argument. His PhD examined the conditions under which logic can be reliably used to evaluate reasoning, and he has published in the areas of logic, philosophy of language and informal reasoning, as well as computer and cognitive science.

Joel Michell is Senior Lecturer in Psychology at the University of Sydney. His publications include two books, *An Introduction to the Logic of Psychological Measurement* and *Measurement in Psychology: A Critical History of a Methodological Concept*, and papers in the areas of mathematical psychology, philosophy of psychology, and history and philosophy of science.

EVALUATING, DOING AND WRITING RESEARCH IN PSYCHOLOGY

A STEP-BY-STEP GUIDE FOR STUDENTS

PB Bell and PJ Staines
with J Michell

SAGE Publications

London • Thousand Oaks • New Delhi

First published in 2001
by University of New South Wales Press Ltd
UNSW SYDNEY NSW 2052
AUSTRALIA
www.unswpress.com.au

SAGE Publications Ltd
6 Bonhill Street
London EC2A 4PU

SAGE Publications Inc
2455 Teller Road
Thousand Oaks, California 91320

SAGE Publications India Pvt Ltd
32, M-Block Market
Greater Kailash –1
New Delhi 110 048

British Library Cataloguing in Publication data

A catalogue record for this book is available from the British
Library

ISBN 0 76197 174 2 (cloth)
      0 76197 175 0 (paper)

Library of Congress catalog record available

Cover photograph IPL
Cover design Di Quick
Text design Dana Lundmark
Printer BPA, Melbourne, Australia

Contents

Acknowledgments

In writing this book we have had to re-examine both our own earlier work and developments in the discipline of psychology itself. So we have relied on several people for inspiration and encouragement to revisit the issues and authors of our earlier book. John Elliot, Derelie Evely and Nada Madjar kept us focused and tolerated our procrastinations more than we deserved. Andy Rantzen's energetic pursuit of contemporary psychological issues that echoed our earlier examples reassured us that there remained a need for the book. We are indebted to Andy for his intelligent and sympathetic research assistance and for his good humour.

When the original *Reasoning and Argument in Psychology* was written, the typewriter rather than the computer translated our ideas into print. Mandi Snowden, with Rowland Hilder, scanned and corrected a version of the earlier publication for use in the preparation of the present book. We thank them for their patience and energy. Word-processing the current work has been done by Julie Miller to whose skills and grace under pressure we also are indebted.

For helpful comments and discussion of some of the ideas, we would like to thank Phil Cam, Michaelis Michael, Graham Staines, Peter Menzies, Pat Suppes, Peter Godfrey-Smith, Paul Griffiths, Cliff Hooker and Jennifer Hornsby.

Introduction:
The problem

PSYCHOLOGY IN THE ACADEMY

This book is a response to what the authors consider is the most common problem confronting students of psychology. Although common, it is largely ignored by those involved in teaching undergraduate psychology courses. Generally, the difficulty concerns the nature of psychological argument — its conventions and idiosyncrasies. More than any other single aspect of psychology it is this that students fail to understand. Perhaps the best way to emphasise the dimensions of the problem is to look at it from the student's point of view.

One of the obvious initial difficulties which strikes students of psychology is that they cannot classify the subject in a precise way. It cannot be placed neatly into the usual pigeonholes which have served so well in their earlier, secondary education. Psychology, they may feel, is not quite a 'science' (meaning that it appears somewhat different from physics), although it is not like the study of literature or art. And yet at times the subject matter is similar to *both* the sciences and the more conventional 'humanities'. It includes fields as diverse as existentialist theories of man's place in his social world, philosophical speculation about the 'mind–body problem', as well as methodologically rigorous experimental studies of behaviour and physiology. A second aspect of students' initial difficulty is the fact that most undergraduate courses in psychology are not explicitly vocational. There is no single 'practical' or 'relevant' body of facts or techniques to be mastered. It is hardly surprising then that many students appear confused as to the most fruitful approach to the course of study they have undertaken.

Failing to find any clearly defined guidelines in these areas of confusion, students may adopt the only approach with which they are familiar. They then regard psychology as similar to, say, high-school physics or biology, assuming that the safest solution consists of accumulating a large body of 'facts', techniques and precisely stated generalisations which can be reproduced on demand (that is, in essays and examinations). They may soon realise that matters are not as simple as this, and become perplexed, hostile or cynical about the lack of 'correct' answers to complex questions which psychology raises. Students may fail to see the situation as a challenge typical of those which tertiary education ideally should provide, and react against the subject by becoming only superficially involved in it.

Such indifference may partly account for the low standard of work that students frequently submit in essays, reports and examinations. When this work is assessed, and critical are comments made, students may become aware that their general approach to psychology is inadequate or misguided. But in most instances there is no provision made for properly rectifying such inadequacies or redirecting students' efforts.

In the large, rather impersonal institutions in which psychology is quite often taught, contact between student and assessor is usually only superficial and may be entirely lacking. Even as an assessor goes to the trouble of writing copious notes on an essay or report, the advice is frequently directed only at the most obvious shortcomings and may be expressed in quite vague terms. Comments such as 'poorly organised', 'badly argued' or 'you have not supported your case' do little more than suggest general areas in which some (quite unspecified) improvement is needed. They certainly do not demonstrate specific ways of improving the student's ability to present extended psychological arguments. In short, comments pointing out what is wrong with an essay do not show how to construct a well-argued case.

Perhaps more importantly, other fundamental problems may be overlooked in such comments. Much of the students' difficulty may be that they simply cannot comprehend or critically evaluate the literature relating to the topic at issue, or they lack the ability to organise what they have read according to a coherent plan. There is little an assessor can do to alter this.

We believe, therefore, that one of the major aspects of studying psychology which students fail to appreciate is the need to present, analyse and evaluate sophisticated scientific argument. This is so at all levels of psychological study, but is particularly obvious in the introductory years.

We do not wish to suggest that all the blame for this state of affairs should be laid at the door of the psychology student. On the contrary. Only a small minority of these students receive any formal training in the basic concepts and techniques of argument relevant to their course of study. If a student does not happen to study logic or general philosophy as part of their degree course, they will probably fail to acquire any real sophistication in this basic area, at least until late in their course. Moreover, many students appear not to recognise the need for such skills, while those who do frequently come to the realisation only when it is too late for any real improvement to be possible. Then, during the later stages of their degree, they find theoretical questions intruding into their complacent acceptance of what they have previously been taught. Yet such theoretical questions are not integrated into the student's general understanding of psychology; theoretical controversy is compartmentalised as something additional to, or separate from, the ordinary concerns of the discipline. It might be added that psychology departments frequently confirm and extend this compartmentalisation by teaching distinct subcourses called 'Theory', 'History and Philosophy of Psychology' or 'General Issues in Psychology' as though such issues do not naturally develop within particular areas of study. Other departments do not make even this concession to theoretical discussion, ignoring such questions altogether.

PSYCHOLOGY IN THE PUBLIC DOMAIN

Psychologists are expected to know the evidence relating to a variety of complex questions, ranging from what causes differences in school performance to how people choose partners, to whether machines can 'think'. The popular media broadcast and publish on topics which psychologists study, but often produce only weak arguments or question-begging analyses. Yet psychology graduates are not usually prominent in criticising constructively these popular misconceptions. In the mid-1990s, for instance, the complex question of whether adolescents who commit acts of violence could have been influenced by the representation of violence in films and on television has arisen in the dramatic and traumatic context of mass killings in Australia, the United Kingdom and the United States. The arguments relating to the evidence for particular causal factors are, of course, complex. They may be theoretical or methodological, not just a matter of describing the 'evidence'. Of course, these more conceptual issues seldom find their way into the media. So psychology may remain relatively silent on such significant matters, even though the discipline has researched the problems consistently and extensively for more than 40 years.

Similarly, what was called 'sociobiology' in the 1960s and 1970s has re-emerged in several popularising, as well as in many academic, publications in the late 1990s under the label 'evolutionary psychology'. And the question of whether computers 'think' (whether they will develop 'consciousness'!) is again (or still) being debated in the pages of non-specialist publications, including the *New York Review of Books* (1999). A tertiary education in psychology ought to equip the graduate to argue constructively and clearly about these kinds of important issues. Similarly, the facile, often narcissistic 'analysis' of interpersonal problems that is the staple of many genres of television 'talk show' and magazine feature, or the rigid and narrow skills taught to Australian matriculation students, to take but two examples, cry out for critical psychological analysis. Not merely differences of 'opinion', but contestable, clearly structured *argument based on evidence, interpreted theoretically.*

We believe that psychology students need to be more aware of, and more confidently able to propose and defend, arguments, including explanations, which are central to their discipline. As well, they should be able to criticise and show the inadequacy of putative explanations in their own field of study and in public discourse.

A third reason for developing critical analytical and argument skills is more general than the above. If we may be a little pretentious, we could say that it is to allow psychology specialists to enter into conversation with the proponents (or purveyors) of conceptual confusion and ignorance, from the religious zealot to the astrologer, the moralist and the racist. Many social or political 'world views' (perhaps we could call them 'ideologies') are maintained in the face of evidence and argument from psychology which could refute or invalidate them. Indeed, many psychology students seem able to believe, say, astrological 'explanations' for human behaviour *and*, without noticing the contradiction, to accept empirical causal accounts of the *same* behaviour. So a third reason for developing the analytical skills presented in this book is to allow readers to evaluate the logical consistency and empirical assumptions of their own (and others') view of the causes of social and individual behaviour, beliefs, attitudes and values — to be more logical psychologists or 'psych students'.

To conclude, students need to develop the ability to analyse and to present various kinds of arguments if they are to succeed in their chosen discipline of psychology. A second reason for gaining confidence in these methodologically difficult competencies is that public debate is frequently carried out in psychologically naïve or tendentious ways. Third, the social knowledge which students rely on in their daily lives ought to reflect the logic and subtlety of the discipline.

ARGUMENTS STRONG AND WEAK: SOME EXAMPLES

When experts present and criticise psychological arguments in the popular press and in general intellectual magazines, they assume a readership that is able to think methodically about, and thereby to evaluate, various kinds of competing explanations of behaviour. Below we consider some recent examples of arguments from journalists and book reviewers writing about psychology. We will draw attention to features of these arguments which also arise in more formal contexts, and which will therefore be the subject of more detailed discussion in relevant chapters of this book.

First, you will notice that, in these excerpts, the **definition** of a technical term ('intelligence' or 'IQ') may be crucial to the argument presented. Second, the **evaluation** of **evidence** may be at issue. The author may point out potentially 'confounded' (or co-varying but overlooked) factors, and thereby reinterpret a possible cause of behaviour. Alternatively, the writer may draw out an **implication** from a theoretical position and show that the evidence is **inconsistent** with it. Or they may argue that the proponents of an argument are inconsistent or seem to change their definition of a crucial term in the course of interpreting the evidence relevant to these implications. Each of these 'moves' is a form of argument or counter-argument. So let us look more closely at each.

DEFINITIONAL PROBLEMS

> The concept of general intelligence has often been attacked. Some psychologists have argued that there are a number of different kinds of intelligence which are not in any way interdependent. That people of high intelligence can vary widely in their mathematical and verbal abilities is well known. But in general, it can be said that a high IQ is a good predictor of ability to complete a university course, at least in science, maths and other genuinely demanding disciplines. But it says nothing about character, stability, sanity, altruism or even commonsense. (*Sydney Morning Herald*, 6 February 1999, p 41)

We consider the complexities of defining psychological terms and 'concepts' in Chapter 4. But at this point we draw attention to the implicit definition of 'intelligence' in this journalist's argument. First, it equates 'IQ' with intelligence; second, it asserts that intelligence is a *general* ability (a contested claim in the psychological literature, as the author himself states). Third, he proposes that intelligence can be inferred from the ability to complete a university degree, but only in 'demanding' subjects. It is possible to argue that such an implicit definition of intelligence is inconsistent with the notion of 'general' intelligence which he, himself, has previously endorsed.

So, one way to begin to analyse arguments is to spell out the precise interpretation or assumptions which an author makes about the concepts *at stake* in their proposed argument. In the present case, the argument is very weak because it relies on a vague or inconsistent (largely implicit, not explicit) definition of its key term.

'CONFOUNDED' FACTORS

In an elegantly argued review of Judith Rich Harris's book, *The Nature Assumption: Why Children Turn Out the Way They Do* (Harris 1998), Howard Gardner questions the evidence for the effects of peers as opposed to parents on children's personalities:

> Earlier, I referred to Eleanor Maccoby's pessimistic conclusions about documenting parental influence, and I mentioned some of the studies of it that both Maccoby and Harris seem to have had in mind. But let me reconsider the most ambitious of these studies in a different light. In the 1950s and 1960s, John Whiting, Beatrice Whiting, and their colleagues studied child rearing in six cultures, ranging from a small New England town to agricultural settings in Kenya, India, Mexico, the Philippines, and Okinawa. What emerges from that study is that child rearing practices are distinctly different around the globe: different in treatment of infants, in parental sleeping patterns, in how children do chores, in their helping or not helping in rearing younger siblings, in initiation rites, in ways of

handling aggression, and in dozens of other variables. So differently are children reared in these cultures that no one would confuse an adult New Englander with an adult Gusii of Kenya or an adult Taira of Okinawa — whether in their knowledge, skills, manners, habits, personality, or temperament.

For the social scientist, the analytic problem is to find the source of these differences. Parents behave differently in these cultures, but so do siblings, peers, other adults, and even visiting anthropologists. And of course the adult roles, natural resources, technology, and means of communication (primitive or modern) differ as well. In all probability, each of these factors makes its contribution to the child's 'personality and character'. But how to tell them apart? Harris chooses to minimize these other factors and zooms in on the peers, but her confident choice is not justified. (Gardner (1998, p 21) cites BB Whiting (ed) (1963) *Six Cultures: Studies of Child Rearing*, New York: John Wiley and Sons.)

The core of Gardner's criticism is that potentially influential variables (factors) are 'confounded' — that is, they co-vary and cannot easily be distinguished. This is a common, but important, kind of counter-argument in psychology. We discuss it in detail in Chapter 5.

INCONSISTENCY

'Popular' psychology books often deal with important questions, such as whether biological ('nature') or environmental ('nurture') factors are responsible for, say, gender differences. We will return to this example in later chapters. Here we cite a very informally written argument against the 'evolutionary psychology' view that such differences in contemporary Western gendered behaviour are 'genetic' or evolutionary (that is, biologically caused).

The author questions the conclusion that males are biologically driven to sexual promiscuity by arguing:

And what of the evidence for these male–female verities? For the difference in promiscuity quotas, the hard-cores love to raise the example of the differences between gay men and lesbians. Homosexuals are seen as a revealing population because supposedly they can behave according to the innermost impulses of their sex, untempered by the need to adjust to the demands and wishes of the opposite sex, as heterosexuals theoretically are.

What do we see in our ideal study group? Just look at how gay men carry on! They are perfectly happy to have hundreds, thousands of sexual partners, to have sex in bathhouses, in bathrooms, in parks. By contrast, lesbians are sexually sedate. They don't cruise sex clubs. They couple up and stay coupled, and they like cuddling and hugging more than they do serious, genitally based sex.

In the hard-core rendering of inherent male–female discrepancies in promiscuity, gay men are offered up as true men, real men,

> deep men, men unfettered, men set free to be men, while lesbians are real women, ultra women, acting out every woman's fantasy of love and commitment without the fuss and slop of sex. Interestingly, though, in other theoretical instances, gay men and lesbians are not considered real men and real women, but the opposite: gay men are feminine men, halfway between men and women, while lesbians are posited as mannish women [emphasis added]. (*Sydney Morning Herald*, *Good Weekend*, 22 May 1999, p 31)

The author criticises the proposed argument by asserting that it is internally inconsistent in its interpretation of gay men's sexuality as 'masculine', so that the argument's assumption of what is 'invariant' about male behaviour is not sustained.

If we ignore the informal language of these journalistic examples, we can see that each engages in a particular argument strategy to support a conclusion about important, perennial issues in academic psychology — the nature of 'intelligence', the effect of parents or peers on children's personality, the biological determination of gender differences. Psychology students need to be able to analyse arguments like these (to take them apart and exhibit their structure). Equally, to be critical, they need to develop the ability to present arguments and to propose alternative explanations of psychological phenomena in clear, precise language.

To conclude, the popular psychology examples of explanation and counter-explanation discussed above show that:

1 **Arguments** in psychology (as in all discourse) have a discernible **structure.** Some **propositions** are advanced to imply, or to claim the likely truth of, other proposition(s), the **conclusion(s)** of the respective argument. In Chapters 1–4 especially, we consider these structures, showing how to **analyse** (to take apart the elements) and to **evaluate** such arguments (to judge them as sound or unsound, 'valid' or 'invalid', supporting their conclusions or not).

2 **Explaining** individual behaviour, some generality about human 'nature', or people's capacities — in short, any psychological phenomena — involves **evaluating competing arguments.** Chapters 1–3 and 5–7, especially, deal with this task. They outline general principles and practices to follow when evaluating competing explanations, and they present examples of the kinds of mistakes and omissions most commonly made in psychology.

3 The **definition** of concepts is an important part of all sophisticated psychological reasoning and explanation. It must be clear what is being argued about and what phenomena are being proposed or postulated, if an argument is to be unambiguous.

So we spend a whole chapter, Chapter 4, on problems of definition in psychology.

The motivation for this book, therefore, rises from our belief that most undergraduates studying psychology are merely *assumed* to know, rather than explicitly taught, how to construct, analyse or evaluate the kind of argument which is characteristic of psychological discussion. We feel that it is unrealistic to expect students merely to 'pick up' such an ability by some apparently magical process. Rather, the ability requires explicit instruction and practice — that is, familiarity with a variety of arguments, concepts and techniques for analysing these. Therefore, this book presents basic concepts and techniques involved in advanced argument in an informal, practical manner to enable students consciously to develop the ability to construct worthwhile written and oral presentations in the field of psychology.

What follows is entirely informal, requiring no knowledge of logic or allied disciplines. Without assuming that there is a unique, simple approach to constructing and expressing arguments, we have tried to present both general principles and specific techniques, illustrating these by numerous examples and exercises.

chapter 1

Understanding and evaluating statements

If you want truly to understand something, try to change it.

Kurt Lewin

INTRODUCTION

Two main skills are required of the psychology student: *comprehension* and *evaluation* of verbal material. In most courses on psychology, students attend lectures, participate in seminars and tutorials, read texts and references, write theses, essays and reports, and conduct or observe experiments. In each of these areas, almost all the psychological ideas to be considered will be provoked by the written or oral offerings of psychologists. This is transparently the case when students are attending lectures and reading the literature, but it is also true when they are conducting experiments. Even if the ideas formulated on the basis of the results of experiments do not derive directly from what someone else has said or written, the ideas or theories which prompted the experiments and which give these results significance almost certainly will be derived from someone else.

Two major features of this situation put a premium on understanding or comprehending verbal statements. First, most of the material considered is presented linguistically, being written or spoken; second, most of the ideas come from other people (which is not to deny that students are required to think in an original manner!). For both these reasons, quite sophisticated skills are required at the receptive end of linguistic communication. Students are required to *understand* — literally, to make sense of — psychological theories and facts received in the form of (often complex) verbal statements. This can be particularly difficult, as these theories and facts are sometimes presented in idiosyncratic language, using unfamiliar terms or, if not, employing familiar terms in unfamiliar ways. *Evaluation,* the second skill, presupposes the first: students cannot properly evaluate what they have not properly understood. Evaluation is particularly important in the social and behavioural sciences, including psychology, where alternative theories compete for acceptance. Faced with this situation, students are forced not merely to understand but to evaluate theories — to consider reasons for and against accepting them, to judge them true or false, well supported or unsupported, and so on.

Accordingly, in this chapter we undertake the deceptively simple task of introducing certain fundamental distinctions between the types of statements that are the elements of all argument. We emphasise the need for students to understand thoroughly and evaluate carefully these statements if they are to appreciate the complex and subtle verbal detail of psychological literature.

UNDERSTANDING STATEMENTS

Understanding what someone has said or written is the everyday ability of coming to know what they mean. It is an ability we all share as users of the same language. Someone who can understand English is someone who, in general, can understand what people are proposing or 'getting at' when they use English. Why, then, should we devote a section of this book to discussing something that everybody who is able to read it can do already?

The answer is: first, even though we all understand English, we do so with differing degrees of competence, at different 'levels'; and second, more than the routine ability to understand informal or colloquial English is required of someone tackling abstract material presented in technical language. A number of quite special demands are made of someone who is trying to understand the technical discipline of psychology.

We will distinguish two levels of understanding. The first, which we call the *linguistic level,* concerns the comprehension of statements to the extent of being able to paraphrase them — to 'translate' them into one's own words. This level is concerned with identifying what is being communicated. The second, deeper or *conceptual level,* involves seeing the significance and implications of what has been communicated. This second level presupposes the first.

What, then, are 'statements'? Clearly, they are to be contrasted with questions, requests or orders. Put very simply, statements say or assert something to be the case (that is, true), while questions ask whether something is the case, and requests ask that it be made the case. Since ideas, or theories and facts, are presented in the form of statements, our concern is with understanding these, not with questions or requests. (However, as we shall emphasise later in this chapter, understanding questions also plays an important part in studying a discipline like psychology.) Thus we might contrast the statement 'More boys than girls were tested' with the question 'Were more boys than girls tested?' and both with the order 'See to it that more boys than girls are tested.' A statement is typically made by producing a simple declarative sentence, although a single word uttered in reply to a question may also constitute a statement. (For example, 'Yes', in reply to 'Were more boys than girls tested?' asserts the corresponding statement above.) Similarly, two different sentences can make the same statement. The sentence 'Fewer girls than boys were tested' can also be used to make the statement that more boys than girls were tested. Sometimes such sentences are said to assert or express the same *proposition,* but we shall adopt the more familiar 'statement' and speak of different sentences being used to make or express the same *statement.*

The statement expressed, because it depends on the meaning of the sentence, is a difficult notion to make precise and is best referred to via the sentence that expresses it. As we have pointed out above, it is the statements, *not* the sentences expressing them, which are taken to be true or false, plausible or implausible. Hence, if the meaning of a sentence is understood, then what was meant can usually be reformulated in other words: being able to put what someone has said or written into one's own words is central to the task of understanding what they said (that is, what they meant).

For the purposes of illuminating some of the difficulties involved in understanding verbal material, let us briefly outline a simple, commonsense account of what is involved in communication. We will exemplify it by discussing the communication between a psychologist and someone studying what she has written.

The psychologist has an idea in mind that she wishes to share. She formulates or 'codes' it into words forming sentences which she then writes. Her reader 'decodes' the words, and if he does so properly 'gets the idea' — or understands what the psychologist means. The sentence she wrote is said to express the idea, 'proposition' or 'statement' she had in mind. She could have used another sentence, but only if it had the same meaning as the original. On this account, successful communication occurs when the reader understands what statement or proposition the writer is expressing.

TECHNICAL LANGUAGE

Since the words used in sentences are the common coin of communication, we need to distinguish what the author means by them from what they are conventionally taken to mean and from what the reader takes them to mean. This is particularly important where the author and reader do not share the same theoretical predilections although they may use similar words that also have a conventional, 'non-technical' use (for example, a behaviourist and a psychoanalyst discussing 'anxiety'). For communication to proceed smoothly, the writer's intended statement and the statement the reader takes her to have made must coincide. Unfortunately, in technical disciplines it is often difficult to tell if this has happened. Although the psychologist may assume that her words are conventionally understood and not idiosyncratic, they may mean something radically different to the student just beginning to learn the 'language of psychology'. We have mentioned the word 'anxiety', but any number of other examples might be cited: 'intelligence' has a (vague) conventional meaning as well as a number of technical ones, as do terms such as 'instinct', 'drive', 'introversion', 'identification' and 'neurotic'.

The differing interpretations of the words used by author and reader mean that the former's words may need to be, quite literally, *translated* from her English to the reader's. This is not to say that the grammar or form of technical language is necessarily obscure — it is the vocabulary that causes the problems. This may include everyday words used in a precise, technical sense, or coined words or phases (such as 'cognitive dissonance', 'eidetic imagery' or 'negative reinforcement').

Since word or phrase meaning is the major source of trouble in this special form of communication, we shall now consider it in more detail. Perhaps the best way to begin is to ask what motivates psychologists to use a technical vocabulary. Oddly enough, for something that causes trouble in communication, one of the main reasons for using technical terms is that they facilitate communication. They, at least, serve as abbreviations for longer phrases. Thus, if a learning theorist uses the term 'operant extinction' for 'the process during which a response becomes less and less frequent when reinforcement is no longer contingent upon that particular response', they will save a great many words.

More troublesome, perhaps, than cases like the above in which no non-technical meaning is apparent, are those words or phrases taken from day-to-day discourse which are adopted by theoreticians for a more restricted use. The word 'authoritarian' is a good example. In everyday language this means, roughly, 'inclined to be dogmatic, aggressive and assertive of one's authority'. However, the technical meaning proposed by Adorno et al (1950) in their book *The Authoritarian Personality* is much more complex and, in some respects, quite paradoxical. For instance, being submissive to authority is said to be a characteristic of being generally authoritarian. This is certainly not part of the word's more common meaning.

Given that the special vocabulary of psychology can lead to serious misunderstanding, how can the reader detect if their interpretation of an author's words is inconsistent with the writer's intended meaning? Unfortunately, sometimes you cannot tell. Although at other times it is possible to know that you have misunderstood, the clues usually lie outside the sentence or passage that is misinterpreted. For example, if a Freudian author states that 'the young boy, during his Oedipus complex stage, wishes to possess his mother sexually, and is jealous of the father', then the reader might regard this as absurd, depending on what they understand by the phrase 'possess his mother sexually'. If they interpret this to mean that the child consciously desires sexual intercourse with his mother, then this is to misunderstand the statement. However, they can only realise that this is so if they compare the statement with the whole paper or theory of which it is part. The reader, having associated one interpretation with the sentence, will need to be alerted to their error by clues they can gain about both the author and her ideas independently of the disputed statement. In our Oedipus complex example, they may learn that the child's desire is hypothetically unconscious and relates to sexual (or 'sensual') possession of the mother in a way that need not include any idea of copulation. Hence the original unreasonable interpretation of the statement was really a misunderstanding.

The problems involved in communicating technical ideas require that special care is taken to make meanings explicit. This is why considerable space is often devoted to defining, analysing and clarifying the meaning of words in psychological literature. We will discuss this topic further in Chapter 4. Here we concentrate only on those aspects that are of general importance for understanding statements.

TRUE 'BY DEFINITION'; TRUE 'IN FACT'

One way of misinterpreting an author is mistakenly to take some statement which she proposes as *trivially true* to be a significant factual claim, or, conversely, to confuse a factual statement with one that she takes to be true by definition. In other words, even though each word of the sentence may be understood, the reader may not be clear as to the status or significance of the statement it expresses. Even if they understand each word of the sentence, and can satisfactorily paraphrase it, they will still not fully understand the intended statement until they are clear which of two alternative purposes the sentence was intended to serve. The sentence may either specify how the author wishes to use words (that is, it is essentially definitional), or be intended to make some claim about the world, not merely about the use of language. For example, a behaviourist might state that 'a reinforcer is any event which increases the probability of a response after which it occurs'. This statement is readily understood at the linguistic level. However, it is also important to understand what *type* of statement this is. Is it intended to be true merely as a result of the way the proponent chooses to employ words, or does it express some fact about the nature of learning? Is the statement *true by definition* or *true in fact*? This is a critical distinction if the reader is to understand the statement in relation to others that the author makes.

Despite its importance, this distinction is not difficult to understand in principle, as the following pairs of statements indicate. Read each pair carefully and attempt to define the way in which the members of each pair differ from each other.

1 (a) A bachelor is an unmarried male adult.
   (b) Bachelors are happier than non-bachelors.
2 (a) The shortest distance between two points is a straight line.
   (b) The distance between Sydney and Melbourne is
      1000 kilometres.
3 (a) No surface can be both wholly red and wholly green
      simultaneously.
   (b) Green apples are less sweet than red apples.

As the heading of this section suggests, for the first of each pair of statements knowledge only of the meaning of the words is sufficient to determine its truth. By contrast, for the second statements in each pair, further information is needed. (We will assume for argument's sake that each is true.) Their truth depends as well upon the state of the non-linguistic world. Let us try to clarify this distinction. The former statements cannot be denied unless we contradict ourselves or misunderstand the conventional meanings of the component words. In that sense they are *tautologies,* or are true *by virtue of their verbal formulation alone.* If someone denies that a bachelor is an unmarried male adult, there may be nothing that can be done to correct their error except to reiterate that, in English, the words of this statement are conventionally used to make a statement that is unquestionably true. No evidence (examples) is relevant. On the other hand, the sentence 'Bachelors are happier than non-bachelors' would be conventionally used to assert a statement which may be denied or affirmed according to factual evidence. Unlike a *tautology,* denial of this statement does not involve self-contradiction. It is an empirical question whether bachelors are happier (although a very difficult one about which to gain reliable evidence).

Although this distinction is a matter of some philosophical controversy, and there are some cases where classification is controversial (even for those who accept it), an understanding of the contrast between statements 'true by meaning' and 'true in fact' is important in understanding the functions of language. Members of the former class are more accurately referred to as **analytic statements**, and of the latter class as **synthetic statements**. The truth or falsity of synthetic statements is an empirical matter requiring evidence, typically from experiment or observation, and hence these are the main subjects of scientific debate. Analytic statements are also important, although mainly as part of theoretical analysis or definition. Let us consider these in more detail.

Since the main function of definitions is to help in the understanding of other sentences, it is important to be able to distinguish which statements are definitions and which are not. It is usually clear when someone is defining a word or phrase. They will write sentences like 'We will use the word ... to mean ...', or 'Let us define ... to be ...'. Sometimes, however, it is not clear whether or not authors intend a sentence merely to indicate the way *they* are using words. This is because the same linguistic form can be used to provide definitions, as well as to make significant empirical statements. Thus, instead of saying 'I will define X as Y', authors may write 'All and only Xs are Ys'. Here it is not clear whether they are telling us that Xs (as we would use the term) are the same things as those we call Ys, or whether they are implicitly telling us that they intend to use the word 'X' to mean 'Y' —

that is, to make it trivially true that 'All Xs are Ys'. If the former is their intention, we can meaningfully ask if the claim that all Xs are Ys is true or false. But this is not so in the second case. Here, instead, we will use the statement as an indication of what the author means by 'X', to help understand other sentences in which they have used the word.

There are two main classes of definition: *descriptive* and *stipulative*. These correspond to what might be called 'conventional meaning' and 'writer meaning', respectively. When proposing a **descriptive definition**, writers attempts to spell out the usual meaning of a term they are using (for example, after referring to a psychological or conventional dictionary), whereas in a **stipulative definition** they specify the meaning they intend for the word or phrase, regardless of more usual or less technically precise possible interpretations. They use a stipulative definition when they give a familiar word a new meaning or introduce a new term. For instance, Cattell (in Sahakian 1965, p 398) defines 'sentiments' as 'major acquired dynamic trait structures which cause their possessors to pay attention to certain objects or classes of objects, and to feel and react in a certain way towards them'. The word 'sentiment' is thereby stipulated to have a special (although perhaps rather vague) meaning within Cattell's Theory of Personality. A descriptive definition of 'sentiment' might be quite different — for example, 'mental feeling or emotion'. Of course, the stipulated and described (conventional) meanings of a word will often be related. But they may differ in precision, emphasis or scope. In this case, it is important for the writer who adopts a term to be consistent in its use: alternating between using the term as stipulated and as it is more conventionally used can generate considerable confusion.

An instance of such confusion arises in Mitchell's book *Psychoanalysis and Feminism* (1974) in which the Freudian notion of hysteria (and hysterical neurosis) is discussed without explicit definition of what Freud meant by the term. To the contemporary reader who is unaware of Freud's stipulated meaning for 'hysteria', Mitchell's account might be quite misleading. Conventionally, hysteria refers to an extremely excited, agitated, even 'giggly' state (for example, one laughs or cries hysterically). But to Freud the concept of hysteria had a more subtle meaning, referring to the somatic (bodily) manifestation of 'repressed' fears or wishes. Hence it would include frigidity and hypochondria, as well as various amnesic or paralysed states. Mitchell's failure to state explicitly how Freud (and she) use the word 'hysteria' undoubtedly confuses some of her readers. In particular, they would be confused about the function of 'anxiety' in hysteria. The Freudian hysteric is *not* overtly anxious, in contrast to the conventional meaning of the term for which overt anxiety is an essential characteristic. The issue is not whether Freud's (or Mitchell's, or our commonly accepted) definition is *true* or *false,* for the analytic statement which implicitly defines hysteria for each author is intended to be trivially true by that writer.

It is worthwhile adopting another term to refer to such implicitly definitional statements. We might say or stipulate that they are 'writer-analytic'. More fully, a statement is **writer-analytic** if it is, or is an obvious consequence of, statements whose truth depends only on the way the writer intends to employ words. So, for Cattell, the statement expressing his definition of 'sentiment' (above) is writer-analytic. In contrast, as we have seen, a statement is generally analytic if it is true as a consequence of the way its words are conventionally used. Writer meaning determines whether or not a statement is writer-analytic. Conventional meaning determines its general analyticity. For Cattell, the statement 'Sentiments cause feelings' is writer-analytic, since, as may be checked above, it follows from his definition of 'sentiment'. The statement 'No maiden aunt is an only child' is analytic in the general sense. Its truth is an immediate consequence of the way the words of the sentence expressing it are conventionally used.

We have highlighted the difference between what a writer means by his or her words and what they would be conventionally taken to mean, and we have mentioned some of the difficulties this can cause. For example, sentences that conventionally express synthetic statements can be intended to express writer-analytic statements. Sometimes, however, the converse happens: sentences that conventionally express analytic truths are used by a writer to assert a synthetic statement. A surprising instance would be the statement 'All women are female', which has been deemed false at least for the purpose of classifying athletes as 'male' or 'female' at the Olympic Games. To understand what is meant in cases such as this, readers must reinterpret the words used in the sentence. They cannot rely on their conventional meanings.

Finally, it is worth emphasising that despite what has been said above, a writer's definitions are not sacrosanct. Sometimes he or she may be inconsistent or fail to justify their choice of definition. The former point concerning inconsistency is particularly noticeable when authors purport to give a familiar word a new technical meaning. To a careful reader, it sometimes becomes apparent they have slipped back into using the word with its older, conventional meaning.

This is highly likely in psychology, where many words are *value laden*. That is, they are used not merely to describe, but to express judgments about, behaviour. Sometimes authors assert what they assume is a fact, and in doing so use a word in a non-evaluative way. But this statement may then be used as the basis for an evaluative judgment which employs the same word and relies on its more usual, evaluative meaning. Good examples are 'intelligence', 'creativity' and 'femininity'. Clearly, whenever familiar terms like these are given novel interpretations which purport to ignore the words' conventional evaluative connotations, we should be careful not to revert to their original meanings or socially accrued connotations of value.

STATEMENTS, QUESTIONS AND IMPLICATIONS

We have suggested that the reader's ability to express in their own words an idea which someone else has stated is the mark of successful understanding. This is surely a minimal requirement. However, even if the reader can paraphrase sentences in this way, it does not follow that they fully understand the original sentences as their author did, for there are degrees or depths of understanding beyond the essentially linguistic level discussed already. Ideally, it is some evidence of such 'deeper understanding' of psychological material that teachers strive to find in their students. How, then, are students to know if they understand psychological material at a level beyond the purely linguistic? Let us suggest an answer by discussing some relatively trivial examples which are not of an explicitly psychological nature.

We have all been asked to explain some matter to a friend or acquaintance. It may be the theory of relativity, or why we were late home. The explanation may require a number of statements each of which elicits a nod of comprehension. And yet a later event, possibly a question the listener cannot answer, shows their lack of understanding. Even though each statement seemed to be understood, some more global or conceptually abstract comprehension was lacking. Each statement may have been understood at the linguistic level, but the deeper 'conceptual' level, which requires the more active manipulation of ideas, has not been achieved. There are two important aspects of this ability: ideas understood at the linguistic level must be capable of being employed to solve problems beyond those covered by the original statements (that is, we must be able to go 'beyond the information given'); and second, the relationships *between* the statements must be understood. We need to understand, not only what each individual statement means, but also what questions or problems the set of statements collectively provides information about.

It may even be said that a statement can only acquire significance (and hence be fully understood) if we understand which questions or problems it answers. To illustrate, consider the statement 'Mary wore her red hat'. Viewed as an answer to the question 'Did Mary or June wear her red hat?', it differs from the same answer to the question 'Did Mary wear or carry her red hat?' Other questions that alter our interpretation of the statement could be constructed. There is an important sense in which the different questions highlight different aspects of the statement. One moral that can be drawn from this example is that reading the same material with different questions in mind can give it very different significances. And to read material without seeing it as an answer to any questions at all is to read, in effect, uncomprehendingly.

Regarding statements as answers to questions not only helps to resolve doubts about what an author means; it can also serve to deepen our understanding of the total significance of a passage because it may relate that passage to the author's ideas advanced elsewhere. If we read Freud's *Three Essays on the Theory of Sexuality* in isolation, ignorant of the questions to which Freud's general theory addresses itself, then much of the essays' import may be lost. But if we read the essays after we have been introduced to the general issues which Freud addressed, the essays 'fall into place'. Sexual aberrations, for instance, are considered as part of the answer to questions about the origins and nature of neuroses, not merely as explorations of the nature of sexuality *per se*.

It can also deepen our understanding of what someone says to consider what they did not say and why they did not say something different. Contrasting what was said with what might have been said can help us to see the significance of what was said. For example, if someone makes a statement of the form 'Most As are Bs', we get a better sense of the significance of that if we consider why they did not say 'All As are Bs' instead — are there any As that are not Bs? If, for example, the claim was some behavioural generalisation about most primates, did they mean to include humans among the primates or were they implicitly talking about non-human primates? Trying to change what the author has written in some small way and judging the plausibility of the result will frequently enhance the reader's understanding of the author's original statement.

A second, related requirement for deeper understanding is that we see the *implications* of what we read. Put briefly, the more **implications** we are able to draw from a statement, the better we might be said to understand it. Since the idea of 'implication' is one that will recur frequently in later chapters, we will attempt to make it precise.

To see the implications of a statement is to understand what difference or differences it would make if it were true. That is, assuming the statement is true, what else must also be true? A criminal suspect may say 'The victim took the glass off the table'. A detective may notice that this implies that the glass was on the table. If this is not consistent with other evidence, then the implication may incriminate the suspect. Part of the detective's understanding of the statement involved seeing one thing that it would mean or imply if it were true. We may say that one statement implies another if it is impossible for the first to be true while the second is false; or if the truth of the first statement guarantees that the second statement is true as well. (For example, the truth of the statement 'The victim took the glass off the table' would guarantee the truth of the statement 'The glass was on the table'.) It is important to notice that implication is a relation between statements which holds irrespective of whether the statements are, in fact, true or false.

We may usefully broaden the idea of implication so that not just one, but a number of statements may imply another. Thus, we may say that a group of statements implies another if it is impossible for all the statements in the group to be true while the other statement is false — that is, if the truth of each statement in the group would jointly guarantee the truth of the other statement. For example, it is impossible for the two statements 'All psychotics are disturbed people' and 'All disturbed people are unhappy' to be true without the statement 'All psychotics are unhappy' being true as well. Again, note that the actual truth of the statements is immaterial; what matters is that *if* they *were* true, the implied statement would also be true.

The ability to see the implications of a statement, therefore, is an aspect of understanding that carries us beyond individual statements; a deeper understanding of statements is achieved if their implications are known. A number of statements made by an author may be combined to see what other statements are implied by them, or these may be combined with additional statements in order to examine their further implications. The statements implied may serve to answer some previously unanswered questions.

EVALUATING STATEMENTS

Psychology students are called upon not merely to understand the material that they read or hear, but also to evaluate it. Assuming that the material to be evaluated has been understood, we shall focus on evaluation in terms of the truth value (that is, the truth or falsity) of the statements being considered. This is not to deny that we can evaluate aspects of statements other than their truth or falsity, but only to emphasise that this is the critical aspect of any statement in an empirical discipline like psychology.

As we shall see below, statements vary widely in the ease with which they can be judged as true or false. Indeed, for many statements we might be reluctant to assert that the judgment can reasonably be made, and may be content with the 'weaker' evaluation in terms of plausibility. We sometimes content ourselves with judging, not whether a statement is true, but only whether, in the light of available evidence, it is likely to be true. Sometimes we are even more cautious, comparing only the relative plausibility of two (usually incompatible) statements.

We have already mentioned that evaluation is part of the process of understanding a statement. In many cases, it is fair to say that understanding a statement involves knowing how to evaluate it (that is, test its truth or falsity). For example, someone who understands the statement

'Fred is taller than Bill' would know that one way to evaluate it would be to stand the two men back-to-back on a level surface. If we are considering a statement made by someone else, then disagreeing with them over the conditions under which it could be evaluated is a sign that we have not understood what they meant. We might then ask them to propose a test that would allow the statement to be evaluated. We will see, in Chapter 4, the importance of explicit criteria for evaluation of psychological statements. Let us merely reiterate here that, often, to know what someone means at least involves knowing how they would evaluate the statement as true or false.

Not all statements can be judged true or false in a simple way. In fact, some statements are such that, if they are false, then this may sometimes be readily shown, but, if they are true, there is no effective way of ascertaining that this is so. Consider the statement 'All dogs are carnivorous', where this is intended to mean that every dog — past, present and future — is naturally carnivorous. It can be contrasted with 'All the cats in the present experiment are male'. If it is true that all dogs are carnivorous, then there is no direct way of determining this (for example, we cannot observe dogs of the future). If, however, the statement is false, one observed instance of a non-carnivorous dog is sufficient to establish this. On the other hand, there are statements where the converse holds. 'This object is breakable' can be readily known to be true (if the object has been broken), but there is no comparably direct way of knowing that it is false. (There may always be unanticipated tests that will prove the statement true.) Hence, failure to break an object does not prove it is unbreakable any more than the failure to find a non-carnivorous dog guarantees that none will ever be found. We mention these otherwise trivial examples to emphasise that not all statements can be conclusively evaluated as true or false, even though their truth or falsity is often mistakenly believed to have been established. A number of psychological statements fall into these two classes: most commonly held empirical generalisations ('All learning involves reinforcement', 'All biologically normal humans can acquire language') fall into the first; while statements such as 'Earthworms are capable of discrimination learning' exemplify the second.

Leaving aside these essentially logical features of general statements, let us now consider whether there is any general method of judging individual (and sets of) statements as true or false.

The key to the general evaluation of statements lies in their interconnectedness. Individual statements that seem difficult to evaluate can often be unambiguously evaluated because of their connections with other statements whose truth or falsity is more easily judged. The question that arises concerns the nature of these 'connections' or relations between statements. Although there are many possible relations, two stand out as important for the present task. The first is the case where one or more statements *implies* another. This is the relation given prominence at the end of the previous section. The second holds between two statements when one is *evidence for the truth of the other.* Unlike implication, this deceptively simply relation is difficult to define and its exact nature is relatively controversial. We will deal with each type.

IMPLICATION

Recall that one statement implies another if they are so related that the truth of the first would ensure the truth of the second: if the first were true, the second could not be false. This is sometimes expressed by saying that the second is a logical consequence of the first. Knowing that this relation holds between statements facilitates evaluation in two main ways: first, if when trying to decide whether a statement is true or false, we find a true statement or group of statements that implies it, then our difficulties are over. The statement must be true. (Remember that all statements implied by true statements are themselves true.) This is the logic of the method constantly adopted by mathematicians. In geometry, for example, this method is used when constructing a proof of a statement (theorem). In this case, the proof establishes that the statement is implied by a number of statements (axioms) which are known, or taken to be true.

The second way in which implication allows statements to be evaluated is of particular importance in empirical disciplines like psychology. If, in trying to evaluate a statement, we can find among the statements that it *implies* just one that is *false,* again the matter is settled: the statement itself must be false as well. It cannot be true, since a true statement implies only statements that are true (see earlier definition), and the statement in question has been found to imply a false statement.

This second method also applies when not just a single statement but a group of statements implies a false statement. If such a group collectively implies a false statement, then *at least one* of that group must be false. Notice that this establishes only that at least one is false, not that all the statements in the group are false; nor does it identify which one is false. Hence, to anticipate later discussion, if a theory is regarded as a group of related statements, and if that theory implies a falsehood, some part of the theory is false. Moreover, should a single statement, in conjunction with a set of statements all of which are known to be true, imply a falsehood, then the original statement must be false. Thus, individual statements (which may include psychological hypotheses) can be evaluated in conjunction with established statements by means of this second use of implication.

We have examined two methods of evaluating one statement in relation to others: first, any statement implied by a true statement is true; and second, any statement that implies a false statement is false. Notice that these rules do *not* state that if a statement is implied by a false statement it must be false, nor that any statement which implies a true statement must itself be true. There is an important asymmetry in the logic of implication which is all too frequently misunderstood. People often mistakenly believe that a result predicted by a theory (or group of statements) will not occur because the theory is false, or they assume that they can evaluate as true any theory which makes true predictions. Yet both types of judgments violate the rules of implication, despite the fact that they sometimes *appear* to be the methods employed by the empirical sciences. We shall have more to say about these points in later chapters. Here, we wish to emphasise that it is only when the statement being evaluated is implied by a true statement (or set of true statements) or implies a false one that the rules of implication allow a rigorous true/false decision. In other cases, different criteria are required.

EVIDENCE

We previously identified the second connection between statements as the 'evidence relation'. Although easy to illustrate, this is difficult to define. We all make assertions about the evidence for or against statements such as 'The rods of the retina respond to white light', 'Imprinting occurs in all mammal species', and so on, yet we seldom analyse what statements constitute evidence for these claims. In Chapter 3 we examine the connection between evidence and explanation. Here we wish to make only some general, but quite important, remarks.

By comparison with implication, the **evidence** relation concerns not whether a statement is unquestionably true or false, but rather whether it is plausible or not; whether it is *likely to be true,* given the truth of other statements (evidence). It is a matter of degree: we may say of certain statements that they offer slight or good evidence for some other statements. There is considerable disagreement about the exact nature (or even the existence) of this relation, but it is frequently taken to hold where a theory has successfully predicted the outcome of an experiment or other observation, and where the theory seems best to explain that outcome. The statement describing this outcome is said to be evidence for the theory that predicted it.

In this respect it is like the converse of the implication relation. As we have noted, however, it is a mistake to think that the outcome implies the truth of the statements that predicted it. The most that can be concluded, and then with some caution, is that one statement provides evidence for the other. Unlike the implication relation, the degree of evidence is conditional on additional information. Further facts can alter judgments about the status of what initially appeared to be weak or strong evidence. Hence, in saying that the evidence renders a statement plausible or likely, we leave open the possibility of changing our judgment. The statement is not '*proved*' although it may be '*supported*' by the evidence. This is an important distinction that will arise frequently in later chapters.

It is worth adding one way in which the evidence relation between statements is connected to the implication relation between statements. If a statement *p* implies a statement *q*, then any evidence that *p* is true is equally evidence that *q* is true. Similarly, any evidence that *q* is false will be evidence that *p* is false. Notice some of the consequences of this interaction. If there is considerable evidence that *p* is true and it implies *q*, then there is also considerable evidence that *q* is true. If there is some evidence to suggest that *q* is false, then if *q* is implied by *p*, there is some evidence to suggest *p* is false as well.

OBSERVATION

We have considered some ways in which statements that are difficult to evaluate individually can be judged in relation to other statements that are more easily evaluated. For this comparative process not to continue indefinitely, for it to be 'anchored', some statements are required which can reasonably be judged as true or false on other grounds. What kinds of statements might these be?

To return to one example we mentioned when illustrating comparative evaluation, elementary mathematical truths are capable of unambiguous evaluation, as are reports of simple observations made in, say, experiments. Although these statements belong to quite different classes, they can be evaluated without recourse to further, related statements. The central difference between the two is in the role of *observations* which are irrelevant to the first class yet critical for the second. Of the two, the second is considerably more important for evaluating psychological statements, but we will briefly discuss the first for the sake of contrast.

The first class, to which elementary mathematical truths belong, is what we previously called simple *analytic statements* — statements like 'All human primates are primates', 'Bachelors are male' and '2 x 3 = 6'. Put another way, they are those simple statements whose truth or falsity is due only to the meanings of the words involved, regardless of any observations or experiences of the person making such statements.

However, as mentioned previously, apart from definitions and statements they directly imply, few interesting psychological statements are of this type. Psychology is concerned with statements to which *observations* are relevant, knowledge of whose truth or falsity makes a direct difference to specific predictions. Not only do simple analytic statements by themselves say nothing about what will or will not happen, but statements they imply fail to do so also.

The second class of statements, those that report observations, are of more direct importance to psychology. Reports of experimental phenomena are generally regarded as *observation statements,* although even some of these may be controversial. This is because statements vary widely in their degree of 'observability'. Hence, we shall begin by treating statements as though their truth or falsity is either verifiable or not, and define a fairly narrow class which shall later be expanded as we consider various functions of such statements. Just as simple analytic statements are those about which everyone who understood the language would agree, so **observation** statements are those about which there would be agreement from anyone who both understood the language *and* observed the circumstances to which the statements applied. Put loosely, they are statements that can be evaluated by being compared, not with other statements, but with observable phenomena.

Consider the statement 'The subject was seated in front of the TV monitor'. This is an observation statement. In normal circumstances, everybody able to observe the subject (and able to understand the statement) would agree on its truth or falsity. By contrast, however, 'The subject was an only child' is not a statement whose truth could be determined by merely observing the subject. Being without siblings does not 'show on one's face', so to speak; it is a characteristic which is not directly observable in the sense that applies in the first example. Despite this, the truth or falsity of this type of statement can usually be confidently determined.

However, if these examples suggest that the contrast is simple, others complicate the picture: deciding if a statement is observably verifiable can be quite difficult. Contrast the pairs 'The subject was smiling' and 'The subject was happy' with 'The subject's face was red' and 'The subject's face was sunburnt'. All four may be true, but in both pairs the second goes beyond what is immediately observable in any direct sense. Although someone who understood the language and saw the subject could agree that she was smiling or that her face was red, agreement could not be guaranteed concerning the causes of these observable characteristics. People are more likely to disagree about the causes of smiling or having a red face than about those more directly observable characteristics. Hence, the second statement of each of the above pairs goes beyond the first and is less likely to be judged as 'observational'.

In these examples, the second statements express what could be *inferred* from the first of each pair. In this respect, they are rather like statements that are not admitted as legal testimony. Eyewitnesses are generally required not to draw inferences from what they have seen.

They are asked not to 'read anything into' what they report they have observed. However, this distinction is difficult to maintain, for what a person 'sees' may itself be influenced by factors such as their expectations and biases — in short, they may infer as part of the process of 'reporting' observations.

In view of this, it is possible that there may be no statement upon which literally everyone viewing the evidence would agree. But this does not mean that we should completely despair of specifying a class of observation statements. For there are certainly some statements which involve relatively few controversial inferences. Earlier we argued that understanding a statement involved knowing how it might be tested, and there is clearly a class of statements for which general agreement can be found concerning appropriate methods of evaluation. Should someone disagree with one of these, they, not the proponent of the statement, would be called on to justify disagreement.

Let us briefly expand on this point. As the examples we have discussed show, observation statements take less for granted, or rely on fewer inferences, than other statements. When a person questions the truth of an observation statement, it is usual to expect them to justify their doubts. On the other hand, people are more likely to accept differing interpretations when statements more clearly involve inferences. Hence, if we question a report that 'the rat turned left at the junction in the maze', we will probably need to justify this stand. However, it would not be so peculiar to question the truth of a statement such as 'The patient had a weak ego', as this involves terms about which there is less consensus than those in the rat example. In other words, a statement that is less likely to be questioned on observational grounds alone provides a greater onus to justify disagreement than a statement involving controversial inferences or assumptions.

Notice, however, that even observation statements can be questioned. To qualify our original definition, an observation statement is one whose truth in most circumstances is relatively easily and uncontroversially assessed; but there is no guaranteed infallibility. Sometimes when such statements clash with a widely held view, they are questioned. Facts that appear supernormal present an interesting case in point. Consider the feats in the 1970s of Uri Geller, who has been 'observed' to bend metallic spoons by moving his hands over their surfaces without applying force. This apparent phenomenon clashes with modern physical theory. Despite the testimony of literally thousands of people that 'Geller bent a spoon by stroking it', there are good reasons for a sceptic to reply that what was observed was Geller stroking a spoon and the spoon bending. That is, there is some reason not to infer, or read into what was observed, a *causal relationship* between the two events.

In the last paragraph we spoke of statements whose truth can be 'relatively easily and uncontroversially assessed' — leaving implicit who it is that is doing the assessing. It is worth adding that whether a statement used in a particular group is an observation statement will often depend on the training of the group doing the observing. Trained radiologists, for example, viewing X-ray negatives can 'observe' tumours or broken bones where the rest of us can only see various shadows.

Given this brief introduction to some of the subtleties of ostensibly simple observation statements, let us now make some points concerning the general issues these raise for understanding psychological argument. First, if we accept that many observation statements involve implicit inferences, then it follows that they are likely to reflect the conventionally accepted psychological theories of the day insofar as they would be accepted unquestioningly by most psychologists. But in psychology there is frequent disagreement over what are acceptable observation or 'fundamental' ('bottom-level') statements. One important way in which psychological 'schools of thought' differ from each other is in their criteria for accepting or rejecting various statements as observational. For example, behaviourists, cognitive psychologists, psychoanalysts and existentialists allow different types of inferences to be implicit in the 'descriptive' statements on which they base their respective theoretical interpretations. Hence, some maintain that only physical movements, not 'behaviour' (and certainly not 'actions'), can be observed. To such theorists, behaviour which is described by statements like 'The rat ran the maze to the goal box' or 'The man climbed the stairs' carry the inference that the organism in question *intended* the described movement. They might argue that, since intentions cannot be directly observed, such descriptions are inappropriate as the basis of an empirical science. Therefore, even the statement 'The rat in the Skinner box pressed the lever' might be regarded as a statement involving unwarranted inferences (ask yourself why).

To avoid such inferences, it might be necessary to describe only the muscular and other movements of the rat in a totally 'physical' manner. Otherwise, should the rat press the bar with its left paw or its nose, these will be classed as the same response, which, in a very strict observational sense, they are not. This example is not an extreme one. Many psychologists dispute whether subjects' verbal reports (for example, of an after-image or dream) should be considered legitimate 'scientific data' for similar reasons. Hence, even putative observation statements may not merely reflect 'the facts' — they may be **'theory-laden'**, reflecting the general theoretical presuppositions of their proponent.

SUMMARY

Understanding a statement is an essential preliminary to evaluating it. In this chapter we have distinguished two important levels of understanding — the linguistic and the conceptual. The former was explained in terms of being able to express the statement in your own words. The latter, deeper notion was most importantly connected with seeing its connection with other statements via implication and evidence. We also saw that it was important for understanding to know if an author intended a statement to be true by definition (analytic) or have its truth depend on the world (true 'in fact').

The key to evaluating statements (once they are understood) is their interconnectedness — the relations of implication and evidence they stand in to other statements. Statements implied by true statements are true. Statements which imply false statements are false. We looked at two classes of statements that are less dependent on others for their evaluation — analytic statements and observation statements. The latter group are particularly important for an empirical study like psychology, and we considered some of the difficulties in identifying them when they may depend on developed expertise (as with radiographers) and when schools of thought differ over which ones are fundamental.

KEYWORDS

STATEMENT • TRUE BY DEFINITION • TRUE IN FACT • TAUTOLOGY • ANALYTIC STATEMENT • SYNTHETIC STATEMENT • DESCRIPTIVE DEFINITION • STIPULATIVE DEFINITION • WRITER-ANALYTIC • IMPLICATION • EVIDENCE • OBSERVATION • THEORY-LADEN

EXERCISES

1 Suppose someone proposed the following as a law of human nature: 'Given a choice, people always choose to do what they most want to do.' (The proponent may add: 'Therefore, people are basically selfish.')

When you present them with a purported counter-example — Mary spending an afternoon with her grandmother when she most wanted to go to the beach — they reply: 'That's what she may have told you she wanted to do, but actions speak louder than words. What did she freely do? She visited her grandmother — that's what she most wanted to do.'

You offer another counter-example — a mother throwing herself in front of a car to save a child. They reply: 'Just a reflex response — so not a free action.' Or perhaps they reply: 'Yes, she couldn't have lived with herself afterwards if she hadn't done it.'

Through this process, you are learning something about how the person understands their statement; it does not seem to be empirically testable in any of the ways you might have imagined and yet it is not analytic — it is not true by definition. It does not seem to be part of the meaning of 'what you most want to do' that it is something you always end up doing. Discuss how the statement is being protected from refutation.

2   Child development researchers, animal ethologists and connectionist theorists often speak of the systems they study as acquiring concepts. However, Rosenberg (1997, p 297) argues:

> the mere exercise of a discrimination capacity, however complex, is not yet an example of *cognition*. A magnet quite efficiently discriminates between ferrous and non-ferrous materials, but that does not put it in the running for the title of 'cognitive system'. Just as one can 'train up' a modest connectionist network regularly to respond differentially to sonar echoes from mines and those from rocks — or, more precisely, as it turns out, to sonar targets made of metal and those that are not metallic — I can (by stroking it with a strong magnet) 'train up' a screwdriver regularly to respond differentially to brass and steel screws.

Discuss what may be needed for the term 'acquired a concept' to be applied so that it does not have these counterintuitive results.

chapter 2

Understanding and evaluating arguments

... our powers of reasoning are nothing but powers of critical argument.

Karl Popper

UNDERSTANDING ARGUMENTS

Even if students can understand and evaluate individual statements in the ways discussed in Chapter 1, there are still a number of different issues which need to be understood when arguments are presented, analysed and evaluated. As we shall see, an argument is not merely the assertion of an individual statement. In general, the difference between the two lies in the fact that an argument does more than merely tell us that something is the case: it *provides reasons* in support of one or more statements. It follows that an argument must involve at least two statements — one putting forward a particular view, and at least one other specifying reasons for that view. When someone argues sincerely, they do not merely say what they think; they also say *why* they think it. It is this that allows listeners and readers to make critical judgments as to whether they should agree with what was argued. This process is the essence of all intellectual activity. Let us see what it involves.

Arguing, like speaking, is something we all do well enough in day-to-day life without any formal knowledge of logic. But when we move to a less familiar, theoretically abstract domain like psychology, some more explicit analysis of argument is necessary if naive confusions are to be avoided. The purpose of this chapter, then, is to provide some of the means for becoming more aware of the nature and value of the arguments found in psychology. Accordingly, it is necessary to introduce a number of mildly technical concepts. We believe that a thorough grasp of these will better enable the student to analyse and construct sophisticated psychological arguments. We have already discussed different types of statements; below we introduce the concepts of 'premiss', 'conclusion', 'argument', 'induction', 'deduction', 'validity' (and 'soundness'). In considering these, we will outline some of the argument forms on which scientific reasoning is based, pointing to some of the more common misconceptions and fallacies found in this area.

THE ELEMENTS AND STRUCTURE OF ARGUMENT

An **argument** can be defined as that totality consisting of a number of statements advanced jointly in support of another statement. More generally, it is a connected series of statements, each of which is either advanced in support of one or more of the others or is presented as supported by one or more of the others, or both. It can be noted immediately from this definition that although arguments consist of statements, they are not themselves statements. Clearly, as was mentioned previously, an argument must consist of at least two statements, one put forward in support of the other. Hence, the headlines of a news bulletin are not an argument, although they are a connected series of statements. What is lacking is the intention that some of its constituent statements support, or are supported by, others. In the headlines of a news bulletin, any statements that might be said to support others are usually rare and generally not explicitly intended to do so.

Another way of characterising the difference between arguing and merely stating or describing something can be seen with respect to understanding. To understand an argument, we have to both understand its component statements, and to identify which of these are intended as support for which others. We must understand the intended relationships *between* the constituent statements of an argument. Perhaps the best way to make this point clear is through an example. Let us analyse the following simple argument into its component elements and express the way these relate to each other in the encompassing structure of the argument. (Of course, arguments rarely display their structure at a level that will permit such an immediate analysis; more often than not, the elements must be abstracted from the general flow of written or spoken language in which they inhere.

> Furthermore, on this question of instincts, I want to make it clear that instinctual behaviour in humans is not supported — humans do not display instinctual behaviour. As we saw earlier, instincts involve rigidly stereotyped, unmodifiable behaviour, but all human behaviour is characterised by plasticity.

The preceding passage has provided the vehicle for a very simple argument, and it is now our task to analyse this argument into its basic elements. We can begin this process by bracketing out superfluous parts of the passage that expresses the argument. This is part of a process that is sometimes called 'taming' an argument, since it makes a naturally occurring (or 'wild') argument more manageable. Clearly, there are some phrases in the passage which simply act as padding and add nothing to the real force of the argument. For example, phrases like 'Furthermore, on this question of instincts' and 'I want to make it clear that' merely serve to maintain continuity and cohesion in the prose passage. The result of this process is:

> (Furthermore, on this question of instincts, I want to make it clear that) instinctual behaviour in humans is not supported — humans do not display instinctual behaviour. (As we saw earlier,) instincts involve rigidly stereotyped, unmodifiable behaviour, (but) all human behaviour is characterised by plasticity.

The elements of the argument which we hope to uncover in our analysis are statements, and it is helpful to list the component statements of an argument in the form of a dictionary where each statement is represented by a letter. For example:

A: Instinctual behaviour in humans is not supported.

B: Humans do not display instinctual behaviour.

C: Instincts involve rigidly stereotyped, unmodifiable behaviour.

D: All human behaviour is characterised by plasticity.

Having analysed the argument into its component elements, we can proceed to distinguish between its *premisses* and *conclusions*. Every argument must contain both a conclusion and at least one premiss. The **premisses** of an argument are those statements that are advanced to support others, and the **conclusions** are those statements that are intended to be supported. In our example using the above letters to represent the component statements and an arrow to reflect the relationship of 'support', with brackets to indicate that a conjunction of statements is considered as a whole, we have the following structure:

That is, the statements *D* and *C* are offered jointly in support of the conclusions *A* and *B*; or, in other words, it is intended that *A* and *B* be inferred from *D* and *C*. As the original argument stands, however, the intentions of the author are not entirely clear. From what he has written, he could have intended to express the following argument:

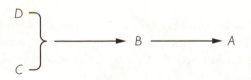

If this was so, then *D* and *C* jointly are intended to support *B*. which is then an **intermediate conclusion**. *B*, in turn, is intended to support *A*. As this example illustrates, it is not always clear which of a number of alternative structures an author intends.

At this point we might distinguish **unitary** from **extended arguments**. **Unitary arguments** have no **intermediate conclusions** — that is, no component statement serves the dual role of being both a premiss and a conclusion. Consequently, their structure diagrams will contain only one arrow, linking premisses to conclusion. A common, alternative way of representing unitary arguments — one that we shall use later — is to indicate premisses and conclusion by writing the premisses, or letters that stand for them, in a vertical list. A line is then drawn beneath the list under which the conclusion is written preceded by a triangle of dots, the conventional symbol for 'therefore'. Thus, any two-premiss argument with premisses A and B and conclusion C which we would represent as:

$$A \left.\begin{array}{c} \\ \\ \end{array}\right\} \longrightarrow C$$

$$B$$

can also be represented as:

$$\begin{array}{c} A \\ \underline{B} \\ \therefore C \end{array}$$

Extended arguments contain intermediate conclusions and have a chain structure linking together a series of otherwise unitary arguments. Hence the structure diagram (or skeleton) of an extended argument must contain at least two arrows. An example of such an argument would be:

> Introspection must really always be retrospection, since it takes time to report on a state of consciousness. Forgetting is rapid, especially immediately after having an experience, so that some of the experience will perhaps be inadvertently lost.

Let us begin to analyse this verbally complex argument by setting out a dictionary of its component statements. This time we use as our abbreviations the first letters of a key word in each of the statements.

I: Introspection is always retrospection.

R: It takes time to report on a state of consciousness.

F: Forgetting is rapid, especially immediately after having an experience.

E: Some of the experience will be inadvertently lost.

In this argument, R is a premiss which is intended to directly support the intermediate conclusion I. I and F are then intended to provide support for E. It can be seen that I, rather like B in the second interpretation of the previous argument, has the dual role of an intermediate conclusion and a premiss in that it is intended to be supported by R and provide support for E.

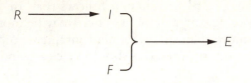

Even this example is not very complex when compared to the types of argument that one continually finds in advanced discussion in psychology and other scientific disciplines. However, the basic structure of even the most complicated argument is amenable to analysis in essentially the way illustrated here.

ARGUMENT INDICATORS

As these examples illustrate, it is sometimes quite difficult to identify an argument. It is often unclear how the component statements are related, even though each is understood. Fortunately, there are a number of key words and phrases which are often used both to signal the presence of an argument and to identify its premises and conclusions.

These include 'therefore', 'so', 'since', 'thus' and 'consequently', while common phrases to the same effect include 'hence it follows that', 'from this it may be seen' and 'from this it can be concluded that'. Such phrases not only alert us to the presence of an argument but also help to reveal its structure.

If A and B represent statements, then the following are some ways of expressing the same argument:

A, therefore B

A, so B

Since A, B[1]

A, hence it follows that B

A and consequently B

Each has the structure:

$A \rightarrow B$ or $\underline{A\quad}$ or $\underline{A\quad}$
$\qquad\qquad\quad \therefore B \qquad$ So B

---

[1] 'Since' does not always indicate an argument: Since Jo turned two she has spoken three languages fluently. 'Jo turned two' is not being offered in support of her tri-lingualism. 'A because B' sometimes indicates an argument, but sometimes it is just used to make a statement telling you that B caused A: His car stopped because it was out of petrol.

As a general rule it is best to begin your analysis by identifying the main conclusion — what the argument is 'getting at' or 'trying to show'. As we have seen, this will usually be clear from the use of words such as 'therefore', 'so' or 'thus', or phrases like 'it follows that' or 'it can be seen that' preceding the relevant statement. There may be more than one conclusion (that is, more than one statement intended to be supported by relevant premisses). If so, then this should be clearly indicated in any analysis.

Given that you have identified the conclusions of the arguments being analysed, you should ask what each is intended to be supported by, or on what grounds (of evidence, for instance) the arguer makes these statements. To answer this, the interrelationship between the relevant supporting premisses will need to be specified. Thus, are certain premisses to be taken conjointly, as alternatives, or as intermediate sequential steps in the argument? As our examples show, it is possible for a number of independent lines of evidence to support one conclusion:

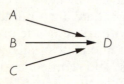

Or, for a number of premisses to form a chain of inference:

$$A \longrightarrow B \longrightarrow C \longrightarrow D$$

Or, for some combination of statements jointly to lead to an intermediate or final conclusion although neither statement is intended by itself to yield that conclusion:

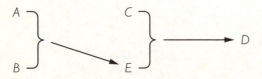

Clearly, therefore, the relations intended to hold *between* the statements of any argument must be understood if that argument is to be criticised in any way. For instance, in the example concerning introspection, *I* and *F* together are intended to lead to conclusion *E*. Neither *I* nor *F* by itself provides strong reason for asserting *E*, but together they do. A very common structure in argument is that the conjunction of two (or more) premises is intended to support a third, otherwise unexpected, statement. This kind of structure leads to conclusions that might not have been anticipated by examining the premisses in isolation from each other.

We should comment briefly on something you have already seen us do in the examples above, identifying the structure of arguments. We have defined arguments as a special kind of series of statements. You may have noticed in the above examples that there can be quite a difference between the sentences that express the argument in the passage where the argument occurs and the statements we have used in diagramming the argument. For example, we turned 'Introspection must always really be retrospection' into 'Introspection is always retrospection' — dropping the 'must' and the 'really'. In this particular case, 'must' is signalling that the clause it is in expresses a conclusion.

In discussing the above examples we have assumed that the form in which arguments are found in the literature is complete, containing all the premisses that are intended to support the conclusion. However, such complete detail is seldom explicitly specified. Nor is it always clear from the verbal form of an argument which, if any, statements are intended as premisses or conclusions. For example, it is not entirely clear in the following whether an argument is intended, and certainly, if one is intended, it is only incompletely presented:

> Not all primates are monogamous. Humans are sometimes polygamous.

Presumably the second statement is intended as a reason for the first, although there is no obvious sign that this is so (for example, no words like 'hence', 'therefore' or 'so'). Moreover, the second statement would be intended as support for the first only if it is taken in conjunction with at least one tacit (unstated) premiss in the original presentation. (What is one likely candidate?) This example raises an important problem in the identification and analysis of arguments. Authors frequently are content to leave, unstated, premisses which they regard as obvious or generally assumed. Alternatively, they may occasionally not formulate a conclusion, should it be otherwise clearly implied. Such incomplete arguments are called **enthymemes**. Most informally presented arguments are enthymemes; it is rare for someone to state explicitly all the components of a particular argument. Indeed, it is often the most controversial or important premisses which remain tacit. As we shall see when discussing evaluation, if you are to criticise an argument adequately, it is vital to spell out these assumed premisses.

How can you tell what premisses have been omitted? In general, the best method to use is to assume that the proponent of the argument is arguing well — and to consequently read in any extra premisses needed if those offered explicitly are, in fact, to support the conclusion. Thus, on this approach, in

> Jones is a student, so she is likely to have an above-average IQ.

it is plausible to take 'Most students have an above-average IQ' as a tacit premiss. Since it assumes the arguer is arguing well, this method is sometimes unduly sympathetic. However, it does lead to a higher standard of criticism of arguments, for it saves a 'strawman' argument from being set up only to be easily demolished. Sometimes knowledge of the theoretical position the arguer has adopted will guide you in making plausible guesses about exactly which premisses are being assumed.

INDUCTIVE AND DEDUCTIVE ARGUMENTS

There are two main types of argument which it is important to distinguish, because they are evaluated according to very different criteria. What distinguishes them is the different ways in which their premisses are intended to support their conclusions.

So, before turning to the task of evaluating arguments, it is necessary to distinguish these broad classes. The first — **deductive arguments** — are those in which the premisses purport to *guarantee the truth of the conclusion*. These are arguments in which it is the intention of the proponent that the conclusion be so related to the premisses that if the latter are true the conclusion *must* also be true. The remaining class includes all those arguments whose premisses purport to *support* their respective conclusions, but not to guarantee the truth of those conclusions. These are called **inductive arguments**.

The distinction is meant to reflect the difference between arguments that purportedly offer (conclusive) proofs of their conclusions and those not aiming so high.

As can be seen by examining their definitions, the two classes exhaust the complete class of unitary (or 'one step') arguments. In colloquial speech, the one term 'deduction' is sometimes employed indiscriminately to cover *both* types of argument. Arthur Conan Doyle's Sherlock Holmes uses the terms indiscriminately. On the other hand, the term 'induction' is often used in technical contexts more narrowly than we have done, requiring the premisses and conclusion to be

empirical statements or for the conclusion to involve some kind of generalisation of information contained in the premises (see, for example,
Blackburn 1994, p 192). The term 'non-demonstrative' is sometimes
reserved for the arguments we are calling 'inductive'. However, our
broader definition also includes these as inductive arguments, an example of which follows:

> There is reason to believe that the attachment of young children to
> their mothers is instinctive, since many other species (most notably
> mallard ducks and rhesus monkeys) show instinctive attachment
> behaviour.

In this example the arguer does not intend his premiss to guarantee the
truth of his conclusion; he merely intends that it lends support to it. In
contrast, the following is a deductive argument:

> The neuroses are invariably the result of infantile sexual trauma,
> no matter how apparently non-sexual their symptoms. Necessarily,
> therefore, persons suffering from agoraphobia (a form of neuro-
> sis) must have suffered some emotional upset related to sexual
> experience.

In this case it is not intended that the premiss(es) merely lend some
support to the conclusion. In this argument, it is intended that if the
premiss(es) were true, this would be sufficient to ensure or guarantee
that the conclusion was true.

Since quite different criteria apply when we judge the worth of
deductive and inductive arguments, it is imperative to know what type
of argument we are analysing. Just as we have distinguished arguments
from non-arguments with respect to the intentions of the proponent,
so we use the same grounds for distinguishing deductive from inductive arguments. A number of words and phrases distinguish these
intentions. For example, the occurrence of the word 'necessarily' in an
argument of the form 'A, therefore necessarily B' is a reliable sign that
the argument is deductive, while the occurrence of qualifying phrases
like 'so it seems plausible that', 'it is likely that', 'it is reasonable to conclude that', or even 'so, probably' regularly indicate that the arguer
does not intend to guarantee the truth of the conclusion relative to his
premises, but merely to lend it support.

If no stock phrase like 'plausibly' or 'necessarily' occurs, a simple
test for distinguishing the two types of argument is to see if adding the
word 'necessarily' prior to the conclusion alters the force of the argument. If it does not, then the argument can be interpreted as deductive. If it does, then it is likely to be an inductive argument. An
argument of the form 'A, so B' would become 'A, so necessarily B';

which, if both are not considered to express the same intention, means that the original was not deductive. A converse test would be to prefix the conclusion by 'it is likely that'. Should this distort the argument, it can be taken to have been intended as deductive.

It is most important to know which of these two types of argument was intended, because almost all inductive arguments will be found to be very poor if judged by the criteria applicable to deductive arguments. Clearly, if someone merely intends the premisses to lend some support to the conclusion, it would be surprising if they actually guaranteed its truth. This would clearly be judged a bad deductive argument, although it might be quite acceptable as an inductive form of reasoning. Two important practical consequences follow: first, to assess someone else's argument fairly, we must determine whether or not it was intended as inductive or deductive; second, to have our own arguments clearly understood and fairly evaluated, we must make clear whether or not we are arguing inductively or deductively.

EVALUATING ARGUMENTS

We have discussed three aspects of understanding arguments. The first was the need to understand the component statements; the second, identification of premisses and conclusions; and the third was recognising whether an argument was intended to be deductive or inductive.

As we mentioned, the last issue is important because the standards for judging inductive arguments differ markedly from those applicable to the deductive variety. In this section we will consider only the evaluation of deductive argument for which criteria are relatively well defined, leaving the evaluation of inductive arguments until the chapter on explanation (Chapter 3).

To argue is to propose a number of statements in support of one or more further statements. When the components have been understood and their functions as premisses or conclusions identified, two questions arise:

1 Are the component statements true or false?
2 Does the intended relation between premisses and conclusion (or conclusions) actually obtain? Do the premisses support the conclusion or not?

We have considered ways in which we may try to evaluate the truth of statements, but how can we judge whether the argument succeeds in its intention? How can we determine if the premisses (deductively) support the conclusion?

Let us begin by returning to our definition of deductive argument.

Recall that in such cases the arguer intends the premisses to guarantee the truth of the conclusion: assuming the truth of the former, the latter must also be true. But this is a relation we have already encountered — it is *implication*. We discussed it in relation to the evaluation of individual statements. Hence, deductive arguments are those in which it is intended that, if the premisses are true, the conclusion must also be true: that the premisses *imply* the conclusion. When the premisses imply the conclusion, the argument is said to be **valid**. If, additionally, the premisses are true, the argument is termed **sound**.

So, the two important considerations in the evaluation of deductive arguments can be expressed by the questions:

1 Is the argument *valid*? (Do the statements that are the premisses imply the statement that is the conclusion?)
2 Are the component statements *true*?

Notice that the relation of implication is important for the evaluation of both individual statements and the deductive arguments of which they are part. This is hardly surprising, for one of the main purposes of an argument is to express, and thereby show others, how a statement (the conclusion) can be evaluated. When one person presents another with an argument, they are showing how the conclusion can be evaluated. Those arguing sincerely make public their reasons for believing the conclusions to be true.

Although arguments consist of statements, as we have emphasised, they are not themselves statements, and although their component statements can be true or false, arguments themselves can be neither true nor false. Whereas the key feature of statements is their truth (or falsity), the key feature of arguments is their validity (or invalidity). Conversely, just as arguments cannot properly be described as being true or false, statements cannot properly be described as being valid or invalid. This is because what determines the validity of an argument is the relation that holds between premisses and conclusion. The argument is valid if that relation is one of implication, and is invalid otherwise. Yet, whether this relation holds or not is almost entirely independent of the actual truth of the premisses and conclusion. For example, some valid arguments have true conclusions, whereas some do not; some have true premisses, whereas some do not. There is only one combination that is definitely ruled out: *no valid argument with true premisses can have a false conclusion*. All other combinations of true and false premisses and conclusions are compatible with an argument's being valid. Remember, an argument is valid if the premisses are so related to the conclusion that it is impossible for the premisses to be true and the conclusion false.

How can we tell if an argument is valid? That is, how can we judge if the premisses imply the conclusion. In general, ascertaining whether or not an argument is valid involves the careful application of our knowledge of the subject matter of the argument and the use of our imagination. *In short, it involves asking of the argument in question whether there are any conceivable circumstances in which the premisses could be true while the conclusion was false.* Consider the very simple argument

> Schizophrenics all come from families with a history of psychotic disorder, and Jones's family has such a history, therefore Jones will exhibit schizophrenia.

That this conclusion is not implied by the premisses is clear, for it is possible to think of circumstances in which the premisses are true while the conclusion is false — namely, circumstances in which, although every schizophrenic comes from such a family and Jones does too, nevertheless Jones is not schizophrenic.

Sometimes, of course, our inability to imagine circumstances in which the premisses are true but the conclusion false does not mean that there aren't any. There may be some conceivable, but not yet conceived, circumstances. The fault may lie in our imagination. It is tempting to think the following argument is valid:

> No one is greater than Ali. So, Ali is the greatest.

Surely if the premiss is true, Ali must be greater than everyone else and so be the greatest? No. On careful inspection, the premiss does not even imply that Ali is greater than anyone. But it is easy to overlook (or fail to imagine) how this might be possible.

Are there any *other* guides to determining the validity of an argument? Fortunately, there is a fact that greatly facilitates the determination of implication, and hence judgments concerning an argument's validity. This is the fact that there is a connection between the implication relation and some recognisable patterns in language.

Thus, for example, in general, any premisses having the patterns

All *F*s are *G*s, and
All *G*s are *H*s

will jointly imply a conclusion having the pattern

All *F*s are *H*s.

For example,

> All dogs are mammals (and)
> all mammals are vertebrates,
> so all dogs are vertebrates

fits this pattern.

Thus, if an argument turns out to have premises and a conclusion that fit this pattern, then it will be formally valid. Indeed, such patterns (or forms) are the subject matter of much of formal logic, and below we shall look at a few very elementary patterns. Unfortunately, the patterns that most formal logicians study are patterns in artificial invented languages, and have limited immediate applicability to the wide variety of arguments presented in everyday English. In addition, to apply the patterns of formal logic, we need to translate or symbolise ordinary English into these invented languages. This process is often as hazardous as the aforementioned method of creatively assessing the possibility that the premises can be true in certain circumstances in which the conclusion is false.

However, if you know a number of reliable patterns in natural language, like the one above in English, you can show that an argument is valid by the relatively easy process of showing it fits one of these reliable patterns. If it does not fit exactly as it stands, you may be able to paraphrase its premises or conclusion so that it does. Here is another place where your ability to understand the component statements in an argument will prove useful — if you can express them in other words which *do* fit a reliable pattern.

In its original linguistic form, the pattern of reasoning which underlies an argument may not be obvious and so some ability to compare arguments with forms that are well understood can facilitate critical evaluation. We now look at some patterns of argument containing conditional statements.

ARGUMENT AND CONDITIONALS

Conditional statements play an important role in many arguments. A conditional, or **conditional statement,** is one having the pattern 'If ... then ...' or 'If p then q' where 'p' and 'q' stand for clauses which, were they to stand alone, would themselves be statements. The clause in the 'p' position before the 'then' is called the **antecedent;** the one coming after 'then' in the 'q' position is called the **consequent**.

There is evidence that people frequently misinterpret conditionals, so we shall take a moment to look at certain aspects of their logic. We shall use a variation of a task used by psychologists in the study of reasoning to make a number of points. It is called the selection task or four-card problem (see Evans et al 1993). In our version of it, you are presented with four cards each of which (you know) has a number (strictly speaking a numeral) on one side and a letter on the other. The cards are presented to you as follows (resting on a table) with only one side visible.

You are given a conditional statement: 'If this card has an even number on one side then it has a vowel on the other.' You are then asked: if this statement is taken in turn to be about each of the four cards, which card or cards (if any) would you need to turn over to see if the statement is false as applied to that card?

Before reading on, you may like to try this yourself.

Almost everyone says you need to turn the '4' card over. Many people suggest that you also need to turn the 'E' card over. Only a few notice that you need to turn the 'K' card over. The correct answer is '4' and 'K'.

The conditional statement 'If this card has an even number on one side then it has a vowel on the other' as applied to the '4' card would not be true if there was a consonant on its other side. It would have an even number on one side and not have a vowel on the other. If you did not turn this card over, you would miss a chance to see if the statement is false. This illustrates a general truth about conditionals.

Any conditional statement having the pattern 'If p then q' is false if p is true and q is false.

Similarly, the 'K' card needs to be turned over because, if it has an even number on the other side, it will be a card with an even number on one side without having a vowel on the other. (It has a 'K' instead.)

The 'E' card does not need to be turned over to see if the statement 'If this card has an even number on one side then it has a vowel on the other' is false. Whatever was on the other side — whether an even or an odd number — would be compatible with the statement being true. The statement does not say 'If this card has a vowel on one side then it has an even number on the other'.

In general, statements of the form 'If p then q' make a different statement from those of the related but different form 'If q then p'. (But not, of course, when p and q stand for the same clause.) Two statements so related are called *converses*. So, putting this another way, *a conditional statement and its converse are not in general equivalent*. It does make a difference which of p and q is the antecedent and which is the consequent.

It is worth noting in addition that, in general, statements of the form 'If p then q' also differ from statements of the form 'If not-p then not-q'. On the other hand, it is true generally that statements of the form 'If p then q' and 'If not-q then not-p' are equivalent. (Here, and in the following pages, 'not-p' stands for the negation of the statement p — that is, a sentence or clause equivalent to 'It is not the case that p'.) So, 'If this card has an even number on one side then it has a vowel on the other side' is equivalent to 'If this card does not have a vowel on one side then it does not have an even number on the other side'. We can add that in the context of the four-card problem this amounts to: 'If a card has a consonant on one side then it has an odd number on the other'. It is instructive to note that if the four-card statement had been expressed this way instead, almost everyone would have realised they must turn the 'K' card over and probably have missed the need to turn over the '4' card. This is further evidence that our comprehension of a statement can be affected by the way it is expressed. (And, of course, is a selling point for a knowledge of some of these patterns!)

Alerted to some of the hazards surrounding conditionals and our comprehension of them, we consider now three elementary reliable argument patterns that use conditionals. These underlie some common forms of scientific prediction and evaluation. A **reliable pattern** is a pattern of sentences expressing arguments with the following attractive property: every sequence of sentences that fits the pattern expresses a valid argument.[2] What is attractive about this is that if we know that a pattern is reliable and we can see that the sentences expressing the argument fit the pattern, then we know that there is a valid argument expressed by those sentences. We also look briefly at some corresponding unreliable patterns — patterns not to trust.[3]

Asserting the antecedent (*modus ponens*)

Consider the argument:

If the ability to learn a language is largely innate, then children will all learn to speak at about the same age.
The ability to learn a language is largely innate.
Therefore, children will all learn to speak at about the same age.

---

[2] Notice that we have not said every argument expressed by the sequences of sentences that fit the pattern is valid, since sentences are often ambiguous. A special case we will mention in Chapter 4 is equivocation. It is not always clear what argument is expressed by a sequence of sentences.

[3] An unreliable pattern is only a pattern that is not reliable — at least some sequences of sentences that fit the pattern do not express a valid argument. It is not a pattern with the property that every argument expressed by a sequence of sentences fitting it is invalid. The argument 'This is red. If this is coloured, then this is red. So this is coloured' is valid, since the first premiss alone implies the conclusion. Yet it fits an unreliable pattern we consider below, showing that valid arguments can fit unreliable patterns.

This fits the reliable pattern

If p then q

p
_____

$\therefore q$

as can be seen by replacing 'p' by 'the ability to learn a language is largely innate' and replacing 'q' by 'children will all learn to speak at about the same age'.

Arguments fitting this pattern are said to *affirm or assert the antecedent* — the antecedent of the conditional is affirmed or asserted in the second premiss.

We should note that when using reliable patterns of valid argument to show the validity of an argument, it is important to be sure that the clauses the pattern elements (in this example, 'p' and 'q') stand in for have the same meaning at all of their occurrences. The language learning example above satisfies this condition.

Asserting (or affirming) the antecedent is, however, sometimes confused with an unreliable form of argument that appears to follow a similar pattern:

If p then q

Not-p
_____

$\therefore$ Not-q

Invalid arguments fitting this pattern are said to commit the *fallacy of denying the antecedent*. Notice that the second premiss denies — is the negation of — the antecedent of the conditional. Here is an example:

> If the ability to learn language is largely innate, then children will all learn to speak at about the same age.
> The ability to learn a language is not largely innate.
> Therefore, children will not all learn to speak at ab out the same age.

Clearly, this conclusion does not follow. Actual matters of fact aside, if it were not the case that the ability to learn a language were largely innate, it could still be true that children learned to speak at about the same age (for other reasons). Invalid arguments that happen to fit this pattern are surprisingly common and may be due to their proponents mistakenly taking sentences of the form 'If p then q' to imply sentences of the form 'If q then p'.

These examples illustrate the important asymmetry between asserting and denying the antecedent in a simple conditional argument. When you have argued from premisses you find plausible to a conclusion you also find plausible using a conditional statement that connects the two in some way, it can be tempting to suppose the premisses imply the conclusion. This may be another source of the mistaken view that arguments like this are valid. *But having true premisses and a true conclusion is no assurance that an argument is valid.* All too often, for example, if both the simple statements (*p*, *q*) in a conditional seem untrue, the denial of the antecedent is taken as grounds for the denial of the consequent. The following is a relevant case:

> If computers can 'think' in a genuinely creative manner, they could be programmed to write a poem. Computers cannot 'think' in a genuinely creative manner, therefore it is ridiculous to think that they could be programmed to write a poem.

Leaving aside the controversial questions concerning the meanings of words like 'think', 'creative' and 'poem', this argument is deceptively appealing because the relevant statements are widely believed (that is, both the conclusion and the denial of the antecedent are widely believed). The same might be said of another (oversimplified) argument:

> If the unconscious mind exists, people's dreams are capable of being analysed and understood. However, the concept of unconscious mental processes is simply ridiculous, so there is no likelihood of ever comprehending people's dreams.

Both of these arguments are invalid as they stand.

Denying the consequent (*modus tollens*)

In a sense, this form of argument is the converse of *modus ponens*, and may be illustrated by expanding our example concerning language acquisition:

> If the ability to learn language is largely innate, then children will all learn to speak at about the same age.
> Children do **not** all learn to speak at about the same age (or, **It is** not the case that children all learn to speak at about the same age).
> Therefore, the ability to learn language is not largely innate (or, It is not the case that ...).

Formally, this can be represented simply as:

If *p* then *q*
Not-*q*
∴ Not-*p*

Notice that the second premiss denies the consequent of the conditional. Denying the consequent (or *modus tollens*) is a particularly common underlying form of argument in science where, as shall be seen in later chapters, predictions from theories are often formulated in a manner that allows refutation of the theory by means of denying the consequent or consequents. Thus, in the above example, a 'theory' of the biological foundation of language development predicts a phenomenon that is denied. Its denial is taken to be sufficient to refute the original (theoretical) statement. Although the issue of falsification of theories is extremely complex and will be discussed at length later, let us make some general points about the importance of this reliable pattern of argument.

First, it might be said that this form of argument captures the spirit of the critical method of the sciences. We begin with a hypothesis or theory (p) to test which one formulates observationally testable statements that it implies (including, say, q). This is then empirically evaluated, and, if found to be false (Not-q), is used as the basis for concluding that p is false — that is, as the basis for rejecting the original hypothesis or theory. This is one of the methods that we suggested in Chapter 1 could be used for evaluating individual statements. Hence, *denying the consequent* makes explicit, in the form of an argument, the reasoning that is implicit in that procedure of evaluation.

In contrast to this pattern of argument, not all arguments fitting the following pattern are valid:

If p then q
$$\underline{q}$$
$\therefore p$

Invalid arguments that fit this pattern are said to commit the *fallacy of asserting the consequent*. To continue our example, although it might appear valid to argue that if all children learn language at approximately the same age, then the ability is largely innate, this is not so. Another example that makes this point might be:

> If the Freudian theory of dreams is correct, then men will have dreams with accompanying sexual excitation. Men do have such dreams. Therefore, the Freudian theory of dreams is correct.

Or, even more trivially,

> If all rats are white, then all the rats in this Skinner box will be white. All the rats in this box are white, so all rats are white.

Clearly, each of these arguments is invalid. Yet, arguments like these are sometimes passed off as valid under camouflage of complicated language.

Chain argument (hypothetical syllogism)

A generally reliable pattern of argument in which all the components are conditionals is the following:

> If p then q
> If q then r
> ∴ If p then r

Called chain argument (or hypothetical syllogism), arguments fitting this pattern can be used to establish conditional statements.

An unreliable pattern of argument sometimes mistakenly taken to be reliable is the following. Consider:

> If p and q then r
> Not-r
> ∴ Not-p

Although it resembles the pattern of denying the consequent, arguments fitting this pattern are not all valid; in general, all that can be relevantly concluded is that either it is not true that p, or it is not true that q. As we noted in the preceding chapter, if a number of statements (here p and q) imply a false statement, then it cannot be determined from this information alone which of the former is false. In the absence of any other information (for example, that q *is* true), it cannot be concluded that p is false. It is the whole set of antecedent statements which implies the consequent, not just one, as in denying the consequent.[4]

We have been looking at a number of simple argument patterns using letters, like 'p' and 'q' to stand for clauses of English in which one or more of the statements is a conditional. There are, of course, many other reliable patterns. A simple, frequently used one in theoretical reasoning is called denying a disjunct (also called disjunctive syllogism). A statement of the form 'p or q' is called a disjunction and the component clauses are called disjuncts. **Denying a disjunct** is the following reliable pattern

> p or q
> Not-p
> ∴ q

---

[4] A theory p about the behaviour of some system may be supplemented with some statement q describing the initial conditions of the system to deduce some testable consequence r about the state of the system. This could be expressed by a statement of the form 'If p and q then r'. When, say, experiment reveals Not-r is true, you should be wary of concluding that the theory is false. q may be false instead (or as well). Adding q as a premiss will permit deducing that Not-p.

Here is an argument that (with a little taming) fits this pattern:

> The subject's memory disorder is anterograde amnesia or the subject's memory disorder is retrograde amnesia. (But the present study established that) the subject's memory disorder is not anterograde amnesia.
> So the subject's memory disorder is retrograde amnesia.

DIAGRAM METHODS

So far we have concerned ourselves almost exclusively with patterns of clauses, but as our first example of a pattern of valid arguments shows:

> All Fs are Gs, and
> All Gs are Hs,
> So All Fs are Hs

there can be helpful patterns that do not depend upon the simple clause structures we have considered so far. This pattern picks out features inside clauses. We now introduce a simple technique for identifying reliable patterns like this one.

Here are four particularly useful elementary patterns of English sentences. Aristotle noticed patterns corresponding to these in Ancient Greek.

> All Fs are Gs
> No Fs are Gs
> Some Fs are Gs
> Some Fs are not Gs

Statements that can be expressed in these patterns are called **categorical statements**.

The letters 'F' and 'G' (we will use 'H' and 'I' as well) stand in positions where (count) nouns could naturally be placed — for example, 'Some farmers are not graziers' is a statement that fits the fourth pattern. Replacing 'F' with 'farmer' and 'G' with 'grazier' takes you from the pattern to the statement. Correspondingly, replacing the words in the statement by the letters takes you from the statement to the pattern. Words like 'farmer' and 'grazier' are called 'terms' and their important characteristic for our purposes is that they identify *kinds of things or things with a certain property*.

Statements of these four patterns can then be seen to tell us about whether or not there are things of certain more complex kinds, or equivalently, whether or not there are things with certain combinations of properties. Thus, statements of the form 'No Fs are Gs' tell us that nothing is both an F and a G. Statements of the form 'Some Fs are not

*G*s' tell us that there are things which are *F*s but not *G*s. A statement of the pattern 'All *F*s are *G*s' is taken to tell us that there is nothing which is both an *F* and not a *G*.

There is a simple graphical technique called **Venn diagrams** that exploits this way of interpreting categorical statements and gives us an easy pictorial way of checking for validity. A circle drawn on a plane separates it into two regions: inside the circle and outside the circle. Associate the inside of the circle with a certain property — say, *F*— and the outside with its complement, non-*F* (the property possessed by everything which does not have the property *F*). A pair of intersecting circles on a plane separates the plane into four undivided regions. Consider the diagram in which the left circle represents the property *F* and the right circle the property *G*. The region 1, which is the intersection of the *F* and the *G* circle, represents the property of being *F* and *G*. Region 2, being inside the G circle but outside the F circle, represents the property of being *G* and non-*F*, and region 4 outside both circles represents the property of being non-*F* and non-*G*.[5] (What property does Region 3 represent?)

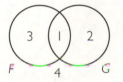

Now that we have regions associated with properties, we just adopt two simple conventions which enable us to represent the categorical statements (and others as well).

The first convention is to shade (or cross-hatch) an area on the diagram to represent the statement that there is nothing with the combination of properties corresponding to that area. The second convention is to put a cross or 'x' in an area if there is something with the properties corresponding to that area. Thus if we shaded the area 1 in the above diagram, it would represent the statement 'No *F*s are *G*s' because it says there is nothing with the property of being both *F* and *G*.

---

[5] The labels for these circles 'F' and 'G' are outside them (in area 4) It would have been more natural to have them inside their respective circles but each of the circles is subdivided into two areas. The labels would have had to straddle the internal boundaries, making them difficult to read.

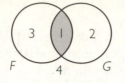

No Fs are Gs

If instead we put an 'x' in area 3 (inside the '*F*' circle but outside the '*G*' circle), that would represent the statement 'Some *Fs* are not *Gs*', since the cross in **3** says there is at least one thing which is *F* but not *G*.

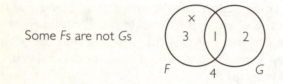

Some *Fs* are not *Gs*

The other categorical statements can be represented as follows:

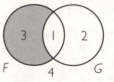

All *Fs* are *Gs*

That is, nothing is an *F* and non-*G* — the area shaded is inside the *F* circle but outside the *G* circle.

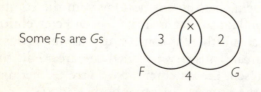

Some *Fs* are *Gs*

Putting an 'x' in area 1, the intersection of the two circles, says there is something with the property *F* and *G*.

If an area representing a property is subdivided, as in the above diagram, the circular area corresponding to the property *F* is subdivided into areas 3 and 1, then we put an 'x' in each sub-area and link them together with a line. So, linked crosses in areas 1 and 3 represents the statement 'Something is an *F*'. This is equivalent, after all, to 'Something is an *F* and a *G* or something is an *F* and a non-*G*'.

Notice that this diagrammatic technique can also be used very widely to represent *any* statements that can be expressed or paraphrased in sentences fitting the four patterns we have identified here. For example, the sentence 'Only adults are voters' does not fit any of these patterns but it can be expressed as 'All voters are adults' which does. Incidentally, don't confine yourself to labelling the circles with '*F*', '*G*' and '*H*'. To represent 'All voters are adults', it would be natural to use '*V*' and '*A*', so the pattern it fits can be written as 'All *V*s are *A*s' and the circles labelled accordingly.

You may have noticed we have already loosely used '*F*' and '*G*' as pattern holders not only for nouns but adjectives as well. For example, 'All geniuses are eccentric'[6] has a noun in the '*F*' position and an adjective in the '*G*' position. Letters like these can also be used as patterns for quite complex noun and adjectival phrases. For example, 'Some psychics exploit the superstitious' can be paraphrased as 'Some psychics are exploiters of the superstitious' and its pattern can be represented on a diagram with circles labelled '*P*' for 'psychics' and '*E*' for 'exploiters-of-the-superstitious'. As this example illustrates, the wider use of these logical methods depends on your ability to paraphrase sentences into sentences exemplifying the four basic patterns. This ability is related to the basic aspect of understanding a statement we mentioned in Chapter 1 — the ability to express a statement in your own words with the constraint that for these purposes your words are (mostly) restricted to the four basic patterns.

Many statements cannot be expressed in sentences fitting the patterns 'All *F*s are *G*s', 'No *F*s are *G*s', 'Some *F*s are *G*s' and 'Some *F*s are not *G*s'. The simple conditional statements discussed in the previous section are examples, as are statements fitting the pattern 'Most *A*s are *B*s'. 'Most subjects in the experiment are bilinguals' is not equivalent either to 'Some subjects in the experiment are bilinguals' or to 'All subjects in the experiment are bilinguals'. Nevertheless, the attempt to express a statement in one of these ways can often clarify its meaning. For example, when you see a statement of the form 'All *F*s are not *G*s', it can be instructive to ask whether what the author means can be expressed in the form 'No *F*s are *G*s' or 'Some *F*s are not *G*s' (or neither). When a statement can be expressed in one of these ways, we may be able to use simple diagrammatic methods to guide our judgments of the validity of arguments it occurs in.

---

[6] Notice that 'All geniuses are eccentric*s*' does not have exactly the same meaning as 'All geniuses are eccentric'.

The general principle, the **Venn diagram principle**, for using these diagrams to check the reliability of a pattern of argument is:

> Represent the premisses successively on a single Venn diagram and then check to see if either the conclusion is already represented or information is represented which implies it. If so, the pattern is a reliable pattern.

For example, the following pattern is reliable:

> There are *F*s.
> No *F*s are *G*s.
> So some *F*s are not *G*s.

The first premiss is represented by putting linked crosses in areas 1 and 3. The second premiss is represented by shading area 1. The result is a diagram with a cross in area 3 which represents the conclusion and so the pattern is reliable.[7]

There are *F*s

No *F*s are *G*s

Notice that the shading over the top of the linked cross in area 1 tells us that there is nothing with the property represented by that area (being both *F* and *G*). The upshot is that the cross in area 3 is not now linked to anything and is treated as standing alone — that is, as an unlinked cross in area 3.

Similarly,

> Some *F*s are *G*s
> So some *G*s are *F*s

is a reliable pattern. The premiss 'Some *F*s are *G*s' is represented by putting a cross in area 1 and this is the very area where a cross would be put to represent the conclusion 'Some *G*s are *F*s'.

---

[7] Despite the suggestion of plurality, we are taking statements of the form 'Some *F*s are *G*s' to be true if there is only one *F* that is *G*, and we take 'There are *F*s' to be true when only one thing is an *F*. We are also taking 'Some *F*s are *G*s' to be compatible with 'All *F*s are *G*s'.

The following pattern, however, is not reliable:

All *F*s are *G*s

So all *G*s are *F*s

Representing the premiss shades only area 3, but the conclusion requires area 2 shaded.[8]

By way of introduction, we have considered diagrams with just two circles representing the possible presence or absence of combinations of two properties. We now consider more interesting and useful cases with three terms represented by three intersecting circles. Look at the diagram below. As before, the area on the inside of circles represents the property associated with that circle — so that associated with the inside of the *H* circle is the property of being *H*.

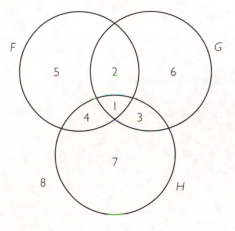

Notice that the H circle subdivides each of the four areas we have considered, leaving us with eight undivided sub-areas. Each of these sub-areas corresponds to combinations of the presence or absence of the three properties. We have numbered them starting with 1 in the middle and spiralling out to 8. Area 1, which is the only area inside all three circles, represents the property of being *F* and *G* and *H*; while area 8, being outside all the circles, represents the properties of being not-*F* and not-*G* and not-*H*. Area 2, for example, being inside the *F* and *G* circle but outside the *H* circle, represents the property of being *F* and *G* and non-*H*.

---

[8] Statements of the pattern 'All *F*s are *G*s' are sometimes taken to imply statements of the form 'Some *F*s are *G*s'. So far we have taken 'All *F*s are *G*s' to be equivalent to 'There is nothing which is both *F* and non-*G*' which is (trivially) true simply if there is nothing which is *F*. If in the context of a particular argument it seems clear to you that a statement of the form 'All *F*s are *G*s' would be false if there were no *F*s, then it should be represented by shading area 2 *and* putting a cross in area 1.

To represent the categorical statements, we use the same principles as above for diagrams with only two circles. Continue to think of areas being inside and outside circles. Don't be distracted by the fact that now, with three circles, these areas are subdivided. For example, to represent 'Some *F*s are *G*s' in the following diagram, we put an 'x' in the area common to both *F* and *G*. Since it is now subdivided, we do this by putting linked crosses or 'x's into its sub-areas: areas 1 and 2.

Linked crosses or 'x's in areas 5 and 2 ,which comprise the area inside the *F* circle but outside the *H* circle, will represent 'Some *F*s are not *H*s'.

The following diagram represents 'All *G*s are *H*s' using darker shading. The portion of the *G* circle outside the *H* circle is shaded — areas 2 and 6. Lighter shading represents 'All *F*s are *G*s' by shading the area inside the *F* circle, but outside the *G* circle (that is, areas 4 and 5) the resulting diagram has areas 5 and 2 shaded.

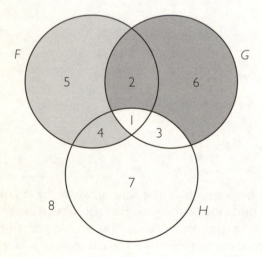

These areas make up the area inside the *F* circle but outside the *H* circle. Shading of this area represents the statement 'All *F*s are *H*s' and by the Venn diagram principle we have shown that the pattern

All *F*s are *G*s
All *G*s are *H*s
So All *F*s are *H*s

is reliable.

Two more examples will suffice to illustrate the technique. First an example in which we use this method to show a pattern to be unreliable.

Consider the pattern

No *F*s are *G*s.
No *G*s are *H*s.
So no *F*s are *H*s.

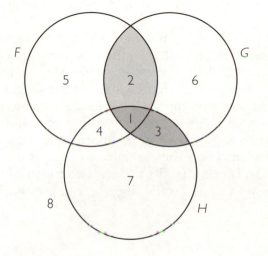

As you can see after representing the premisses, areas 1, 2 and 3 are shaded. (Area 1 is doubly shaded.) But to represent the conclusion, we need both 1 and 4 shaded. But 4 is unshaded, so it fails our Venn diagram principle. So, it is an unreliable pattern — not every argument fitting the pattern is valid.

We finish this section by applying the diagrammatic method to the argument:

> No fluent English speakers are younger than six months old.
> Some of the subjects in the experiment are fluent English speakers.
> So some subjects in the experiment are not younger than six months old.

The following pattern fits this:

No *F*s are *Y*s.

Some *S*s are *F*s.

So some *S*s are not *Y*s.

With *F* = <u>f</u>luent English speaker

Y = (person) <u>y</u>ounger than six months old

S = <u>s</u>ubject in the experiment

Represent the first premiss on the diagram by shading the area common to the *F* and *Y* circle — nothing is both *F* and *Y*. So we have areas 1 and 2 shaded.

To represent the second premiss, we put a cross in the area common to the *F* circle and the *S* circle — that is, the area consisting of areas 1 and 3. But 1 is already shaded, so the cross can only go in area 4. At this stage the premisses have been represented on the diagram. Now, representing the conclusion requires a cross inside the *S* circle but outside the *Y* circle — that is, in the area consisting of 4 and 7. Since there is a cross in 4, there is a cross in the more inclusive area and the conclusion is represented on the diagram, so the pattern is reliable. This reliable pattern is one that fits the sentences expressing our argument, so we know there is a valid argument expressed by these sentences.

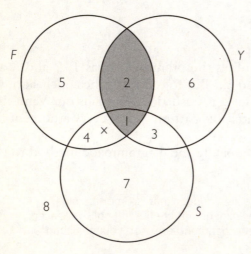

We have just seen an easy graphical technique for determining the reliability of many patterns in language. There is another way of taking advantage of the link between implication and patterns in language. In general, if you can find an obviously invalid argument that has the same form as one that you wish to criticise, then that suffices to show the pattern is unreliable. You may hear someone reply to another's argument by saying, 'You might just as well argue that ...' and give an argument with a similar pattern to the first, but with clearly true premises and a clearly false conclusion. To adapt an example from Lewis Carroll, if the first person argues,

> 'I mean what I say, therefore I say what I mean',

a second person may reply,

> 'You might as well argue: "I see what I eat, therefore I eat what I see."'

Notice that although this shows that the pattern is unreliable it does not prove that the argument is invalid. What the invalid analogous argument shows is that not all arguments fitting that pattern are valid. It does not show something different — namely, that all arguments fitting that pattern are invalid. However, even though the 'You might as well argue ...' method does not prove invalidity, it can serve to usefully challenge an arguer to show how, if at all, their argument differs from an analogous invalid one.[9]

Here is a pattern that some people seem to rely on:

Most *A*s are *B*s.
Most *B*s are *C*s.
So most *A*s are *C*s.

But this pattern can be shown to be unreliable by giving an invalid argument that fits it. To someone who has produced an argument fitting this pattern, the reply could be: you may as well argue that the following is valid:

Most Sydney neonates are Australians.
Most Australians are literate.
So most Sydney neonates are literate.

---

[9] For a detailed discussion of this, see Staines (1996).

If you are dealing with an argument that fits none of the reliable patterns we have considered in this section (including those assessable using diagram methods), this method may be helpful, even if it provides no guarantees.

Here is one last method that may help in assessing the validity of an argument. We could call it the 'method of mathematicians' because we see it most clearly used in mathematics but it is widely applicable elsewhere. One stereotype of mathematical reasoning is that it consists of long chains of argument — what we have called 'extended arguments' above — that start with some premisses (axioms) and take you step by step to a conclusion. (Frequently, in mathematics, this will be a theorem.) At first you cannot see how a unitary argument from those premisses to that conclusion is valid (that is, you cannot see how the conclusion follows), but after you see an extended argument leading to that conclusion with several intermediate conclusions along the way, you can see that the argument is valid. Here is an entertaining non-mathematical example:

> Everyone is afraid of Dracula.
> Dracula is afraid only of me.
> So I am Dracula.

At first sight you probably cannot see that the argument is valid. (Can you?) But turn this unitary argument into the following extended argument and its validity becomes much more obvious.

Since everyone is afraid of Dracula, it follows that Dracula is afraid of Dracula. But Dracula is afraid only of me. So I am Dracula. In diagrammatic form:

The attractive feature of this method is that in general it is easier to see that the individual steps (that is, the sub-arguments) are valid. If each step in the extended argument is valid and uses only the initial premisses and intermediate conclusions in the sub-arguments along the way, then the initial unitary argument is valid as well.

---

[10] You may feel cheated a little by this first step because you took its premiss to mean everyone *else* is afraid of Dracula. But it does say *everyone* is afraid of Dracula. The example comes from Richard Cartwright via Raymond Smullyan, Simon and Schuster, 1978, p 212).

The practical advice this turns into is a recommendation: where you cannot tell that a conclusion follows, look for intermediate conclusions that do follow and see if these can lead in a sequence of valid steps to the conclusion. There is no guarantee you will succeed. But the process can be instructive in its own right. Along the way, you may become aware of some unexpected implications or consequences of the position expressed by the premisses and thus reach a deeper understanding of it.

EVALUATION AND UNDERSTANDING

A number of aspects of the evaluation of arguments go beyond the questions of the truth of premisses and the validity of the argument. For example, there are some arguments that are unsatisfactory even though they have true premisses and are valid. Such an argument may be defective because it fails to show how to evaluate its conclusion — perhaps because the conclusion is little more than a *restatement* of the premiss(es) of the 'argument'. Hence, in evaluating the components of the argument, the same questions are raised by the premisses as by the conclusion. To take a blatant example, 'Monday follows Sunday, so Monday follows Sunday' is clearly valid, although uninformatively 'circular'. The premiss and conclusion are identical and, although the argument is valid, it gives no guidance in evaluating its conclusion. Although sound, it is unhelpful — someone in need of help in evaluating the conclusion is equally ignorant when confronted by the premiss. In this case, the argument assumes exactly what it seeks to prove. Although not as blatant as our illustrative case, examples of these deficient arguments are quite common. We will further examine arguments like this from the psychological literature when we consider circular explanation in the next chapter.

It is important to distinguish between evaluating a person's argument and judging their motives for proposing it. Psychologists can be particularly prone to attributing motives to their opponents, rather than assessing the soundness of their arguments. But whether someone's argument is due to their 'peculiar' childhood, 'distorted' beliefs, class background or empty stomach is irrelevant to the validity of what they write or say. It is the argument, not the arguer, that must be evaluated.

Finally, it is worth mentioning the relation between *evaluating* and *understanding* an argument. As we argued with respect to statements in Chapter 1, if what someone says appears patently false, then we should re-examine our interpretation of it. Similarly, in the case of arguments, we may make premature judgments unless we are certain which components are premisses and which conclusions (or both), and whether a particular argument is intended to be deductive at all. Moreover, authors frequently omit statements they think are particularly obvious. Consequently, if an otherwise reasonable author appears to argue in an invalid manner, this might best be taken as an indication that something (that is, some statement) is being taken for granted, without stating it. They may be arguing enthymemically. Here the problem becomes one of explicating and evaluating the missing premisses. Similarly, if we find that an argument is obviously invalid, it may be that we are expecting more from it than was intended. In particular, we may have mistakenly applied the standards of a deductive argument (validity) to an inductive argument.

SUMMARY

The key idea linking this chapter on argument to the previous one on statements is that arguments can serve to show us how to evaluate statements. As with statements, evaluating arguments presupposes understanding them and this goes beyond understanding their component statements. Arguments consist of premisses and conclusions. We distinguished unitary or simple arguments from extended arguments which have intermediate conclusions, and hence more than one step, and we looked at some techniques for extracting and making clear what someone's argument is.

We distinguished two kinds of unitary arguments — deductive arguments that aim to have their premisses imply their conclusions, and inductive or non-demonstrative arguments where the premisses are intended to support the conclusion but in a weaker way than by logical implication.

In the evaluation of deductive arguments, two questions were central: are the component statements true? and do the premisses imply the conclusion?

If the answer to the second question is 'yes' we say the argument is *valid*, and if the answer to both is 'yes' the argument is *sound*.

Determining that an argument is valid can be quite difficult: you need to show that it is impossible for the premisses to be true while the conclusion is false — so we looked at a number of reliable patterns in language which can make the task easier. If you can express the argument in language that exemplifies these patterns, then the argument will be valid. We also introduced a simple and memorable technique — the method of Venn diagrams — for checking the reliability of many patterns of language, the 'you might as well argue' method which shows that a pattern is unreliable, and the 'method of mathematicians' for showing that an argument is valid.

KEYWORDS

ARGUMENT • PREMISS • CONCLUSION • UNITARY ARGUMENT • INTERMEDIATE CONCLUSION • EXTENDED ARGUMENT • ENTHYMEME • DEDUCTIVE ARGUMENT • INDUCTIVE ARGUMENT • VALIDITY • SOUNDNESS • CONDITIONAL STATEMENT • ANTECEDENT • CONSEQUENT • RELIABLE PATTERN • ASSERTING THE ANTECEDENT • DENYING THE CONSEQUENT • CHAIN ARGUMENT • DENYING A DISJUNCT • CATEGORICAL STATEMENTS • VENN DIAGRAM • VENN DIAGRAM PRINCIPLE

EXERCISES

1   Identify premisses, intermediate conclusions and conclusions in the following arguments, and lay out their structure in diagram

form. Where possible, identify the argument steps as inductive or deductive.

a   The pattern of problem-solving found in this study reflected the knowledge the subjects had from their architecture classes regarding how to solve this kind of problem. So, although the collaboration looks very situated, it is, in reality, shaped and guided by the collaborators' individual knowledge of the task. (Vera et al 1997, p 1079)

b   Mean IQ test scores have been rising steadily, all around the world at an average of about 3 points per decade (the 'Flynn Effect'). A person who scores 100 on an IQ test today would have scored about 115 on the tests that were current 50 years ago. One might think that such a rise would have been obvious, but the fact that most intelligence tests are periodically 're-normed' (to keep the mean at 100) has made it hard to see. The steady rise of IQ scores around the world is a truly remarkable demonstration of environmental influence on mental process. More complex environments may just produce more complex minds. (Adapted from Neisser 1997, pp 254–56)

c   Results from the first experiment show greater activation in ventro-medial frontal areas in the *self* relative to *other* condition. Results from the second experiment show greater activation in dorsolateral prefrontal areas for *rational judgment* relative to *self* or *other* conditions and greater activation in ventro-medial frontal areas in *self* and *other* condition relative to the *rational judgment* condition. The different activations may reflect either that the information retrieved from memory in order to make a judgment is different for the three kinds of judgments, or the mechanism for making judgments is different. (Stone et al 1997, p 1061) The work of Smith (Smith et al 1996) suggests it is not the former, so there is evidence that the mechanism for making judgments is different.

d   People do not think and behave in the same way when in social groups as they would as isolated individuals. So the properties of social situations cannot derive solely from the thoughts and actions of single individuals. (Papineau 1978, p 8)

e   Classical and operant conditioning both produce an appropriate expectation in a learner, but they differ in what the learner discovers about control. In classical conditioning a subject learns an association between two kinds of events, neither of which are interventions or actions of the learner.

In operant conditioning, a subject learns an association between two kinds of events, one of which is an action of the learner. In classical conditioning, unless there is other relevant knowledge, all that can be learned is an association, not a causal relation, because the causal process responsible for the association is underdetermined by the association itself. Pavlov's dogs could not know whether the bell ringing caused dinner, or dinner the bell ringing, or something else caused both. Neither could we in circumstances comparably bereft of information. In contrast, in most cases the proposition describing what is learned in operant conditioning is that an action of a certain sort *causes* an event of a certain kind, and the learner acquires the capacity to control or at least to influence the occurrence of the relevant events. (Glymour 1998b, p 44)

2   Use the method of Venn diagrams to check the validity of the following arguments which we have adapted from two examples earlier in this chapter. When you are drawing the diagrams, label the circles with suitably mnemonic letters.

a   All humans are primates.

Some humans are monogamous.

So some primates are monogamous.

b   All instinctual behaviours are rigidly stereotyped unmodifiable behaviours.

No human behaviours are rigidly stereotyped unmodifiable behaviours.

So no human behaviours are instinctual behaviours.

3   The following is an excerpt from a reply by its authors to a review of Spirtes, Glymour and Scheines, *Causation, Prediction and Search* (1993):

Humphrey and Freedman denounce us for having the temerity to criticise both statisticians and epidemiologists in the debate over smoking. (pp 118–19) They offer not a single substantive point on which they disagree with our account. They denounce us for saying we appear not to believe the epidemiological evidence that smoking causes lung cancer. (p 118) However, we never said the *evidence* did not support the conclusion: we said the *arguments* offered did not support the conclusion. (Spirtes et al 1997, p 566)

Clarify the nature of their distinction between evidence and argument.

chapter 3

Explanation

I don't understand you, Sir.
I have found you an argument. I am not obliged to find you an
understanding.

Samuel Johnson

INTRODUCTION

Psychology is sometimes defined as the *science* of behaviour — a definition which obscures as much as it reveals. In particular, it does not specify what a 'science' is — especially in relation to complex human behaviour. However, it is conventionally assumed that psychology attempts to *explain* why animals (including or especially, humans) behave as they do, and hence ideally allows the prediction of the conditions under which specific behaviour will occur. Although there are some who would argue that human behaviour is inherently inexplicable, and that psychology cannot, therefore, be a genuine science at all, it is clear that to understand complex, empirically significant arguments in psychology, some analysis of 'explanation' and 'prediction' is essential.

We take the view that science is continuous with 'common sense'. The activities of the scientist are extensions of, not essentially different from, the activities of the sensible layperson, although they may be carried out with more care and thoroughness. Reasoning, we noticed in the previous chapter, is not the exclusive domain of the scientist. Argument, the public expression of reasoning, is similarly not peculiar to science. Indeed, people present, identify and evaluate arguments well enough for everyday purposes without any special study. For scientific purposes, however, some explicit attention to the nature and evaluation of scientific arguments has proved valuable.

The case is similar with respect to explanation. Each of us is both familiar with, and readily able to provide, explanations for a wide variety of everyday matters. Yet, despite this everyday familiarity and capacity it is necessary, for the purposes of scientific or disciplined thought, to become better acquainted with the nature of explanation and, in particular, with criteria for distinguishing better explanations from worse ones.

In the preceding chapters we discussed what is involved in understanding and evaluating statements and arguments. As we shall see, explanation has connections with each of these four concepts. Explanations can be of very different kinds. In this chapter we discuss two central general kinds of scientific explanation — *causal explanations* and *law-based explanations*. Our aim in this chapter is to give a general view of explanation. Later chapters look at some special kinds.

After presenting the law-based and causal view of explanation, we consider the question of how explanations can be assessed. Finally, we look at an important connection between explanation and inductive reasoning. But first we outline some general features of explanations.

Let us begin by locating some of the general features of **explanations**. One can ask for an explanation by asking, 'Why?' For example, the questions 'Why does forgetting occur more rapidly at first?', 'Why is there a bigger standard deviation in IQ in the male population than in the female population?', 'Why do humans dream during sleep?', 'Why did John fail his exams?', 'Why did he try to run away from home?', and so on, all ask for explanations as answers. Another way of requesting an explanation is to ask for the cause of a particular occurrence or phenomenon. Thus, 'What is the cause of schizophrenia?' also asks for an explanation. However not all 'why' questions ask for an explanation as an answer. Some such questions, in context, express doubt about the truth of a statement and ask for reasons for believing it to be true. They ask not for explanations but for justifications. In contrast, someone using a 'why' question to ask for an explanation typically accepts the truth of the statement describing the event or state of affairs they want explained and expresses puzzlement as to why it is true.

Indeed, explanations are generally required only of statements that have *already* been evaluated as true. For if they are false, there is nothing to explain (although sometimes we are not sure whether a statement is to be judged true or false and we may ask how it *would be* explained if it were true). Thus a request to explain why males are brighter than females could be completely answered by saying 'They're not'. That is to say, there is nothing to explain. Frequently, the statement to be explained has been judged true as a result of some observation, and the explanation offered shows how the event it describes could have been expected (or could have been predicted). Although the explanation is not needed to show how to evaluate what it explains, for the statement is already held to be true, the explanation does serve to integrate what has happened into the belief structure of the (otherwise) puzzled person by showing how it could have been evaluated. It increases the coherence of their beliefs. Explanations help to systematise a body of knowledge.

Requests for explanations can be answered in a number of quite different ways. Some questions, like the one above about dreams, can be answered by showing what (if any) *function* dreaming serves. Others, like the one asking for an explanation of John's running away from home can be answered by citing his motive or the purpose he had in running away — perhaps to hurt his parents. We shall look at aspects of these and other types of explanation in Chapter 7. In this chapter we shall restrict our discussion to the two broad patterns of explanation mentioned above.

Requests for explanations can be put in the standard form: 'Why is it the case that *p*?' — where '*p*' can be replaced by a declarative sentence characterising some event, phenomenon or state of affairs. Thus, our first illustrative question can be put into this form — 'Why is it the case that forgetting occurs more rapidly at first?' It is worth noting something that is not apparent when explanation-requests are written down rather than spoken: explanation-requests often have a contrastive force, which is signalled by the way a particular word or phrase is stressed in the request. Thus, if the word 'more' is stressed in the above request, then we are being asked to explain specifically why forgetting occurs *more*, rather than *less* rapidly, at first. If the word 'first' is stressed, then we are being asked to explain specifically why it occurs more rapidly at *first* rather than later. Many explanation-requests do not ask simply why a particular state of affairs is the case: they ask more specifically why some particular aspect of it is 'this way' rather than 'that way'.

In everyday usage, the word 'explanation' is ambiguous. Sometimes it is used to refer to sentences, sometimes to statements, and sometimes to the events, phenomena or states of affairs they describe. Sometimes it is used to refer only to the part that does the explaining; at other times, it is used to refer to the composite of explainer and explained — what does the explaining, together with what it purports to explain.

In this chapter we will, in most cases, leave the first three different meanings for the context to determine. In particular contexts it will be easy enough to tell whether we are referring to sentences, statements or states of affairs. However, it is worth introducing some special terminology to help with the second ambiguity. Since we are concerned in this chapter with the structure of explanation, we will be constantly referring to the different parts of an explanation — the part that does the explaining and the part that is to be explained. To save a lot of words, we call the first part the *explanans*. The second part — what is to be explained — we call the *explanandum*. These words, taken from Latin, are widely used with this meaning in the literature on explanation. The nearest single English word for the explanans is 'explainer', but this is usually used to refer to the person who does the explaining. Perhaps the closest in meaning to explanandum is 'explained', but this is more typically used to describe the process rather than to describe what is explained. (A better word would be 'explainee'.) Since we will be using them constantly in the rest of this chapter, it is worth checking that you know what each means. The **explanans** is the part that does the explaining (or purports to); the **explanandum** is the part that is (purportedly) explained. We shall reserve the ambiguous word 'explanation' for the composite consisting of explanans and explanandum.

CAUSAL AND LAW-BASED EXPLANATIONS

In this section we consider what some have taken to be the central form of scientific explanation. After a brief discussion of the nature of laws we describe, first, law-based explanations and, second, causal explanations. The first view relates explanations more to argument and evaluation, while the second relates them more to statements and understanding. Accordingly, we shall call the first the *Argument Model* of explanation, and the second, the *Statement Model*. The Argument Model, as we have termed it, has been the most influential and widely accepted view of the nature of explanation and is associated with the work of the eminent philosopher Carl Hempel (1965, 1966). The Statement Model is sometimes known as the causal model (Lipton 1991, p 32) and elaborates the work of David Lewis (1986).

LAWS

When someone studies high-school physics they often memorise a number of 'laws' (Newton's laws, Charles' laws, Boyle's laws, and so on). These are universal, apparently immutable principles that subsume widely diverse physical phenomena in a most parsimonious manner. It is therefore tempting to expect psychology (a science) to revolve around similar universal principles. It may come as a surprise to the student to discover that (a) psychology does not appear to include 'laws' of such general character, and (b) physical laws are themselves subject to much controversy. One of the controversies, which we will only mention in passing, is over whether or not laws are merely statements. The usual view is that they are not only statements, but true statements correctly describing regularities in the universe. This is the position we shall adopt here. One of the opposing views is that laws, particularly theoretical laws, are not statements at all, but solely devices or instruments for ordering and organising experience. Their value is as mere instruments, making internally coherent a set of otherwise unrelated phenomena. This alternative 'instrumentalist' position does not hold that laws are true (just more or less useful).

As the divergence of the views above indicates, there is considerable difference of opinion as to the nature of laws. Since our concern here is with the place of laws in explanation, in this section we focus only on two aspects of a widely agreed-upon property that laws must have — namely, generality.

Laws are true synthetic (Chapter 1) general statements, but not every true synthetic general statement is a law. For instance, general statements like 'All the animals in the study show retardation in discrimination learning ability' and 'The cases of schizophrenia studied by Laing all come from repressive isolated families' are not law-like. Although they are generalisations, they are insufficiently general. They just summarise what could be expressed in a finite number of specific statements. Thus, 'Case 1 studied by Laing came from a repressive isolated family', 'Case 2 studied by Laing came from a repressive isolated family', and so on.

There is a further property associated with generality which is taken to be characteristic of laws. A generalisation of the form 'All *A* are *B*' is a law only if it implies or supports the truth of certain statements of the form 'If x were an *A*, x would be a *B*'. This later statement is called a counterfactual conditional and says that whether or not anything is in fact an *A*, if it were an *A*, it would be a *B*. Put generally, the property required of a law is that it imply or support the truth of the corresponding counterfactual conditionals. That the generalisations in the preceding paragraph fail this condition can be illustrated as follows: the generalisation 'The cases of schizophrenia studied by Laing all come from repressive isolated families' does not imply or support the truth of the claim that if Smith were a case of schizophrenia studied by Laing, he would have come from a repressive, isolated family. Loosely put, laws have to be so general that they apply not only to things with a certain property but to things lacking it: of things lacking the property *A*, they say that, *had they been A,* they would have been *B*. A law does not simply say that all *actual A*s are *B*s; it says that *any A* would be a *B*.

The great generality of law statements makes it difficult to establish their truth. Consequently, it is often difficult to tell if a statement that resembles a law in other ways really is a law, for one of the conditions for a statement to be a law is that it be true. Such candidates for law 'status' are called naturally enough, **law-like statements** — a term we shall use later in this chapter.

THE ARGUMENT MODEL OF EXPLANATION

The nature and logic of scientific explanation is the subject of an extensive philosophical literature, so no pretence is made of considering all the alternatives or of covering the more technical details in this elementary discussion. However, the concept of explanation is central to nearly every theoretical controversy in psychology and requires some detailed analysis.

We follow Hempel (1966), with whom this model is most closely associated, in distinguishing two major classes of explanation:

- *deductive-nomological* (D-N); and
- *probabilistic* or *inductive-statistical* (I-S).

As the names suggest, these are closely related to deductive and inductive argument forms, respectively. Arguments, we saw in Chapter 2, are a means of showing how statements can be evaluated, and, as we mentioned above, the argument model is linked to evaluation. Indeed, Hempel takes, as the main requirement that scientific explanations must meet, the condition that 'the explanatory information adduced affords good grounds for believing that the phenomenon to be explained did, or does indeed occur' (1966, p 48). If we link the explanatory information (explanans statement) with the premises of an argument, and link the statement describing the phenomenon to be explained (that is, the explanandum statement) with the conclusion, then the above condition is the condition that the premises should support the conclusion. This is the link the argument model makes between explanation and argument.

In our view, although explanations are not arguments as we have defined them, they are sufficiently like arguments for the argument model to throw useful light on them. Like arguments, explanations show how a statement could be evaluated, but unlike arguments they are not typically offered with the main intention of supporting the statement which they show how to evaluate. To the extent that they are like arguments in showing how their conclusions (analogously — explananda) can be evaluated, they are only like a very restricted class of arguments. It is the special restrictions that throw most light on the nature of explanation. To these we now turn.

DEDUCTIVE-NOMOLOGICAL EXPLANATION

The name of this model of explanation, 'deductive-nomological', is a helpful description of its main features. It represents an explanation as a special kind of *deductive* argument with the explanandum as the conclusion and with premises (explanans) which must include at least one law (for which the Greek word is *nomos*, hence the English adjective, *nomological*).

Scientific explanation has generally been analysed as a process of subsuming particular 'facts' under general 'laws' of nature. However, sometimes one attempts to explain, not only particular 'facts', but also other generalisations or laws, or the general properties of certain classes of objects. So the D-N (deductive-nomological) model covers cases where some deduction from a more general law-like generalisation is present (that is, a generalisation of broader scope or range of application than the phenomena or regularity being explained). Consequently, D-N explanation might be briefly characterised as 'deduction' from a 'law', or 'subsumption under a law'.

For example, we might explain why humans suckle their young by stating that this practice is common to all mammals, adding if need be that human beings are mammals. If the request was not to find out what *causes* humans to suckle their young, this form of explanation might be quite adequate. Of course, it might be asked in turn why mammals suckle their young, but that is a different question that does not effectively reduce the explanatory adequacy of the former account. An explanation can be evaluated only in terms of the phenomenon being explained; there is no universal, 'all-purpose' explanation, only explanations of particular phenomena or particular generalisations. This point is sometimes overlooked by people who persistently ask 'why', whenever a putative explanation is proposed (for example, 'Why do people eat?' — 'Because they want to survive'; 'Why do people want to survive?', and so on). There can be no answer to such questions which may not itself lead to other questions. For that reason, explanations seek only to provide information about the phenomenon being explained, and insofar as they achieve this aim, can be regarded as adequate.

Hempel (1966, p 61) outlines the D-N model thus:

> The explanations ... may be conceived, then, as deductive arguments whose conclusion is the explanandum sentence, E, and whose premise set the explanans, consists of general laws, $L1$, $L2$, ... Lr and other statements, $C1$, $C2$, ... Ck, which make assertions about particular facts. The form of such arguments ... can be represented by the following scheme:

$$L1, L2, ... Lr \qquad \text{Explanans sentences}$$
$$\underline{Cl, C2 ... Ck}$$
$$E \qquad \text{Explanandum sentences}$$

The D-N model is sometimes called the Covering Law approach, while L^1, L^2 ... L^r are often called 'covering laws'. C^1, C^2, ... C^k would include all relevant antecedent conditions (called initial conditions) — particular conditions relevant to the possible application of the covering law (such factors as the species of animal referred to, relevant experimental conditions, and so on). To illustrate this pattern, the following explanation:

> Each member of an identical twin pair has eyes and hair which are the same colours as those of his co-twin. This is because eye and hair colour are genetically determined (develop from the same genetic material).

could be schematically represented thus:

L^1: Eye and hair colour are genetically determined in humans.

L^2: Each member of an identical twin pair develops from genetic material that is the same as that of his or her co-twin.

C^1 C^k: Although not included in the original, essentially incomplete explanation, antecedent conditions which might be assumed could include: no administration of artificial colouring agents to the hair or eyes; intra-uterine environments constant across twins within pairs, and so on.

E: Each member of an identical twin pair has eyes and hair that are the same colour as those of his co-twin.

This type of explanation occurs in the biological and behavioural sciences (although seldom would details be made as explicit as in this example). We might say that an event or state of affairs, and so on, is explained on this approach (involving laws in a particular way and using the implication relation as discussed in Chapter 1) if we are in a position to evaluate as true the statement describing it.

The parallel drawn between deductive arguments and explanations by the D-N model of explanation can guide the evaluation of explanations. On this model, the criteria we discussed in Chapter 2 for evaluating deductive arguments can be applied in assessing the worth of explanations. For deductive arguments, two evaluative questions were raised:

1 Do the premisses imply the conclusion?
2 Are the premisses true?

In this model, these become:

1 Does the explanans imply the explanandum?
2 Is the explanans true?

If the explanans does not imply the explanandum, then the explanation is unsatisfactory, and if the explanans is not true the explanation is unsatisfactory. In the next section of this chapter, we will look in more detail at ways of assessing the worth of explanations.

INDUCTIVE-STATISTICAL EXPLANATION

Not all generalisations are appropriate to deductive explanation, and consequently it must also be acknowledged that by no means all explanation is deductive in the strict sense outlined in the previous section. As anyone who has studied psychology might have quickly noticed, many of the arguments which assert a relationship (for example, a causal one) between psychological phenomena are based on *probabilistic statements*, not universal generalisations. The certainty that appears to characterise laws in the physical sciences often seems lacking in the behavioural and social sciences. Most frequently, particular events in these sciences are explained by means of *probabilistic* or *statistical* generalisations which, for example, might assert that the likelihood of an event is high, given some other occurrence. Inductive-statistical (I-S) explanation, as the name suggests, represents explanations as *inductive* arguments with a statistical law among the premises.

Hempel (1966) schematises such inductive explanations in a similar way to D-N explanations. For instance (p 59):

> The probability for persons exposed to the measles to catch the disease is high.
> Jim was exposed to measles.   (makes highly probable)
> Jim caught the measles.

> A general scheme that this exemplifies is:
> The probability of an event of kind A also being of kind **B** is high.
> This is an event of kind **A**.   (makes highly probable)
> This is an event of kind **B**.

Such a scheme suggests the similarity with inductive arguments. In contrast to deductive arguments, the conclusion is not literally *implied* by the premisses; although highly likely, in relation to them it does not follow from the premisses. Just as inductive arguments do not guarantee the truth of their conclusions, so this type of explanation does not show why the explanandum phenomenon or event *must* have occurred.

In the light of this, some people argue that such potential explanations are not really explanatory. Yet, it would seem difficult to deny that the argument is explanatory, because it brings forward 'good grounds for believing that the phenomenon to be explained did or does indeed occur' (Hempel's main requirement for a scientific explanation — see earlier). In line with this, one of Hempel's specific requirements for inductive-statistical explanations is that, in relation to the explanans (premisses), the explanandum should be highly probable.

One unsatisfactory feature of inductive explanations not shared by D-N explanation is that even though the statements in the explanans may be true, further information may undercut their explanatory force. Thus, in the measles example, if it is discovered that when Jim was exposed to the measles he had just recovered from the disease, the original explanation might not be regarded as adequate. In colloquial language, the following conversation might reflect the shifting confidence in inductive explanations:

A: Why did Jim catch the measles?

B: He was recently exposed to them.

A: But he has only just recovered from measles himself.

B: Well sometimes they can be caught twice in quick succession. This must have been one of those times.

In his second contribution to the conversation, *A* introduces information in the light of which it is highly unlikely that Jim would catch measles even if he has been recently exposed to them — information which undercuts the explanatory force of *B*'s explanation.

In a growing discipline like psychology, it is not unusual to find preliminary I-S explanations undercut in this manner by new information. There is no sure way of avoiding this, but it is important to be aware of the possibility, and to try and anticipate information that may have this effect.

In conclusion, it is worth stressing another difference between the D-N model and the I-S model. The D-N model can be used to explain both specific phenomena and general states of affairs (for example, those described by laws). In contrast, the I-S model is only intended to apply to specific events or phenomena. Consequently, explaining in turn the statistical generalisations that are invoked in I-S explanations (for example, 'There is a high probability of persons exposed to measles catching the disease') is often done in the deductive fashion of the D-N model, from more general laws.

THE STATEMENT MODEL OF EXPLANATION

In our introductory remarks for this chapter, we distinguished two types of 'why-questions': those requesting an explanation, and those requesting a justification. We noted that it was important to separate the two. Yet Hempel's main requirement for a scientific explanation was that the explanans should justify ('give good grounds for believing') the explanandum phenomenon. A major criticism that proponents of the statement model bring against the argument model is that it links explanation too closely to justification, for an argument, as we have noted, is a way of justifying one's evaluation that a statement is true. This criticism is particularly directed at the I-S model of explanation. Put in our terms, these critics hold that explanation has more to do with understanding than evaluation. This is not the only criticism. Another is that the argument model pays too little attention to the requirement that the explanans be *causally relevant* to the explanandum. We shall look at other requirements below.

CAUSAL EXPLANATION

The importance of *causation* for explanation is easy to illustrate with a simple example that shows a weakness of the D-N model. There is a law-like relation holding between the height of a tower, the angle of the sun and the length of its shadow cast on a level surface. Conforming to the D-N model we are happy to explain why the shadow is the length it is by deducing its length from the law, the height of the tower, and the angle of the sun. But equally, we can deduce the angle of the sun from the law and the height of the tower and the length of the shadow. Yet we would be reluctant to claim that this explained why the sun was at a certain angle. (It would *justify* but *not explain* the fact that the sun was at that angle.) The difference in these two cases seems clearly to be one of causation. In the former case, the height of the tower and the angle of the sun *cause* the shadow to be of a certain length and thereby explain its length. In the latter case, the suggestion is that there is no adequate explanation of the angle of the sun because the length of the shadow and the height of the tower are *not causally relevant* to it.

According to the causal view, to explain an event is precisely to provide some information about its causal history (Lewis 1986, p 217). In our terminology, an explanans is a statement (or collection or statements) *providing causally relevant information*. Where what is being explained is not an event but a causal regularity, the explanans will give information about the mechanism linking cause and effect.

The key notion here is causation, so we shall have more to say about it later (Chapter 5). An immediate reaction now is that this approach does not sufficiently constrain what information is explanatory — even though it requires it to be causally relevant. As Lipton (1991, p 34) observes: '... causal histories are long and wide, and most causal information does not provide a good explanation. The big bang is a part of the causal history of every event, but explains only a few.'

One source of constraints on the information required about the causal history comes from **contrastive explanations**. We often explain not merely why P happened, but why P *rather than* Q occurred. For such contrastive explanations — to explain why P rather than Q— 'we must cite a causal difference between P and not-Q, consisting of a cause of P and the absence of a corresponding event in the case of not-Q' (Lipton 1991, p 43). If we want to explain Lewis's visit to Stanford University, it may be sufficient to provide the information that he received an invitation. But this will not do as an explanation of his visit to Stanford rather than Oxford if he has received invitations to both.

One difference between this approach to explanation and the I-S model is that it does not require the explanans to make the explanandum highly probable. It is in this sort of case that the link between explanation and evaluation (and hence prediction) is most clearly broken by this model. It allows an explanans to consist of causal information in the light of which the explanandum may be very unlikely. This model also uses a number of statistical conditions as a guide to which of the statistical relevance relations are causal. But we will not pursue the details here — suffice to say that, as in the I-S model, care must be taken to reduce the chance that omitted information might be relevant and so change the probability of the explanandum in relation to the explanans.

EVALUATING EXPLANATIONS

In the previous two sections we discussed three models of explanation — two law-based argument models and one causal statement model.

Being models, they were meant not only to describe what explanations are like, but also to specify what they *ought* to be like — to provide a model or ideal for scientific explanations. As a result, the models provide *criteria for evaluating explanations* and we shall discuss these in this section. For, despite models being ideal, purported explanations may *appear* to fit these criteria without really being good explanations, so we shall also discuss ways in which such apparent explanations can be distinguished from genuine explanations.

To evaluate an explanation, we must have identified an explanation to evaluate — just as with the evaluation of statements and arguments, the evaluation of explanations first requires that the explanation be identified and understood. As with arguments, so with explanations. One needs not only to identify and understand the component statements, but also to identify and understand the interrelationship (structure) of these statements — that is, which ones are the explanans and which ones the explanandum. Again as with arguments, the exigencies of communication mean that there is often a large gap between what is verbally presented as the explanation and the intended explanation. If something is too obvious to be stated, it may be left unstated, or perhaps only implied but, nevertheless, be an essential part of the explanation.

What is omitted may be some particular claim; or it may be a law that is required for the full explanation. Even citing a cause of a particular event by way of explaining it can be fitted to the D-N model of explanation. This is done by taking the causal claim to imply an unstated law connecting events and circumstances, which are relevantly like the claimed cause, with events and circumstances relevantly like the event to be explained. However, as with enthymemes (elliptically presented arguments), so with elliptically presented explanations — what is left unstated may be very difficult to determine precisely.

Once the explanation has been filled out, if it is elliptical and identified, an important preliminary check to make is to ask whether the explanandum (statement) is really true. If not, as we noted earlier, there is nothing to explain. Beyond being an interesting intellectual exercise, further evaluation of the explanation would be pointless. Where what is being explained is a regularity or even a law, it may be difficult to tell with certainty if it is true, but we should at least have good reason to think it is.

When the explanation has been identified and checked, how is it to be evaluated? How are we to distinguish good explanations from bad? How are we to distinguish better explanations from worse ones? How are we to distinguish genuine explanations from those only masquerading as such? There are two central criteria for judging explanations. They can be formulated as the following questions:

1 Would the explanans, if it were true, explain the explanandum?
2 Is the explanans true?

The first question concerns the relation between the explanans and the explanandum. What we accept as an answer to it will depend upon the model of explanation we are using. Apart from questions excluding trivial explanations, for each model the basic question is:

> *For the D-N model:*
> Does the explanans logically imply the explanandum?
>
> *For the I-S model:*
> Does the explanans render the explanandum highly probable?
>
> *For the causal model:*
> Does the explanans cite factors that are causally relevant to the explanandum?

We take the first question to be asking if the proposed explanation has *explanatory force*. Is it a *possible* explanation? For both the I-S and the causal models there will also be further questions, as we noticed. These concern the availability of further information that might undercut the apparent explanatory force of the explanans.

The second criterion is that the explanans should be true. It is sometimes easy to invent an explanans with explanatory force — for example, one implying the explanandum — but unless it is true it does not explain it. We shall discuss this second criterion under the heading 'Acceptability of the explanans', below.

EXPLANATORY FORCE

We take the force of an explanation, its **explanatory force**, to be the degree to which the explanans would, if it were true, explain the explanandum. It gives some means of assessing an explanation that is independent of the question of the truth of the explanans. Separating these two questions enables us to reject some purported explanations without showing or knowing that the explanans is false or unacceptable. An explanans known to be false can still be judged for explanatory value.

Although there are a number of conditions that an explanation must fulfil if it is to have explanatory force of a non-trivial nature (discussed below), the basic question is whether the explanans logically implies (D-N model), makes highly probable (I-S model), or is causally relevant to (causal model) the explanandum, according to which model of explanation is being used. Thus, each of the three models gives a different account of the required relation between explanans and explanandum — implication, high probability and causal relevance.

Despite the differences between the proponents of the various models, there is quite wide agreement about the explanatory force of a number of types of explanations. Deductive-nomological explanations in which the explanans logically implies the explanandum and in which the law appealed to is a causal law are held to have greater explanatory force than either the I-S or the S-R types of explanation. This might be loosely expressed by saying that explanations that explain *why-necessarily* something is the case, rather than *why-probably* or *why-possibly*, have greater explanatory force. In line with this judgment, some people hold that only D-N explanations are fully explanatory. Because the D-N model is widely held to be the ideal form of explanation, we frame most of the following discussion in terms of it. We discuss some common ways in which explanations can lack explanatory force. We conclude by presenting a more general notion of explanatory force.

Partial or incomplete 'explanations'

Explanations in which the explanans has nothing in common with the explanandum mislead no one. A more deceptive type of pseudo-explanation is one in which the explanans *seems* to imply the explanandum, but in which, in fact, it only implies part of the explanandum. Such explanations are called *partial explanations* and they are quite common in psychology and psychology essays. Instead of explaining the explanandum in full, they only explain part of it. To illustrate this, we will consider an example familiar to most students of psychology — the Muller-Lyer illusion.

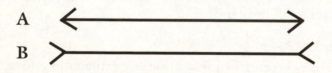

What needs explaining is the illusion. Why, given the associated arrows at the end of each, does the top line look shorter than the bottom line, even though they are the same length? One purported explanation of this illusion can be dismissed without inquiring into the truth of the explanans. It is what Gregory (1966b) calls the 'confusion' theory. Here it is held that the perceptual system is confused by the shapes and this yields the illusion. As Gregory comments, '[This] gives no hint as to why the perceptual system should be confused by these and not other shapes; or why the confusion should lead to distortions only in certain directions' (1966a, p 143). Both parts of this sentence implicitly criticise the explanation for being partial. The first part points out that the attempted explanation does not explain why *these* rather than some other associated lines lead to the error of judgment. The second part shows that if this explanans explains at all, it only explains a *difference* in length. It does not explain the specific illusion, which is that the top line looks shorter.

A useful practical check, to test whether or not a D-N explanation is partial, is to ask: Given the explanans, could the explanandum have been predicted? If the explanation is complete as required, the explanans will imply, and hence allow the prediction of the explanandum. The confusion 'theory' (it does not warrant the term) fails this test. It does not enable us to predict that the top line looks shorter.

It has sometimes been argued that the logical properties of explanation and prediction are identical, and that the only difference between the two is 'pragmatic'. For instance, Hempel (1965, p 249) discusses the difference in terms of the temporal relationship between the explanandum and the proposal of the explanans:

> If the explanandum *E* is given, i.e. if we know that the phenomenon described by *E* has occurred, and a suitable set of statements … is provided afterwards, we speak of an explanation of the phenomenon in question. If the latter statements are given and *E* is derived prior to the occurrence of the phenomenon it describes, we speak of prediction.

This thesis is usually known as the *Symmetry Thesis* and has been the subject of an extensive philosophical debate, resulting in considerable refinement of the original proposal. For present purposes, the thesis serves to emphasise that explanation and prediction are alike in some respects. We are here recommending the prediction test only as a way of unmasking partial deductive explanations.

Circular 'explanations'

Circular explanations also lack explanatory force, but for a very different reason. A circular explanation is one in which the explanans includes the explanandum. In most circular explanations the verbal formulations differ in a way which hides the fact that it is really the same statement expressed in different ways. The classical example of a circular explanation is explaining why opium is a sleep-inducer by citing the fact that it has a 'dormitive' virtue or quality. Since the statement 'Opium has a dormitive virtue' is effectively the same statement as 'Opium is a sleep-inducer', the explanans is effectively identical with the explanandum, and consequently the explanation is circular. In circular explanations, even though the explanans logically implies the explanandum, it does this so trivially that the explanation does not enhance understanding.

Analytic 'explanations'

A related type of deficient explanation to look out for is one in which the apparent law statement, though true, is not an *empirical* law — explanations in which the 'law' statement is not a synthetic statement but an analytic one. An obvious example of this would be attempting to explain why Smith is unmarried by citing the fact that he is a bachelor and all bachelors are unmarried. To illustrate with a more deceptive example: an author who has defined a reinforcer as 'anything which increases the probability of a response', when asked to explain why something increases the probability of a response, cannot explain it as follows: 'It is a reinforcer and all reinforcers increase the probability of a response.' For, as he or she is using the words, the 'law' statement — 'All reinforcers increase the probability of a response' — is an analytic statement, and so is not law-like at all. Of course, as we noted in Chapter 1, exactly the same words might be used to express a genuine synthetic law-like statement, so when criticising an explanation it is important to have fully understood the kinds of statement it consists of. This type of failing is linked with circular explanations, in that if the generalisation in an explanation is an analytic truth, the explanans often amounts to very little more than a restatement of the explanandum.

The preceding discussion has been focused on deductive explanations. We now consider briefly a few points about the explanatory power of inductive (or probabilistic) explanations. Such explanations do not purport to show why the explanandum must be true. They merely purport to show how, in relation to the considerations introduced in the explanans, the explanandum is (highly) probable. Other things being equal, the higher this probability the greater the explanatory force.

We noticed earlier, in discussing the 'measles' example, that inductive explanations run the risk of being undercut by further information. This information, when added to the explanans, can radically reduce the explanatory power of these explanations. Consequently, an important question to ask when assessing (or constructing) an inductive explanation is: How complete is the explanatory information? This question does not ask if the explanans is true; it is a question that seeks to ensure that all the available relevant information is being used, and that consequently the explanans does have, to the best of the available knowledge, the explanatory power it claims.

So far in this section we have considered the explanatory power of an explanation as the relation between an explanans and a *single* explanandum (either particular or general). A more general notion, particularly important in science, has to do with how well a certain type of explanans *would explain a number of diverse phenomena*. If the different law-like statements of a variety of such explanations go together to form a coherent theory, we can investigate the *explanatory power of the theory*. That is, we can ask: How well would this theory (if true) explain these (diverse) phenomena? To answer this question, we at least need to be able to judge individually of each phenomenon, how well the theory (together, where necessary, with the particular initial conditions) would explain it. Of course, that is what we have just been examining. However, extra considerations are involved in this wider question. Here we just mention two of the most important – *generality* and *simplicity*.

Generality is a precondition if a theory is to be able to explain a diversity of phenomena. It has to be sufficiently general either to imply or to bear probabilistically on many different phenomena. Simplicity is an important related notion, connected with the coherence of the theory. Without the requirement that the theory be simple, any heterogeneous collection of law-like statements could be grouped together to form a 'theory' with the desired generality. But they would do so at the expense of simplicity.

As preconditions for the explanatory power of theories, generality and simplicity establish the main link between explanation and scientific understanding. In explaining a wide variety of apparently diverse phenomena, a theory having these properties increases our understanding of the world. Phenomena previously thought to be unconnected are related through the generality and coherence of the theory that explains them. This relationship reveals new similarities, which, in turn, expose new differences, thereby enhancing understanding.

ACCEPTABILITY OF THE EXPLANANS

In this section we consider the other main criterion for evaluating explanations — the truth of the explanans. At first glance, the explanans should not only be true; it should also be known to be so. This accords with a common view of explanations — namely, that they should explain the unfamiliar in terms of the familiar. For familiar truths are mostly ones that people claim to know are true. However, many good scientific explanations do absolutely the reverse. They explain quite familiar phenomena in terms of very *unfamiliar* phenomena. In physics, for example, interactions of subatomic particles with strange properties are used to explain a wide variety of everyday phenomena. Correspondingly, many an explanans used in good explanations is not *known* to be true. So, although it would be a bonus if the explanans were not only true, but known to be true, as a requirement for a good explanans this is too strong.

So, the requirement is simply that the explanans be true. However, requiring that a good explanans be true and determining in practice if it actually is, are two quite distinct matters. Given that the explanans is required to contain law-like statements, and that because of their generality we cannot typically determine conclusively if law-like statements are true (whereas sometimes we can tell more conclusively if they are false), the second criterion, while expressing what is required of a good explanans, is impractical. A weaker, more practical criterion for a satisfactory explanans is that it should be (scientifically) acceptable: that there should be good reason to think it is true and no conclusive reason to think it is false.

Of course, that the explanans is acceptable does not mean that it is true. There can be good evidence for the truth of statements that are, in fact, false. Put another way, having good evidence at one time that a statement is true does not rule out having better evidence, at another time, that it is false, or vice versa. But if we are interested in whether or not a statement is true, having good evidence that it is, is preferable to having no evidence at all.

Although (non-elliptical) explanans sentences consist of both general and particular statements, in this section we will be concerned largely with criteria for the acceptability of general (law-like) statements in the explanans. However, much of what we say applies not only to general statements, but to statements in general. We noted earlier that some explanations are given by citing a cause of the event to be explained. In Chapter 5 we examine more specifically criteria for the acceptability of causal claims.

A minimum requirement for acceptability of a statement is that there should not be conclusive evidence that it is false. If there is conclusive (not merely conclusive-looking) evidence that it is false, then it is false and consequently unacceptable. Putting this another way, the least we can ask is that the statement should not be incompatible with established facts. However, this is a very weak condition for acceptability and many unacceptable statements satisfy it. Irrefutable statements form an important class of scientifically unacceptable statements which, nevertheless, meet this requirement. We shall discuss them later in this section.

A stronger requirement for acceptability of any statement is that there should be some evidence in its favour. If, however, the statement is being used in an explanation, we need to make the requirement stricter than this. For in general, if the explanation has explanatory force and the explanandum is true, there will be some evidence for the explanans — namely, the event or phenomenon it would explain if it were true. (We will discuss this important relation between explanation and evidence in the next section.) Consequently, there will be *some* evidence for the explanans of all such explanations, and so the requirement just mentioned will not distinguish better from worse among those explanations which have satisfied our first criterion (that is, those explanations having explanatory force).

What is needed is not merely that there be some evidence for the explanans, but that there be **independent evidence** for the explanans — evidence independent of the (evidence for the) explanandum.

The important question to ask is whether there is independent evidence for the truth of the explanans. If, in evaluating an explanation, we find no independent evidence for the explanans, then the explanation will, in general, be judged unsatisfactory. Explanations in which the only evidence for the explanans is the explanandum are sometimes called '*ad hoc*' explanations. The 'confusion' explanation, cited earlier as illustrating another common fault of explanations, is also a clear example of an *ad hoc* explanation. If we ask what independent evidence there is for the claim that the perceptual system is confused, the answer is — none. The only evidence of confusion is (the evidence) that the illusion occurs. Many weak explanations can be uncovered by applying this test. If someone attempts to explain a suicide by saying that the deceased had a death wish, they can be asked if there is any independent evidence for the death wish. (They can, of course, also be asked other questions concerning the explanatory force of the explanation; for instance, how would having a death wish explain *this* suicide?) If the suicide is the only evidence, then the explanans is insufficiently supported to be acceptable in an explanation.

The request for independent evidence can also help to uncover another, already mentioned, defect of explanations — circularity. If the explanation is circular, then the explanans will contain a sentence which is simply a different formulation of the explanandum sentence. Since, in such explanations, the explanans is identical with or includes the explanandum, there cannot be independent evidence for (part of) the explanans. Consequently, circular explanations are also *ad hoc*. Even though there may be very good evidence that opium has a dormitive virtue, there can be no evidence that opium has a dormitive virtue which is independent of evidence that it is a sleep-inducer, because these two sentences make the same statement.

We have mentioned prediction as a practical test of explanatory power. As we saw, asking whether a given explanans would have enabled us to predict what it is meant to explain can show an explanation's failure to bear on its explanandum — perhaps through being a partial explanation, or being only an explanation sketch. The prediction test can also be used to indicate whether there is independent evidence for the explanans. If we could not have predicted that a particular result would have occurred *before* we knew it had, that could indicate not only that the right relationship between explanans and explanandum fails to hold, but also that, prior to the explanandum event, there was not sufficient evidence to warrant accepting that particular explanans, and, consequently, insufficient evidence to use it in a prediction. In explaining the Muller-Lyer illusion, the confusion 'theory' also fails the prediction test on these grounds, as well as on those due to lack of explanatory force. Before we knew that the Muller-Lyer illusion had occurred, we could not have predicted, on the basis of the 'confusion theory', that it would. One reason was that the confusion theory does not predict the illusion in full detail (that is, it lacks explanatory force). Another reason is that, prior to knowing that the illusion had occurred, there were insufficient grounds for holding the opinion that such lines would 'confuse' the perceptual system, and consequently insufficient grounds for using the statement to predict the illusion. Another name that is sometimes used for what we have called *ad hoc* explanations is '*post hoc*'. This name for these explanations highlights the fact that too often the explanans can be 'justified' only *after* the explanandum is known to have occurred.

The independent evidence test is important in psychology, because the social and behavioural sciences are especially prone to such *post hoc* explanans sentences. Indeed, there is a whole class of everyday explanations which some have argued are *post hoc,*. These are sometimes called teleological explanations. In psychology, they include attempts to explain behaviour by citing purposes, goals, intentions, motives or desires of the agent. In many such explanations it is possible to be wise only *after* the event they purport to explain, and consequently they may not serve to predict any further behaviour. Hence, they frequently are not readily *refutable,* and for this reason are often rejected as adequate scientific explanations, despite being very common in everyday discourse. We shall consider them in Chapter 7.

Refutability

Recall the confusion theory explanation of the Muller-Lyer illusion. We have been able to use it to illustrate several different faults from which explanations can suffer. Underlying these faults is its vagueness — a vagueness that makes it impossible to test — that renders it unrefutable. In science, despite the sound of its name, *refutability* is a highly desirable property for a statement to possess. Refutability is such an important property for the explanatory statements of an empirical science that some highly developed views on the nature of the science have taken it as their key concept.

Quine and Ullian (1970, p 50), who take a 'hypothesis' to be (roughly) a statement used to explain (that is, part of an explanans), describe **refutability** thus:

> It seems faint praise of a hypothesis to call it refutable. But … some imaginable event, recognisable if it occurs, must suffice to refute the hypothesis. Otherwise the hypothesis predicts nothing, is confirmed by nothing and confers upon us no earthly good beyond perhaps a mistaken peace of mind.

Another word for this property is 'falsifiable'. A less misleading one is 'testable' The terms 'refutable' and 'falsifiable' are misleading because they wrongly suggest that if a statement has this property it must be false, since any statement that can actually be refuted or falsified is false. However, a closer look at the definition shows that it requires only that some *imaginable* event would suffice to refute the statement. If the statement is true, such an event will never actually occur. For a statement to be refutable, the event need not actually occur, but it must be imaginable. Of course, if such an *event does* occur, then the statement will have been refuted.

A useful practical test of refutability, for someone who believes a statement, is to ask them under what circumstances they would give it up. Could they specify an event which, should it happen, would refute the statement and cause them to no longer believe it? Here it is important that the second of Quine and Ullian's conditions be met — that the event be recognisable if it occurs. Otherwise, any generalisation, however unrefutable, would seem to pass the test. Someone who believed that All *A* are *B* (or that No *A* are B) could say that they would count it as refuted if they ever ran across an *A* that was not a *B* (or, correspondingly, an *A* that *was* a *B)*. In this respect, compare the refutability of the two statements 'No cats dream' and 'No cats undergo rapid eye-movement sleep'. The former would be refuted by a dreaming cat and the latter by a cat undergoing rapid eye-movement sleep. But the two events are not equally clearly recognisable.

In this way, an advocate of the 'confusion theory' explanation of the Muller-Lyer illusion might claim that the 'theory' was refutable. They would be prepared to give it up, they might say, in the event that the perceptual system were not confused. But how would they recognise this event if it did occur? That's easy — they would recognise it if the illusion did not occur! If the 'theory' is simply a restatement of the illusion, then they are right, for any statement that amounts to the claim that the illusion occurs would be refuted if it did not. (In this case, using this simple restatement in an explanation of the illusion would be circular.) However, if claiming that confusion has occurred amounts to more than simply claiming that a specific error of judgment has occurred, then recognising an error of judgment (the illusion) is not the same thing as recognising the occurrence of confusion. In its vague state, the 'confusion theory' is unrefutable.

In general, refutability of the explanans is an important requirement for scientific explanations, both for the acceptability of the explanans and for the explanation to have full explanatory force. If the statement is refutable, then it can be tested, and may, as a result, acquire evidence in its favour — one of the requirements for an acceptable explanans. If it is not refutable, then it will not imply the specific event it has been called on to explain and consequently the explanation will lack full (that is, deductive) explanatory force.

Not all statements are directly refutable on their own. Theoretical statements may need to be taken in conjunction with a number of other statements if they are to conflict with 'some imaginable event, recognisable if it occurs'. So, in this case, if such an event does occur it is not always clear which of the statements we should count as refuted. Nevertheless, the principle is important. If the truth of a statement (in combination with others) makes no difference to what circumstances or events to expect, if whatever could happen would not remotely conflict with it, then it may, as Quine and Ullian say, 'confer upon us no earthly good beyond perhaps a mistaken peace of mind'.

INDUCTION AND EXPLANATION

When we distinguished inductive arguments from deductive arguments in Chapter 2 we noted that, unlike deductive arguments, there were no clear guidelines for evaluating inductive arguments. Recollect, that whereas deductive arguments purported to *guarantee* the truth of their conclusions, inductive arguments merely claimed to offer some sort of support and provide weaker non-conclusive evidence or grounds for believing their conclusions.

One very important class of such arguments includes those inductive arguments that express the reasons we have for accepting law-like statements and scientific theories, or for preferring one theory to another. Consequently, any guidelines we offer for evaluating inductive arguments will help in the difficult but important task of evaluating theories in psychology. One guideline is an important link between induction and explanation, and between the evaluation of inductive arguments and the comparative evaluation of explanations, to which we now turn.

We have seen that, typically, explanations are required only for statements that have already been evaluated as true. Although explanations are like arguments in that both show how a statement — the explanandum or the conclusion of the argument — could be evaluated (or what factors bear on it), they are different in purpose. The purpose of an argument is the evaluation of its conclusion, but since any explanandum is already evaluated (as true, and hence in need of explanation), the purpose of the explanans is to reduce puzzlement and increase understanding. It does this by showing how the explanandum statement could have been evaluated and by showing what factors bear on it. It is notable that, for many explanations, we are a good deal more confident of the truth of the explanandum than we are of the truth of the explanans, which includes law-like statements. Although the latter may be regarded as plausibly true, there is no way of being certain that they are not false. Indeed, we are frequently so sure of the truth of the statement to be explained that we take its truth as support for the statements that are advanced to explain it. This is often the reasoning that lies behind the claim that certain evidence supports a theory. The theory, if true, would explain the evidence.

Thus, if a statement p explains why q is the case, then the truth of q can sometimes be offered in support of p. Here, then, is an important link between argument and explanation. We can take explanations of the form 'p explains q' and produce a corresponding inductive (that is, non-demonstrative) argument of the form 'since q, (there is reason to believe that) p'. But we want to know more. We have seen that in this case q gives *some* support to p. What are the conditions under which q gives not just *some* support but *strong* support to p? An illuminating answer to this is: q can be taken to provide strong support to p when p is the *best of competing alternative explanations* of q. This condition provides a way of evaluating the worth of an important class of inductive arguments.

A special case of this occurs when there seems to be no other explanation. If this were true, p, being the only explanation, would trivially be the best. In these circumstances, q will be taken to very strongly support p. The commonly used pattern of reasoning, 'p must be true: it is the only explanation!' illustrates this. An antecedently implausible statement can be strongly supported if it seems to be the only explanation of a particular event. Innocent people have been found guilty and hanged for lack, at the time, of any other explanation of events.

To illustrate more generally this important condition, let us consider some simple examples. First, the fact that most observed As are Bs is often taken as a reason for holding that most As are, in fact, Bs. That is, one inductively generalises from the observed to non-observed instances. One's reasoning could be represented by an inductive argument of the form 'since most observed As are Bs', it is reasonable to conclude that, of all As, most are Bs'. Thus, someone may argue from the evidence that most observed (or recorded) instances of suicide come from lower socio-economic groups to the conclusion that most suicides come from these groups. However, it may *not* be reasonable to draw this conclusion, and the requirement that the conclusion be the best of competing alternative explanations serves to distinguish when it is reasonable from when it is not. In this application, the principle yields: if, in the light of all the available evidence, the best explanation for the fact that most *observed* As are Bs is that most As are, in fact Bs, then the inductive conclusion is reasonable. In our present case, a better explanation for the fact that most recorded suicides come from lower socio-economic groups may be that the families (and doctors) of people who suicide from the higher socio-economic groups conceal the fact, and the deaths are not recorded as suicides. If this is a better explanation in the light of available evidence, then the earlier inductive conclusion is not justified by the evidence — it is not the best explanation of the evidence.

We have already examined some of the considerations that determine whether one explanation is better than another. One is worth emphasising here. Other things being equal, a D-N explanation is better than an I-S explanation. Indeed, a general principle is that, other things being equal, the explanation that renders the explanandum the more probable is the better. This applies even if, on either explanation, the explanandum is highly improbable.

Another example of this type of reasoning can be perceived as a basis for use of the familiar 't' tests found in the inferential statistics armoury that serves the empirical psychologist so well. When an experimental psychologist concludes that the difference in performance between two groups of subjects is statistically significant, they are asserting that the hypothesis that there is, in fact, a particular difference between the parent populations from which the two groups are drawn, is a better explanation of the results than is its competitor.

The competing hypothesis may be that there is no difference between the performance levels of the two parent populations. Given the observed results, the hypothesis that there is a difference is the better explanation of the two. For if it were true, the observed result would be more probable than if its competitor were true.

Of course, statistical inferences like this are always subject to various assumptions — for example, concerning the nature of the distribution in the parent populations of the performance variable compared in the study. But, allowing for these assumptions and the adequacy of the methodology adopted, the direction of theoretical argument is frequently *from* the observation *to* that explanans of the competing alternatives that best explains the observation. To make this point in a more general way, good inductive arguments frequently involve reasoning to a conclusion which, if true, would best explain the premiss(es). Hence, the usual goal of an author in the discussion section of a psychological paper is to show that their theory or hypothesis best explains the results of the research (and, ideally, of other relevant research). They claim their theory has greater explanatory power than competing alternatives in the light of their research evidence. They may express this by claiming that the evidence best supports their theory.

However, if the theory does not really explain the results, or if they are insufficiently knowledgeable to know of, or insufficiently inventive to think of, better competing alternative explanations, they would be wrong to claim good evidence for the theory. This highlights two important questions to be asked in evaluating such inductive arguments and the reasoning they express in favour of theories:

1   Does the theory really explain the evidence cited in its favour?
2   Is there a better alternative explanation for the evidence?

Considerations introduced earlier in this chapter will help in answering the first question. The second question is difficult to answer conclusively in the negative, for there may be a better explanation that no one has considered. That a statement provides the best of the *available* alternative explanations does not guarantee its truth. But this is to be expected. The inconclusiveness of answers to this question reflects the well-known inconclusiveness of inductive arguments.

'UNDERSTANDING' VERSUS 'EXPLANATION': DISCOURSE AS EVIDENCE

From the time of Freud, at least, psychologists have sought to *interpret* or *analyse* what people say as a way of understanding the psychology of the speaker. The process of interpretation involves providing a new (theoretical) context within which to 'read' the person's utterance (their dream report, anecdotes, even non-verbal expressions, like drawings). The name 'psycho*analysis*' captures this interpretive feature of much of the work of clinical or personality psychology where explanation as such is seldom explicitly proposed, at least not in terms described in earlier sections of this chapter.

The interpretive tradition in psychology sees utterances as symptoms or clues to the 'real' or causally relevant motives, attitudes or dispositions of the individual being analysed. This is sometimes called the 'hermeneutic' tradition or school in psychology, linking it to European linguistic, literary or artistic interpretation rather than to empirical generalisation and law-based explanation. Within psychology, the distinction between '*verstehen*' and explanation has sometimes been made with the German word denoting interpretive understanding. Psychologists and laypersons seeking to answer psychological questions have, not surprisingly, asked: 'What does this mean?' ' What does she mean by ...?' or 'What ideological or value-orientation does some utterance express?' — all questions which demand analysis of people's utterances.

Of course, these are all questions that might arise in other academic disciplines (art, literature, politics) but they can also be, clearly, psychological questions. They all seek to explain (to some degree) by contextualising and making less ambiguous the things people say, seeing such utterances as meaningful and, therefore, as revealing the 'truth' of a person's motives, history or 'identity'.

Some of the methodological issues about which you need to be aware when evaluating interpretive explanations can be illustrated by looking at recent uses of **discourse analysis** in social psychology. In the example below, the analysis of a publicly exhibited and recorded utterance (the 'maiden' speech of the Australian MP Pauline Hanson) is used to show how the right-wing politician's words can be read to reveal how she sees herself (her self-identity) and how she positions herself politically or ideologically. In social psychological terms, then, her discourse can be broken down into its components, its underlying binary oppositions (of social category membership, even identification) and its defensive strategies. Rapley (1998) proposes a discourse analysis, beginning with the opening paragraph of Hanson's speech:

> Mr. Acting Speaker, in making my first speech ... I congratulate you on your election and wish to say how proud I am to be here as the independent Member for Oxley. I come here not as a polished politician but as a woman who has had her fair share of life's knocks. My view on issues is based on commonsense, and my experience as a mother of four children, as a sole parent, and as a businesswoman running a fish and chip shop.

Rapley proposes the following analysis:

> With skilful deployment of the two discursive styles ... termed offensive and defensive rhetoric, Hanson actively works, by the deployment of a contrast pair, to construct her in-group ... Hanson's text employs a method of category construction which moves from the particular to the general (*characteristics*, category, context). In her opening utterances she spells out the characteristics of the general social category to come ...
>
> She defines herself, and warrants her epistemological entitlement (claim to knowledge — P.B.), by reference to both a shared social identity (those who have had 'knocks') and also, simultaneously, in terms of a number of self-categories, or personal identities: it is 'my experience' as 'a mother of four children', a 'sole parent', and a 'businesswoman running a fish and chip shop' (p 16 of original manuscript).

Such a discursive analysis (and there are many alternative, linguistically detailed ways of conducting these) illuminates the 'text' (or utterance) and thereby the psychology of the speaker. It provides evidence of the social categories and, perhaps, the psychological strategies used to establish the speaker's 'identity'. (It may be used to show how the text is rhetorically or ideologically structured as well, although that is more sociological than psychological and will not be pursued here.)

In terms of the models of explanation outlined earlier in this chapter, such a discourse analysis is only partially explanatory. But it does provide information about the speaker and her 'self' or 'identity' which, if allied with general theories of personality or identity formation, for instance, would be conventionally explanatory. However, the understanding given by analysing utterances, stories, dreams (or dream-reports) does purport to be genuinely informative in that it 'reduces puzzlement' about a person's reasons, motives or the 'meaning' of their actions. It is this kind of interpretation which courts of law, for example, might seek to explain an alleged crime (say, of racist aggression). It is the kind of explanation which most day-by-day social interactions assume.

EVALUATING INTERPRETATIONS AND DISCOURSE ANALYSIS

In the Hanson example, above, discourse analysis is used to make sense of the politician's claims by linking them to social psychological concepts. This helps the reader to understand the (otherwise less clear) function or purpose of the discourse, but it does not 'explain' Hanson's personality or her appeal to voters, for example. Put in the terms of our earlier discussion, the discourse analysis addresses a limited explanandum — one that is not made explicit in the passage we quoted from Rapley. What, then, we need to ask, is the analysis purporting to (help to) explain? If the analysis is not relevant to explanation, then how can it offer any 'understanding'?

In the present case, Rapley formulates the explanans in his abstract as '...the way in which Pauline Hanson's political rhetoric is constructed to emphasise the ordinariness, reasonableness and commonsensical mass appeal of her views'. So, in a sense, his analysis seeks to make clear the strategies of the discourse (her speech) by showing what they mean and how, in the social world, they would be meaningful and appealing to certain kinds of people. This may sound a little vague, but it would be unduly restrictive to deny that this is, in some sense, an explanandum worth explaining.

To evaluate such analyses, one might begin by asking: Can the text in question be analysed by other means to produce a more coherent and comprehensive interpretation? That is, the understanding generated by an interpretation needs to be judged against alternatives. Second, it needs to be comprehensive — to include all, rather than to exclude arbitrarily, elements that the analysis proposes *in advance* as relevant to the social context of the utterance or text in question. The resulting analysis can then be judged as more or less plausible — coherent, non-circular and non-arbitrary. The best test for these criteria is to use the analysis to make predictions about the meaning of other related utterances to which the analysis used could also be applied. So, evaluation concerns how informatively and precisely the interpretation links an utterance to a social context: its purpose, its likely audience, and so on.

Interpretation, then, is preliminary to, or an alternative to, explanation based on laws or generalisations. But it should also meet the conditions of non-circularity and empirical adequacy (that is, be non *ad hoc*) like other forms of explanation. Only then will an 'interpretation' be informative.

The important question to ask of any interpretation is: Precisely what does the proposed analysis seek to give information about? How might you characterise the explanandum? Then you can break down the proposed analysis to see if it is comprehensive, coherent and informative (non-circular). Ask whether the analysis could be used to predict other features of discourse in new contexts with similar purposes to that already analysed.

DISCOURSE AND 'SUBJECTIVITY'

Discourse analysis is usually practised as part of disciplines other than psychology. Yet, the past decade has seen the boundaries between disciplines break down and the questions of traditional concern to psychology have been increasingly addressed by sociologists and by cultural studies or feminist writers, especially those concerned with the causes of what are conventionally called 'personality' differences or (as the new question is posed) the 'construction of identity and subjectivity'.

The relations between 'discourse' and 'subjectivity' have become a theoretical preoccupation of cultural studies, which has reinterpreted Freud via the work of the French psychoanalyst, Jacques Lacan. Sociologists, such as Michel Foucault, are also invoked to explain (or to interpret, at least) differences between individuals' subjectivities which are seen as ever-changing and even contradictory, rather than as fixed sets of psychological dispositions resulting from different early experiences. 'Subjectivity', in these debates, refers to the experienced sense of self and self-definition/identity of people in their social lives. 'Discourses' might be seen as sets of ideas, statements and linguistic terms which embody ways of thinking or making meaning associated with social institutions (education, the media, religion and science, for example).

An accessible and clear account of the main lines of the main approaches to these issues can be found in Shirato and Yell (1996). They argue that 'identity' is a product of socially powerful discourses (around gender, age, taste and patriarchal values, for example) and of the 'performance' by which individuals reiterate and continually re-enact the norms of these discourses. So, bodies are given identity and subjects are produced by means of normalising, if shifting, discourses that incorporate or give effect to social power. Instead of using psychological concepts such as 'motive', 'drive', 'wish' or 'anxiety', these ways of understanding subjectivity use sociological concepts: they externalise and relativise the causes of differences between individuals and see psychological qualities as the effect of socially-constructed meanings that normalise and regulate human 'subjects'.

To the extent that these analyses offer would-be explanations that compete with other, more traditionally psychological explanations, they may be evaluated by identifying precise explanandum statements and related explanans. The precise mechanisms which mediate the process of 'subject formation', for example, can then be sought and evaluated for their empirical adequacy. We discuss this issue in Chapter 5. Of course, the question of possible circularity in the proposed explanation is a critical issue in postulating discourse as a 'cause' or factor in 'identity formation'. If the only evidence for the causal discourses is the characteristics of the identity that they purport to explain, then the putative explanation will be judged circular or trivial.

SUMMARY

The aim of this chapter has been to explain what explanations are, to show how you can evaluate them and, finally, to show how they can help in the assessment of inductive arguments.

We have described two main kinds of explanation: causal and law-based. Law-based explanations treat them as arguments whose conclusions describe what is to be explained (the explanandum) and whose premisses are what does the explaining (the explanans). The deductive-nomological (D-N) model (sometimes called the covering-law model) likens explanations to deductive arguments and requires that the premisses include laws and that the explanandum (conclusion) be implied by the explanans (premisses). The inductive-statistical (I-S) model likens explanations to inductive arguments which include a statistical law among the premisses and whose explanans (premisses) make the explanandum highly likely.

We have also sketched an alternative view of explanations as statements which provide information about the causal history of an event. The relevant causal information can be guided by contrastive explanations which attempt to explain not merely why P, but why P rather than Q. On this model, there is no requirement that the event explained should be highly probable in the light of the explanatory information as long as it cites relevant causal information.

We looked at some ways in which explanations can be deficient: they may only be partial; they may be circular; they may be analytic and depend upon a premiss which, although apparently law-like, is an analytic truth; they may be ad hoc — the only evidence for a crucial part of the explanans may be the explanadum itself. We highlighted refutability or testability as an important property of explanatory information. We then looked at one view of a link between inductive arguments and explanations: one circumstance in which a premiss p of an inductive argument provides support for the conclusion q is when q is the best explanation for p.

Finally, the use of discourse analysis to explain or to understand (to 'interpret' or 'read') psychological phenomena was briefly outlined.

KEYWORDS

EXPLANATION • EXPLANANS • EXPLANANDUM • LAW • LAW-LIKE STATE-MENT • CAUSAL EXPLANATION • CONTRASTIVE EXPLANATION • EXPLANA-TORY FORCE • PARTIAL OR INCOMPLETE EXPLANATION • CIRCULAR EXPLANATION • ANALYTIC EXPLANATION • INDEPENDENT EVIDENCE • REFUTABILITY • DISCOURSE ANALYSIS • IDENTITY

EXERCISES

1 In the exercise section of the last chapter we cited an argument of Neisser's that 'The steady rise of IQ scores around the world is a truly remarkable demonstration of environmental influences on mental process. More complex environments may just produce more complex minds.' He confidently offers a general explanation for the phenomenon — environmental influences. He is considerably more circumspect about what aspect of the environment has the influence. Consider alternative possible explanations for the rise of IQ. How adequate as potential explanations are the two possibilities suggested by Neisser?

2 (Difficult) Discuss the following criticism of Gregory's own explanation of the Muller-Lyer illusion (refer back to our diagram on p 82):

> Gregory claims that an organism sees arrow A as shorter because it forms the hypothesis that the arrow is the projecting edge of a three-dimensional corner, while it hypothesizes the longer-looking arrow B is a further away receding edge of a corner. If you look at the corner of a room, at the line where the walls join together in a room, they look somewhat like arrow B where the extensions are the lines formed by the ceiling and floor.
>
> What Gregory is doing in this explanation is twofold. He is claiming that in perceiving the Muller-Lyer lines we are forming a hypothesis based on the visual input from the lines plus information gleaned (from) what we have experienced about three dimensional objects such as corners of rooms. This information about corners causes the organism, when stimulated by the lines, to hypothesize that the lines are really edges of three-dimensional (or representations of three-dimensional) objects. After this hypothesis is formed, the organism then further infers that since one set of lines B than the other, A, that B must be larger. So the organism unconsciously makes a size constancy correction to make line B look longer, and then experiences B as longer.
>
> The missing premiss here is that the organism in some sense unconciously saw A and B as being the same size, and then under the three-dimensional hypothesis applied a size-constancy distance correction function in order to experience B as longer. This supplementation of the details of the theory brings out the major fault of Gregory's constructive hypothesis formation theory. There seems to be no consistent or principled description about how such hypotheses are formed. We are never clear what hypothesis is being formulated or whether one hypothesis or a set of them is required.
>
> Gregory's experimental designs most often start with a well-specified illusion or ambiguous object and a well-specified assumption about the organism's prior experiences or relevant behaviors. The hypothesis attributed to the organism is defined, qualitatively,

by what is necessary to map the stimulus so specified into the response so described. This smacks suspiciously of the mentalistic ad hoc method that so irritated Skinner. Indeed many of Gregory's inferences and hypotheses are similar to Moliere's *virtus dormitiva*. (Machamer 1993, pp 355–56)

3 Assume for a moment, if you can, that you know little more about lawn bowls than that it is a game played on a level grassed surface in which players attempt to bowl a number of large balls so they end as near as possible to a target small ball. How would you critically assess the following argument?

Lawn bowls is the most dangerous game people play. It has far and away the highest death rate during play of any game.

What further considerations might lead to a reassessment of the worth of this argument, and what morals might we draw for the assessment of analogous arguments in cases where we lack the information to bring analogous considerations?

chapter 4

Definition and clarification of terms

> 'The question is,' said Alice, 'whether you can make words mean so many different things.'
>
> 'The question is,' said Humpty Dumpty, 'which is to be master — that's all.'
>
> Lewis Carroll

INTRODUCTION

Psychologists analyse mental processes (cognition) and capacities and try to explain human behaviour. The medium of explanation is language, and, as we have seen in Chapters 1 to 3, psychological explanations involve arguments about people's actions, aptitudes, beliefs or behaviours. In this chapter we will concentrate on the important questions that arise when choosing which words to use in the relatively formal contexts of undergraduate study of psychology. These include: the need to be as precise and consistent as possible in using the vocabulary found in this broad field; how to define your terms; and the ways in which you can make unjustified assumptions in defining (or in omitting to define) the words you will rely on in your essays and reports. We discuss the language used in psychology and demonstrate the problems that can arise in defining and employing the technical vocabularies (note the plural) which constitute this field.

Studying psychology involves (amongst other things) learning the language used by psychologists. 'Ego-strength', 'reciprocal inhibition', 'IQ', 'self-actualisation' — these are terms which mean something quite specific when used by psychologists. They may mean nothing, or nothing in particular, when heard by non-specialists. The technical language of psychology is, in itself, composed of many different vocabularies. Such specialist vocabularies, or **registers**, are the building blocks of various theories in the many sub-fields of the discipline. Knowing these (or some of them, at least) is part of what makes it possible to claim that one is a psychologist.

A great deal of psychological literature, as well as informal debate, seems to consist of merely defining and redefining words, preparing for argument rather than actually engaging in more substantive discussion. This is reflected in the fact that participants in psychological debate seem to be continually calling on each other to clarify their definitions, or to justify the choice of a particular term. For instance, in the debate about possible psychological differences between peoples of various 'races', it is common to hear opponents say things like 'It (the outcome of the debate) depends on what one means by "intelligence"', or 'there are many ways of defining and distinguishing "races"'. To the student of psychology, it may appear that answers to the questions in which they are interested will never be forthcoming, because it is impossible to provide and justify reliable, unambiguous definitions. That is, the criteria an author adopts for the use of a word may not be commonly or universally accepted. Hence, unless you explicitly state your criteria, statements may be misunderstood by your readers who may employ different criteria for the use of a particular term.

One tempting solution to this difficulty is simply to ignore the problem in the hope that definitional issues will resolve themselves as more research data are collected. We have probably all felt like saying, in exasperation, that definitions should be put to one side in order for the 'real' issues to be debated or researched. Indeed, many textbooks and journal articles begin with this tactic: the author admits the possible ambiguity or controversial nature of an expression, and deliberately provides only a somewhat arbitrary, 'working' definition to facilitate discussion. In many cases, such tentative definitions suffice. But in other, often quite important cases, the definition of terms becomes a central focus of the psychological debate.

Put briefly, definitions and clarification of meanings are necessary where there is some possibility of misunderstanding between writers and some of their readers. Of course, the writer is also one such reader, so if they reuse the same word or phrase unwittingly with a different meaning the second time, this particular type of misunderstanding can lead to invalid reasoning. When this occurs in an argument, it is known as the **fallacy of equivocation**. The writer is required to be consistent and not to change the meaning of their words during an argument. The patterns that we saw in Chapter 2 can guide our judgments of the validity of arguments. They depend for their use on the assumptions that the recurring word and phrases retain their particular meaning each time they are used.[1]

More generally, in many branches of psychology there is considerable risk of misunderstanding. In Chapter 1, we considered how the same term can be used with different meanings by people working within the conventions and assumptions of different theories. This is the main reason for needing explicit definition in psychology. Unlike physics, in many branches of psychology there is no settled framework or theory within which problems are posed and solved. For instance, psychological theorists concerned with studying language acquisition in young children will define the phenomena to be explained in different theoretical vocabularies, depending on whether their approach derives from a *behaviouristic* background or one that stresses the more abstract '*cognitive*' dimensions of infant language. Lacking agreement about the appropriate way to describe the phenomenon to be explained, theorists from such different backgrounds may find it difficult to comprehend their opponents' arguments unless detailed, explicit definitions are provided.

A second factor that increases the need for defining and clarifying terms is the strong impetus in psychology towards measurement and

---

[1] A blatant example of equivocation occurs in the argument 'Only man is rational. No woman is a man. So no woman is rational.' No one is likely to be taken in by this switch of meanings for the word 'man' (what are they?), but it illustrates a general principle: equivocal arguments are typically unsound. If the word is used with one meaning thoughout the argument, then one of the premises is false. If not, the argument is invalid.

quantification. Not content with statements like 'bright people tend to be tall', psychologists seek to correlate concepts such as intelligence with height in a mathematically precise way. Hence, they need some way of measuring intelligence. And they cannot measure what they have not (at least provisionally) defined. There are already accepted procedures for comparing the heights of any two people, and even accepted procedures for linking these with numerical values. But, until recently, this has not been true for the concept of intelligence. Tests that allow fine-grained comparisons of people's intelligence, although widely used, do not ensure unanimous acceptance of their theoretical rationale. It is still debatable whether a proposed test actually does measure the concept it claims to measure, or at least whether it is *the* only or best way of measuring that concept. (The 'measurement' of psychological attributes or variables is a central practice of the contemporary discipline. We will consider questions of measurement and meaning in relation to psychology in Chapter 9.)

Natural languages such as English embody complex psychological 'theories'. That is, everyday language assumes *causal*, motivational *explanations* of people's behaviour. Everyone is an informal or amateur psychologist. We all explain our own and others' behaviour in more or less sophisticated ways — or at least, we proffer potentially explanatory accounts of such behaviour, using terms such as 'stress', 'hysteria', 'learning', 'dream', or even words that have come into the language from psychology, such as 'neurotic', 'egocentric' or 'introverted'. So, before presenting a formal psychological argument, such as an essay, it is important to ensure that the vague or variable meanings of everyday language are not simply being assumed in the more academic context.

Given these preliminary considerations, this chapter focuses on four main aspects of the problem of definition:

1   We consider various types of definition, especially the 'operational' variety.

2   We emphasise that many apparently simple psychological concepts may be employed in ways which implicitly make theoretically important assumptions. They cannot be coherently employed unless certain statements are assumed true. Failure to examine these assumptions may seriously weaken any critical appreciation of the argument in which they are made.

3   The technical use of psychological terms frequently needs to be distinguished from the use of similar terms in everyday speech.

4   We emphasise the need to distinguish the *definition* of a term from the provision of *criteria* for its use.

So, how do psychologists attempt to ensure that their terminology is adequate for unambiguous argument? Briefly, our answer to this question focuses on two main classes of definition: *stipulative* and *operational*. We then consider some of the most common inadequacies and misconceptions concerning psychological terms (especially what we call *circular definitions* and *reification*).

STIPULATIVE (NOMINAL) AND DESCRIPTIVE DEFINITIONS

We pointed out in Chapter 1 that there are two main kinds of definition: stipulative and descriptive.

In proposing **stipulative definitions**, writers indicate how they intend to use a word or phrase. Thus, they could either accept the conventional meaning of a word like 'sentiment' or, as the pioneering psychologist Cattell did, stipulate a particular meaning for that term. The stipulated meaning then becomes the **working definition** for that writer in their work, until, of course, they alter the stipulated meaning of the term. (If you do this in the course of your writing, you will need to be explicit in telling the reader that you have done so.)

There is an important difference between stipulative and descriptive definitions. Where a **descriptive definition** attempts to describe an existing convention (a conventional meaning of the term being defined, as in a dictionary), a stipulative definition attempts to set up or to establish a new convention. A stipulative definition can be interpreted as a statement of intent. The intention is to use a word or phase in a certain way.

The stipulated meaning of a term or phrase can become conventional among a group of people who use it; researchers, for example, may use a term that has come to have a common value as part of their technical language (what linguists call their 'register').

Where literature is written for a technical audience, it is assumed that the particular conventions are known. In these circumstances, someone who is unwittingly not a party to them can easily be misled. Some of the mistakes purveyed by popularisers of science may result from this situation. An obvious example might be the journalistic use of the word 'intelligence'. This concept is frequently equated with academic ability in the pages of the press, but it may have a more complex or different meaning in the literature on psychometrics or in educational psychology.

It is more obvious that stipulative definitions are used to establish a convention where new words are coined to suit a new theoretical need; it is less obvious where the words are already in use but are adopted for a more specific technical purpose. To take an historical example, 'proactive inhibition' is an instance of the former. This term would carry virtually no precise meaning outside its technical usage to refer to specific interference effects in memory. However, other expressions carry informal or colloquial meaning despite being defined in the context of a particular theory: an example might be the concept which some psychologists term 'learned helplessness'. Whatever the informal **connotations** (associated or non-literal meanings of the phrase), in the psychological literature it is given a particular interpretation. The phrase may be used to refer to the emotional, cognitive and behavioural consequences of punishment that is not contingent upon any particular response. This definition does not describe the *experience* of feeling 'helpless', but defines the concept in terms of its cause, arbitrary punishment. Of course, 'punishment' is also a term with everyday as well as technical psychological meaning. Words 'borrowed' from ordinary language, but given more precise technical interpretations, are quite common in psychology (for example, 'anxiety', 'ego' and 'reinforcement').

'Working definitions' are stipulative, but may still be theoretically complex, as the following attests:

> Factor analysis affords quantitative estimates of the relative degree to which variance on each of the various tests in a particular collection of tests is 'loaded' with the source of variance that is common to all the tests in the collection. This ... can be termed a *general factor*, or simply *g* ...
>
> The *g* factor in a large collection of diverse mental tests is a scientifically and practically useful 'working definition' of intelligence. The *g* will differ somewhat from one collection of tests to another, of course, but by selecting diverse tests with the highest *g* loadings in each collection, one can obtain a battery of tests whose *g* is maximally correlated with the *g* of many other collections of diverse tests ...
>
> The best '*intelligence* tests' for practical purposes are those that are both the most highly *g* loaded and the most appropriate for a particular population and circumstances in which they are to be used. (Jensen, in Sternberg and Detterman 1986, pp 110–11).

Note that this definition stipulates how the author is to use the term 'intelligence'. Note also that he provides what might be seen as a *circular definition*, at least in the sense that '*g*' is equated with unspecified results on 'mental' (undefined) tests. (We will return to the question of circularity and discuss *operational definitions*, such as Jensen provides, later in this chapter.)

Because they are setting up conventions, rather than describing existing ones, stipulative definitions cannot be criticised as being incorrect. They are not true or false. This is not to say, however, that they cannot be criticised at all. Apart from the criticism that the words used to define the term do not themselves have a clear meaning, other special criticisms can be levelled against stipulative definitions. These centre on the way in which definitions can be misleading when an idiosyncratic or narrow stipulation is inadequately distinguished from conventional usage. (Two examples: 'IQ' — the stipulative, precise term is not synonymous with everyday 'intelligence'; and 'superego' — the Freudian concept is not the same as, although it has some meaning which overlaps with, 'conscience'.)

Unlike a stipulative definition, a *descriptive definition* can be either right or wrong. It can accurately describe the conventional meaning of the term being used, or it can misrepresent it. In evaluating descriptive definitions, it is also important to distinguish between the meaning, sometimes called the '**intension**', of a term and its 'extension'. The **extension** of a term is the class of all those entities to which the term correctly applies. Thus the extension of the term 'schizophrenic' is the class of all schizophrenics, since they are the people to which the term conventionally applies. Terms that differ in meaning can, nevertheless, sometimes have the same extensions. Two such terms that come close to having the same extension are 'creature with a heart' and 'creature with a kidney'. The meaning or intension of a term determines, but is not determined by, its extension — the class of those things to which it applies. If the extension of the term you propose to use is more restricted than the actual extension of the term when it is used with its usual meaning, your definition will be *too narrow*. If your term has been defined in such a way that it would apply to a wider class than the term is conventionally taken to apply to, then your definition is said to be *too wide*. To illustrate these distinctions, if an author writes, 'As is well known, the term "behaviourist" means "a person who studies behaviour"', then their definition is too wide, as it could be used to apply to (and hence its extension would include) not only behaviourists but other psychologists as well, since non-behaviourists also study behaviour. Equally, an attempted definition of 'language' as 'a vocal system of communication' is a definition that fails to include in its extension the non-vocal sign languages used by the deaf. Consequently, it would be too narrow.

With these points in mind, you can employ stipulative or nominal definitions in many contexts, provided your terminology is made explicit and you are consistent. For example, you can nominate 'manifest anxiety' as the term to summarise scores on various pencil-and-paper tests concerning fear-arousing situations, and so on. In this case, you use an older, perhaps vague term ('anxiety') to relate to certain objective criteria which you specify for the purposes of your essay or report. Such a procedure is defensible on much the same grounds as 'operational' definitions, which we will discuss later in this chapter. Nevertheless, the stipulative aspect of the proposed criteria should not be overlooked, for the criteria may be questioned by psychologists of different theoretical persuasions.

This example indicates the possible abuse of definitions nominated in a particular theoretical framework. The word 'anxiety' has a more general, conventionally accepted usage than applies in the present case. That is, the nominated interpretation is more restricted than the original meaning of the term. Hence, if you do not adhere strictly to the nominated definition the term will acquire 'surplus meaning' — connotations and implications over and above its narrower interpretation. It is important to be aware of this when employing words such as 'anxiety', for there is the danger that the words will be used even by you, in their vague, original sense, however much you alter their usage by stipulation.

To conclude, there can be no hard and fast rules against providing stipulative definitions, for an argument must begin somewhere. It is therefore better to render your terminology explicit than to leave it obscure. Moreover, many expressions 'borrowed' from common language can quite legitimately be 'tidied up' or more narrowly specified in this way. However, nominal or stipulative definitions need to be carefully scrutinised. This is so whether they are obvious verbal tautologies or whether they involve observational, operational criteria. It is important to realise that what are apparently informative definitions may be, at best, quite preliminary, or at worst, quite restricted and arbitrary when further examined. But many types of definitions are subject to similar criticism: theoretical and empirical justification is always required. However, it is fair to emphasise that purely stipulative definitions are particularly prone to one form of abuse — that of 'circularity'.

CIRCULAR DEFINITIONS

Perhaps the most common abuse of definition is the use of essentially **circular**, and hence non-informative, criteria. In such cases, the proposed definition simply gives verbal analysis or seemingly relevant operations which do not really clarify how the term being defined is to be employed. It is this type of circularity that is so blatant in the often-quoted definition of 'intelligence' as 'that which intelligence tests test'. Obviously, if no further detail is provided, this could be criticised as circular because the word 'intelligence' occurs on both 'sides' of the definition. To such critics, the definition is analogous to defining 'tennis' as a 'game played by tennis players', or 'neurosis' as 'the illness suffered by people who are classified as neurotic'. In the case of 'intelligence', if a test is a test of intelligence, the question of what constitutes intelligent behaviour still needs to be specified.

If we adopt circular, or otherwise vague, definitions of terms, we may preclude any genuine argument about substantive issues. For instance, the person who maintains that intelligence is what intelligence tests test may effectively allow no debate about the nature of intelligence (including the criteria by which we might judge behaviour as intelligent or otherwise). They present, as the premise to their argument, a definition that precludes alternatives, and hence, rules out conclusions that could contradict or qualify the original assumption.

The way in which the choice of definition may effectively **beg a question** can be illustrated by the following hypothetical dialogue on a topic of considerable controversy: the issue of whether non-humans can employ language. (The phrase 'to beg the question' refers to the practice of illegitimately assuming what you need to establish.)

A: There is no doubt that lower forms of life than humans can use language.

B: I don't consider that possible. Only people can speak and create novel sentences at will.

A: Yes, but bees can communicate by means of dances. Their dances convey precise information about pollen sources by indicating both the direction and distance of these from the hive.

B: That is so; but merely being able to transmit and receive coded information in that way is not the same thing as using language.

A: Why not? Any organism which can communicate with others of its species must be able to use language — the transmission of coded information is what defines a language system.

B: How can I argue with you? Your definition of language completely *begs the question* (by assuming the answer).

A: So does yours — but in the opposite direction: for you will only allow as language, systems of communication that are practically identical with human speech.

In this dispute, it is clear that *A* and *B* do not really disagree about the evidence before them and the debate results from two opposed and incompatible assumptions. In effect, the debate is exclusively concerned with the definition of 'language'. The antagonists can only 'agree to disagree' about what language 'really' is, or they can accept one definition for the sake of pursuing a related argument. In the latter case, *B* might accept that a language is a coded system of information transmission and proceed to argue for the existence of different types of languages in different animal species.

Whatever the outcome of our hypothetical debate, it is important for students of psychology to be aware of the issue it illustrates: although many discussions appear to be about 'evidence', they are, in fact, centred on questions of definition.

OPERATIONAL DEFINITIONS

Psychologists define terms in order to avoid having their statements misunderstood. As we noted, this is particularly likely in psychology, where everyday terms are often employed with slightly different interpretations in their more formal contexts. One set of examples of this is concepts that have been given scientific quantification by contemporary psychology. Not content with saying that one person is more intelligent than another, the psychologist wishes to measure and describe, in numerical terms, the magnitude of such differences. To speak quantitatively of human intelligence, some reliable measuring instrument and procedures are presupposed. Although the word 'definition' may be something of a misnomer, psychology textbooks speak of providing **'operational definitions'** in these and other cases. In order to understand the importance of the problem of definition in psychology, it is essential to be aware of the historical background to the controversy concerning operational definitions.

However, before presenting this background, let us clarify what we mean by a 'theoretical' term, for it is **theoretical terms** whose clarification and definition are generally regarded as most controversial. Just what constitutes a theoretical term is itself a matter of dispute in psychology, so let us *stipulate* for the duration of this section that a term is 'theoretical' if its use presupposes a body of statements which are necessary for it to be understood. This may be true in varying degrees of all terms. Some terms are clearly used for concepts that have significance only as part of a body of (non-observational) statements. If we consider some examples, *degrees of theoreticity* can be illustrated: The underlined terms in

1 'This is a <u>human.</u>'
2 'This is a <u>bachelor.</u>'
3 'This is a <u>schizophrenic.</u>'

seem to reflect increasing degrees of theoreticity in that they demand increasing knowledge if they are to be correctly (conventionally) used. The terms of an *observation statement* are relatively uncontroversial and are at the opposite pole from theoretical terms, about which most definitional controversy centres.

In the above examples, the underlined terms are increasingly likely to be interpreted differently by people who adopt different general theories. It would be unusual, although not impossible, for people to disagree whether or not someone (or some thing) was 'human', although there may be much more (theoretically motivated) conflict about whether a person is 'schizophrenic'. It would not be unusual for one psychologist to ask another: 'What are the criteria by which you classify someone as schizophrenic?', or, more conventionally, 'What do you mean by "schizophrenic"?' Later we shall see that these two questions may not be identical, but first let us return to the issue of operational definitions, for it is with the aim of providing reliable, uncontroversial meanings for psychological terms that *operationism* developed.

In the early decades of the 20th century, psychology was emerging as a 'science', relying on observations which were 'public' (as opposed to 'private' introspection). It was rather self-consciously adopting the methods of the natural sciences in place of philosophical speculations about the human mind. Its new-found pragmatism and methodologies, however, did not solve the problem of the nature of psychological concepts. Whereas the theoretical terms of physics and biology appeared well-defined and unambiguous (at least to most psychologists), the ghost of mentalistic terminology still haunted the psychological laboratories. Attempts to exorcise this persistent spectre culminated in two (related) schools of thought — *behaviourism* and *operationism*.

To understand the methods and conventions of contemporary psychology, we must know the basic tenets of these two historically important theoretical orientations, for their combined influence has been, and still is, quite profound in many areas of psychology.

As all students of psychology are aware, behaviourism rejected mentalistic concepts in favour of observable physical behaviour. For example, it replaced the 19th-century concept of the 'association of ideas' with the concept of 'stimulus-response connections'. In so doing, it implicitly ruled out the need to provide elaborate verbal definitions of apparently vague terms like 'image', 'idea', 'intensity of sensation', and so on. Many psychologists must have felt a sense of relief at being able to ignore these seemingly intangible concepts without undue pangs of academic conscience. This security was reinforced by what came to be known as *operationism*. This movement excited psychologists in the 1930s because it appeared to legitimise their radical rejection of mentalistic expressions in favour of behavioural description. Psychologists had not been the only scientists experiencing difficulty clarifying their theoretical constructs. It was the attempt to clarify definitions in modern physics that gave direct impetus to a similar program in psychology. In *The Logic of Modern Physics* (1927), Bridgman proposed operational definitions for various physical concepts.

Bridgman argued that the meaning of a term depended on the operations employed to measure or indicate the presence of the phenomenon or quality under consideration. An example may clarify what this analysis involved: the meaning of the word 'velocity' in the context of a particular physical theory can only be precisely specified by detailing the methods (that is, the *operations*) by which velocity is measured.

This anchors the concept to observable processes and apparently obviates the need for further elaborate verbal definition.

In the original formulation, the meaning of a word was said to derive *directly* from the set of corresponding operations. That is to say, a word is completely defined by means of the set of so-called operations. This is an important point: operationism was not proposed merely as a methodological exercise or pragmatic move, but as an analysis of the way in which adequate definitions could be provided for various theoretical terms which might otherwise be obscure. That is, it attempted to provide a *complete* analysis of the *meaning* of scientific terms.

Although it has been severely criticised by philosophers and psychologists (see Michell 1990), operationism was quickly adopted by a psychology wishing to add rigour to its theoretical constructs and divest these of their mentalistic connotations. The appeal of operationism was very great, especially to behaviouristically-oriented psychologists. Terms like 'drive', 'habit strength', 'expectancy', even 'cognitive map', were analysed in a manner termed 'operational'. The philosophical objections to Bridgman's original formulation were largely overlooked by psychology, which saw in operationism a valuable tool for reducing or eliminating the elements of ambiguity inherent in the mentalistic legacy the new science inherited. The influence of operationism is still apparent today, although many of the original tenets of behaviourism have been considerably eroded.

We have said that the original formulation of operationism equated the meaning of a term with a particular set of operational procedures. As critics were quick to point out, this is a very strong thesis concerning definition, one which may have unacceptable consequences. It would seem to imply that literally any variation in observational procedures for measuring a phenomenon or quality in effect redefines that phenomenon or quality. This conclusion seems clear from Bridgman's (1927, p 5) formulation of operationism:

> We may illustrate by considering the concept of length: What do we mean by the length of an object? We evidently know what we mean by length if we can tell what the length of any and every object is, and for the physicist nothing more is required. To find the length of an object, we have to perform certain physical operations. The concept of length is therefore fixed when the operations by which length is measured are fixed: that is the concept of length involves as much as and nothing more than a set of operations. *The concept is synonymous with the corresponding set of operations.*

But a consequence of this view would be that the 'length' of various objects measured by discrete physical matching procedures (using tape-measures or rulers) and the 'length' of interstellar distances are different concepts, for they involve different measuring operations. This raises the question of whether one is justified in using the one word ('length') for both of these (operationally distinct) concepts. Why not give each a different name to mark the differences between the two? There are two possible replies to this question. First, the operationist might argue that some further set of 'higher-level', more general, or abstract operations could be invoked for relating the two original sets of operations in a manner which made one word appropriate to both. Alternatively, they might accept that different words should be used to indicate concepts defined in operationally different ways. This seems a more plausible suggestion: it is quite common for 'scientific' definitions of words also employed in colloquial language to be quite unlike their informal interpretations.

These considerations held sway with many psychologists during the 1930s and 1940s, although the appeal of operationism was greatest amongst some historically very important theorists — especially those studying human learning (for example, Hull and Tolman), which was the paradigm of objective, 'scientific' psychology until at least the late 1950s. However, despite the frequency and apparent ease with which psychologists employ 'operational definitions', there are many criticisms and qualifications relating both to the general thesis of operationism and to the uses to which psychology may put particular 'operational' definitions.

A typical criticism is that operationism fails as an account of how complete scientific definitions are, or could be, provided. For instance, one operational definition of 'hunger' that has been employed concerns the 'duration of food deprivation'. In some contexts this might be an objective, working definition. But it could be argued that it is by no means a complete definition of hunger. It is possible to be deprived of food without feeling hungry (for example, by taking appetite suppressers). Hence the selection of one operation as the defining condition of a term like 'hunger' appears to be, at best, incomplete and, at worst, quite arbitrary. Ironically, the very goal of operational definitions which were proposed to allow objective and reliable terms cannot be achieved simply by spelling out one or a few operational aspects of an otherwise complex concept. On the contrary, the choice of 'operations' may be just as arbitrary or restricted as the verbal definitions which they supposedly replace. Mandler and Kessen (1959, p 111) make this point in the following way:

> Unfortunately, it is neither particularly scientific nor useful to adopt a word and to define it in terms of some set of operations. This *alone* is obviously possible in the most tender-minded investigation; it is a trivial bow in the direction of scientific respectability and

satisfies only the most primitive notions of scientific communication. However, the use of a term which is *already* functioning in a scientific framework imposes certain limitations on the investigator, and this imposition tends to be a function of the historical and theoretical use of the term. When a new set of operations is employed for a particular term, its definition is extended. At this point an operational analysis will be helpful in specifying new areas of application and new grammatical relationships.

In general, the more abstract a psychological concept is, the more variable will be its attempted definition, whether 'operational' or not. Hence, a word like 'intelligence' creates many definitional problems. Indeed, for a time some psychologists seriously advocated defining intelligence as 'that which intelligence tests test'. Because such tests were widely used and the term 'intelligence' was already functioning when this analysis was advanced, there was a sense in which the slogan was not just a tautology. But as a viable descriptive *definition*, it is none the less somewhat circular or, at best, incomplete. For it merely leaves unspecified the actual criteria for judging something to be an 'intelligence' test (as opposed to, say, an 'aptitude' or 'personality' test). One can still ask: Is speed of mental functioning a dimension of intelligence? Are clerical accuracy or artistic skills to be seen as aspects of 'intelligence' according to some operational criteria? The answers to these questions are not given by the glib 'operational' formula. They will depend on further theoretical analysis of the concept of intelligence to which empirical findings (for example, intercorrelations between tests or test items) will probably be relevant.

Operationism, therefore, offers no simple panacea to the problems of definition. The question that arises is how the student of psychology should regard operational definitions in view of these theoretical limitations. One way of benefiting from this controversy is to see the requirement of operational objectivity from a more general perspective than psychologists originally viewed it. It might be more profitable to regard operational analyses as attempts to specify precise *criteria* for scientific *usage* of terms, rather than as offering complete, unambiguous and unalterable *definitions*. One can then restate the essential insight of operationism in the following manner: *operations can be best employed to determine if and when a term is applicable*. That is, they serve as criteria for using a term. Thus the 'meaning' of a term is left partially 'open' and only the criteria for employing the term in a given context are specified.

This is a somewhat 'weaker', more pragmatic approach to the problem of definition than the stricter versions of operationism. Indeed, contemporary psychologists seldom explicitly refer to operational criteria as such, although they seek to be as precise and explicit as possible in defining their theoretical terms. It is best to err on the side of too much, rather than too little, specification of when a term applies in your writing and research. Communication relies on reliable, empirically viable interpretations of otherwise ambiguous terms.

DEFINITIONS AND CRITERIA FOR THE USE OF THEORETICAL TERMS

The history of operationism shows that there is an important difference between providing a definition for a term and providing criteria for its application. To have criteria for the application of a term is to have some way of telling whether or not the term applies to any entity. An example from chemistry is the litmus paper test for the presence of an acid. Given that a substance is either an acid or an alkali, the test is: if it turns litmus paper red, it is taken to be an acid; if it turns litmus paper blue, it is taken to be an alkali. This criterion provides an observable means of classifying substances — at least in respect of alkalinity and acidity. However, knowing the criterion does not mean being able to define what an alkali or acid is in the sense of being able to specify the essential attributes of each type of substance in a more general way. It would seem fair to say that a person could reliably judge to which of these two classes a substance belonged without knowing how the two differed from each other in general. That is, one may employ a term quite reliably by means of a criterion for deciding when it applies, without knowing what the term 'means' — that is, without being able to provide a general definition which goes beyond that limited criterion. Paradoxically, this may be the case even when a term is very widely used in a discipline like psychology or medicine.

It is relatively easy to specify, and gain consensus about, the criteria for calling someone 'schizophrenic' or 'diabetic', even though it may be difficult to gain general agreement concerning a definition of the term. (This is certainly true of the term 'schizophrenic'.) Indeed, psychologists and doctors might be said not to know what a 'schizophrenic' or a 'diabetic' is, in this sense, at all!

Conversely, it is frequently argued that if we are to know the meaning of a term and be able to use it significantly, then we must be able to judge of any entity whether or not the term applies to it. This view is what appears to motivate psychologists' ready acceptance of operational definitions, for these specify routine, observable procedures for deciding the application of a particular term. However, it can be seen that this underlying view involves too strong a condition for many quite adequate definitions to meet. Although it would seem ideal to have some way of definitely determining whether an entity is or is not correctly described by a term, the lack of such a criterion does not imply that we do not know what the term means. For example, most people know what it means to have conceived a child, but only specially trained persons can spell out decisive criteria for deciding if this has occurred (at least during the early stages). This might also be said of a wide variety of medical and psychological concepts referring to physical conditions or behavioural dispositions. For instance, one may know the meaning of the term 'defensive', as this might be applied to an individual personality, without being able to offer any finite set of criteria for infallibly deciding whether a reaction is defensive. Despite this, the term can be used in a meaningful and precise way within a particular set of theoretical assumptions (in this case, the psychoanalytic theory of defense mechanisms).

Of course, operationists might see this example in a different light. They regard observable criteria as *essential* for the scientifically precise application of a term, and could therefore deny that the person using the term 'defensive' could really be claimed to know its meaning at all if they cannot also provide criteria for its application. Without, at least, the possibility of such criteria, the term is, for all 'scientific' purposes, meaningless. This strong thesis concerning the meaningfulness of terms seems to lie behind the view of many influential psychologists that theoretical terms cannot be employed unless they are capable of being unequivocally related to observable criteria analogous to the litmus paper test for distinguishing acids from alkalis. However, as we have argued above, this seems to be a very restrictive analysis of the meaningfulness of scientific terms.

Theoretical terms are very important in the vocabulary of the social sciences, where there may be no clear criteria to provide guidance concerning usage. Theoretical terms generally refer to unobserved entities whose existence would systematically explain a number of observed phenomena. An example from physics is the term 'electron'; one from psychology is 'unconscious wish'. Their existence could be taken to explain a variety of phenomena. However, the links with the observable processes or events are so diffuse that such terms generally lack decisive criteria for their application, and yet, in the context of their respective theories, they do not lack meaning.

One area where it is reasonable to ask for specific criteria for the application of a term is in the reporting of experimental results. For instance, readers of a learning-experiment report must be provided with information concerning criteria by means of which to infer, say, forgetting of material by subjects, unless there is no doubt that the reader will otherwise understand which commonly accepted criteria apply in that particular type of experiment.

In conclusion, therefore, criteria that are sufficient to justify the application of a theoretical term are not identical to a definition of that term. Yet many types of 'definition' offered within psychology are really more accurately described as attempts to specify unambiguous criteria for adopting a term in a particular context. Operational 'definitions' are essentially of this type. Indeed, to call them definitions at all may be mistakenly to assume that they are complete specifications of a term's meaning. We have suggested that many terms (for example, 'libido', 'hysteria', 'proactive inhibition') derive their meanings from sets of theoretical statements and their underlying assumptions. (It is difficult to understand the concept of libido apart from a general knowledge of Freud's theories, for instance.)

Hence, there are many ways of *clarifying* the meanings of theoretical terms. The procedure that is best called *definition* involves the specification of words or phrases which as nearly as possible have the same meaning as the term defined. Other, perhaps equally important, aspects of clarification include: indicating some of the phenomena to which the term applies (giving examples) or to which it does not apply; specifying some criteria for deciding if it is applicable; or even simply ruling out some of the alternative, confusing meanings with which the term is sometimes used. The methods you should adopt will depend on the degree to which the term is dependent on its theoretical context and on the availability of operational criteria. No single approach to clarifying what psychological terms mean will do the job in every case.

THINGS, PROPERTIES AND RELATIONS

In psychology, perhaps more than in any other science, there is a strong tendency for words to become 'reified'. **Reification**[2] consists of the unwarranted assumption that a noun which labels an abstract concept actually names, or applies to, a discrete physical entity. This can most easily occur when abstract psychological adjectives ('intelligent', 'anxious', 'neurotic') are converted into their noun forms ('intelligence', 'anxiety', 'neurosis') and assumed to refer to specific objects or processes which people possess to various degrees.

The reification of qualities of people into 'things' or entities can be avoided if we specify carefully what we are actually referring to in using a particular term. To do this, it is important not to confuse *relations between or amongst things* with the *properties of things*. Take people's heights as an example. One person is taller than another. This is a relation between the two — the two stand in a certain relation with respect to height. Similarly, one person may perform differently from another on a test of reaction times or of numerical calculation. We may then say

---

[2] Another word frequently used to refer to this process is *hypostatisation* (verb: *hypostatise*), not to be confused with hypothesisation, which does not imply any confusion of abstract concepts and concrete entities.

that one is faster or more computationally competent than the other (or than some proportion of a given population). It is easy, then, to move from this statement about relations between people's respective levels of performance to statements about the qualities or attributes of the people themselves. We might say that one person 'is a quick reactor' or 'has high computational ability'. In taking this step, we are describing the qualities of people (and assuming they 'possess' these qualities to various degrees). This may lead us to speak as though the quality (inferred from a relational observation) is an entity or thing with an independent existence. It is easy to confuse relations between things with qualities of things, and also to make qualities (attributes) into things. A most common example of the former confusion is the use of the word 'difference' itself as though it referred to the qualities of people or of things. 'Ethnic difference' (the differences between two groups of people) may seem to be a quality of one of the groups in question. It is then possible to see this 'difference' as part of the ethnic group's characteristics when, of course, the difference is the relation between it and some other group on some variable(s) or attribute(s).

To see this confusion clearly, we might ask: Can a person be different or only *different from* another in a certain respect? To *reify* 'difference' is to commit a potentially misleading logical error. The interpretation of difference as a quality *of* things, and not as a relation *between* things, may encourage us to think of qualities as things also. For instance, all objects have volume and colour. These are two of their qualities. But their volume or their colour are not entities in themselves: red(ness) or blue(ness) is not usefully considered an object or entity, even though English lets us use such noun forms to refer to such qualities. Such 'thingification' is one instance of what we will mean by 'reification' in this chapter.

Reification is so prevalent in ordinary speech as to go largely unnoticed. For instance, the evaluative adjectives 'good' and 'bad' often are made into nouns. Yet these are *evaluative* words, not *descriptive*. So, there can be disagreement about the criteria that apply in particular cases (what is a 'good' film, for instance) and even about the meaningfulness of evaluative adjectives in general. It is clear that when these adjectives are converted into nouns, reification frequently results. People often speak as though 'goodness' and 'evil' ('badness') were psychological qualities a person possesses in the same way as they possess, say, red hair or blue eyes. We hear it said that a person 'has a lot of goodness' or 'possesses great virtue'. Although it is easy to speak of such qualities in this way and in most cases no serious confusion results, it is only a short step to some very important sources of confusion concerning psychological language. This arises out of a failure to distinguish clearly between *evaluation* and *interpretation* on the one hand,

and *description* on the other. Let us make some preliminary points about the distinction before relating it to the issue of reification.

At a superficial level, the grammatical form of evaluative and descriptive statements is the same, but this is no guide to their semantic roles. We can say '*x* is intelligent', '*x* is good', '*x* is neurotic', '*x* is male', '*x* is blue-eyed', using the same type of sentence. But there are differences between some of these statements that may be quite important. Whether a particular example is regarded as a description or an interpretation of a phenomenon is open to debate, to which the following considerations are relevant. Consider '*x* is intelligent' and '*x* is male'. These two statements can be regarded as strictly descriptive (and hence devoid of evaluative overtones) only if it can be assumed that the criteria by which intelligent behaviour and biological gender can be ascertained are unambiguous and known to all parties to the debate about the issue. There will generally be consensus about criteria relating to gender identification and the statement '*x* is male' can be regarded as descriptive. On the other hand, '*x* is intelligent' need not be regarded as descriptive in this sense. For as we have seen, criteria for its application may be quite controversial. In everyday situations, these criteria probably relate to academic achievement and some vaguely defined dimensions of social behaviour. But such criteria are not the only ones by which someone might be judged 'intelligent'. The choice of criteria will probably involve what must be termed a *value judgment* — either implicitly or explicitly. Such evaluation is also salient in the case of '*x* is neurotic' and, by definition, in '*x* is good'. Indeed, it is not uncommon for one person to regard a certain person as 'neurotic' when another might regard them as morally very worthy (for example, a highly religious person).

These examples suggest that between evaluative predicates[3] (like 'good') and relatively neutral descriptive words (such as 'male'), there is a range of terms (including 'intelligent' and 'neurotic') which require explicit consensus about relevant criteria if the biases of personal preferences are to be overcome.

The importance of the evaluation/description issue for what we have called *reification* should now be fairly clear. It is this: whenever evaluative predicates are wrongly interpreted as *descriptive* of some invariant characteristic of a person whose behaviour is being considered, then an abstraction has been reified. When we make the semantic leap from evaluation (however implicit this might sometimes be) to apparently 'objective' description of 'what a person is like', we may

---

[3] The analysis of the language of evaluation and moral judgments is a very complex area of philosophy. For the purpose of this elementary discussion, we have had to oversimplify, concentrating on some of the most obvious abuses of evaluative terms.

confuse the criteria of evaluation with the person or the behaviour being judged. The next step in the process is the easy transition from adjective to noun, signifying the ultimate 'thingification' of the original term. Although it would be quite pedantic to suggest that all words from everyday English that suggest the possibility of reification should be avoided, you need to be aware of the possibility of using nouns in naive, 'reified' ways.

To return to our (convenient, if rather over-simplified) example of 'intelligence': people do commonly speak of a person's intelligence in much the same way as they discuss, say, their bank account. People have a certain amount of intelligence (in their heads) and a certain amount of money (in the bank).[4] The main danger of this metaphor is that it may lead us to search for answers to questions that we might otherwise not be inclined to formulate. For instance, we might ask (as many introductory psychology texts still do) questions like, 'How much (that is, what percentage) of a person's intelligence is due to hereditary factors and what percentage is due to environment?' Because the question is posed in this apparently simple, quantitative way, it will probably be answered in a corresponding manner: say, '80 per cent heredity, 20 per cent environment'. Taken in isolation, such an issue appears to be as simple as asking which financial interests contributed most to a company's profit — the bonds or the risk capital. If the question can be asked in simple quantitative terms, then, presumably, it can be answered in the same terms. However, the analogy between an individual's intelligence and a commercial company's assets or income is by no means as simple as this example suggests. Although the grammatical form of the questions is similar, it does not follow that their meaningfulness and empirical validity are equally clear. It may only be by reifying 'intelligence' in a very crude way that the analogy appears to be valid at all.

It is examples such as this that have led some psychologists to argue that practically all common-language mentalistic abstractions involve implicit reification. The most radical proponent of this view was BF Skinner who, in his controversial book *Beyond Freedom and Dignity* (1973, pp 13–14), likened many of these would-be explanatory concepts to mythical 'pre-scientific' causes, akin to hypotheses about 'essences' and magical 'forces' — even to possession by the gods. He states:

---

[4] Psychological predicates like 'intelligent', 'honest', 'neurotic', and so on, may also be interpreted as 'dispositions to behaviour' of various kinds. Just as we say that sugar is soluble, meaning that it will react in specific ways in liquids of certain kinds, so, when we say someone is 'intelligent' we imply a disposition towards certain types of behaviour in particular circumstances. Apparent reification may sometimes be merely an abbreviated way of referring to such dispositional concepts. Nevertheless, at other times there is genuine confusion of concepts and what they refer to.

Man's first experience with causes probably came from his own behaviour: things moved because he moved them. If other things moved, it was because someone else was moving them, and if the mover could not be seen, it was because he was invisible. The Greek gods served in this way as the causes of physical phenomena. They were usually outside the things they moved but they might enter into and 'possess' them. Physics and biology soon abandoned explanations of this sort and turned to more useful kinds of causes, but the step has not been decisively taken in the field of human behaviour. Intelligent people no longer believe that men are possessed by demons (although the exorcism of devils is occasionally practised, and the daimonic has reappeared in the writings of psychotherapists), but human behaviour is still commonly attributed to indwelling agents. A juvenile delinquent is said, for example, to be suffering from a disturbed personality: There would be no point in saying it if the personality were not somehow distinct from the body which has got itself into trouble. The distinction is clear when one body is said to contain several personalities which control it in different ways at different times. Psychoanalysts have identified three of these personalities — the ego, superego, and id — and interactions among them are said to be responsible for the behaviour of the man in whom they dwell.

The immediate problem with Skinner's rejection of internal causes of behaviour is that it allows no place at all for 'mental' qualities, capacities or dispositions. He rejects both the crudely reified concepts and many to which this label does not necessarily apply. Rather indiscriminately, he lumps all such postulates together, judging all as 'pre-scientific'. Therefore, it may be fair for him to agree with Isaac Newton, who complained to a contemporary that 'to tell us that every species of thing is endowed with an occult specific quality by which it acts and produces manifest effects is to tell us nothing'. But it does not follow that Skinner should reject all traditional psychological predicates as non-informative — a process he wishes to do (p 15) with the following, heterogeneous set of examples:

Almost everyone who is concerned with human affairs — as political scientist, philosopher, man of letters, economist, psychologist, linguist, sociologist, theologian, anthropologist, educator, or psychotherapist — continues to talk about human behaviour in this pre-scientific way. Every issue of a daily paper, every magazine, every professional journal, every book with any bearing whatsoever on human behaviour will supply examples. We are told that to control the number of people in the world we need to change attitudes towards children, overcome pride in size of family or in sexual potency, build some sense of responsibility towards offspring, and reduce the role played by a large family in allaying concern for old age. To work for peace we must deal with the will to power or

> the paranoid delusions of leaders; we must remember that wars
> begin in the minds of men, that there is something suicidal in man
> — a death instinct, perhaps — which leads to war, and that man
> is aggressive by nature. To solve the problems of the poor we must
> inspire self-respect, encourage initiative, and reduce frustration.
> To allay the disaffection of the young we must provide a sense of
> purpose and reduce feelings of alienation or hopelessness.
> Realizing that we have no effective means of doing any of this, we
> ourselves may experience a crisis of belief or a loss of confidence,
> which can be corrected only by returning to a faith in man's inner
> capacities. This is staple fare.

Not all of these psychological expressions are simple reifications of non-physical concepts. 'Instincts', 'attitudes' and 'frustration' may be terms which are capable of being made sufficiently clear to enable them to be employed in precise scientific study. Although they are sometimes abused in the way Skinner suggests, they need not be so abused. The issue is not simply that of whether a term refers to physical, observable processes (which, for Skinner, means 'behaviour'); it is rather a question of whether, in the context of psychological theory, they are essential for the explanation of behaviour. However, this is a complex problem that raises important philosophical questions concerning the nature of science and scientific constructs which cannot be fully considered here. Suffice it to note that rejecting a concept because it is argued to involve reification may require more justification than that given in arguments like the one quoted above. Certainly we would advise taking each case on its merits within its context.

Having made this point, it must be admitted that the temptation to reify psychological concepts is very great — especially when novel theoretical terminology is being introduced in elementary textbooks. Hence, despite the cautionary statement that the Freudian id, ego and superego 'do not exist as separate real entities and signify nothing in themselves', Lovell (1968, p 87) defines the first of these in the following way:

> The id, which is almost wholly within the unconscious mind, con-
> sists of instinctual drives; it knows neither values nor morality, it is
> non-rational and demands immediate satisfaction, and is essential-
> ly pleasure loving.

It is very difficult to avoid thinking of such constructs as mental agencies or forces, just as Skinner warns against. Hence, when Lovell goes on to state 'When a child acts on impulse and throws a stone though a window he is under the control of the id' (ibid), he is using the Freudian concept to *explain* (at least verbally) the behaviour in question. This is very obviously the type of expression at which objections such as Skinner's are directed.

In conclusion, although psychological terms are subject to two important abuses (circularity and reification), they can be employed in precise theoretical statements if their meanings are carefully clarified and made explicit. Psychological terms, like those from other disciplines, may be employed reliably and consistently by various authors provided that some explicit clarification or definition is proposed. This may consist of a stipulative, descriptive definition showing how an author intends to use a term, or it may involve the provision of operational criteria. In either case, vagueness and inconsistency should be avoided. However, because theoretical terms to some extent derive their meanings from the respective theories of which they are part, their broad justification will normally involve questions which relate to the adequacy of the statements (and assumptions) of such theories. The problems of definition and use of theoretical terms are not distinct from considerations of the general adequacy of theories.

JARGON AND OBSCURANTISM

The technical vocabulary of a discipline, its **jargon**, is, as the preceding discussion attests, what makes specific definition so necessary. It is also what most frustrates students new to a field of study. We discuss in Chapter 9 practical aspects of the problems raised by elaborate technical language that may presuppose specialised theoretical contexts. Here we emphasise that jargon is unavoidable, but that explicit definition is the best defence against obscurity and the deliberately vague, self-important verbiage that is sometimes called 'obscurantist'. Consider the following, noting the many jargon words which non-psychologists would need to have defined before they could understand the paragraph:

> The construct 'personality' may be conceived as a psychic system of structures and functions paralleling those of the body. It is not a pot-pourri of unrelated traits and miscellaneous behaviours, but a tightly knit organisation of stable structures (e.g. internalised memories and self images) and coordinated functions (e.g. unconscious mechanisms and cognitive processes) ... The system *is* the sum and substance of what the construct 'personality' would 'mean'.
> (Milton 1990, pp 339–40)

The technical terms in such a definitional passage would require definition themselves if the obscurity of its claims were to be eliminated. Yet the paragraph is not intentionally opaque, just technical and definitionally incomplete as it stands.

Obscurantism involves using words for words' sake: terms which are used to convey the sense that a passage is technically sophisticated but which are difficult or impossible to understand because they are undefined or undefinable. The following example seems to exemplify this opaque style. We make no further comment, other than to reassure readers that the difficulty of such verbiage should not be allowed to intimidate them.

> Suppose, then, that such a thought is a mental tokening, tokening, that is, of some mental sentence. How do we know the lucid content of the sentence tokened? The answer is that consciousness produces a nexus of metamental ascent and descent, quotation and disquotation, that, combined with our understanding of the sentence, yields our knowledge of lucid content. Consciousness creates a kind of metamental loop from quotation of the token back on itself as an exemplar of a token having a certain kind of function or role. (Lehrer 1996, p 85)

If nothing else, such an example indicates the need for definition within a precise theoretical context.

SUMMARY

Thinking and arguing about psychological issues requires careful attention to the use of words. Defining what you will mean by a term in your essays is an important first step in making a clear argument.

Some definitions merely stipulate how a term will be used; others describe precisely how they are usually used in psychology or in the area of the discipline in which you are writing.

Operational definitions specify the set of operations which can be said to show what a word means (for example, 'length' as different methods of measurement, 'intelligence' as a set of tests). This type of definition is sometimes criticised as circular, or as incomplete or arbitrary. It may be better to think of operations as criteria for applying a term, rather than as complete definitions.

Reification is the name given to confusing abstract words with physical things. We called it 'thingification' and pointed out that many psychological concepts which are postulated to explain behaviour and cognition may involve merely giving a physical-sounding name to cover one's ignorance, rather than providing an adequate explanation of the phenomenon in question.

The main lessons to take away from this chapter are that circular and reified definitions should be avoided and that it is important to be explicit in defining the words (the technical or specialist words) you use when writing about psychological questions.

KEYWORDS

• REGISTER • (FALLACY OF) EQUIVOCATION • STIPULATIVE DEFINITION • WORKING DEFINITION • DESCRIPTIVE DEFINITION • CONNOTATIONS • INTENSION • EXTENSION • CIRCULAR DEFINITION • BEG THE QUESTION • OPERATIONISM/OPERATIONAL DEFINITION • THEORETICAL TERMS • DEFINITION • CRITERIA FOR USE OF TERMS • REIFICATION • JARGON • OBSCURANTISM

EXERCISES

1   Concepts like intelligence are defined in terms of a general theoretical network, and within this network they are given operational definition in terms of some kind of measurement.

Gravitation is a concept we arrive at by measuring certain properties in a network that includes falling apples and circling planets — this is, its operational definition. The same is true of intelligence, and the often used answer 'intelligence is what intelligence tests measure' is neither an attempt to avoid the question nor a mere tautology. In a very real sense, the question 'What is electricity?' can be answered by enumerating the experiments we use to measure electricity. Electricity is that which turns a magnetic needle when passing over it; it is that which makes iron magnetic when passing around it (Eysenck 1971, p 51).

a   Is the analogy between intelligence and gravity or electricity as direct as Eysenck argues here? Why or why not?

b   Is it likely that intelligence will ever be other than operationally defined? Does this apply to electricity or to gravity?

   (See also the questions relating to Eysenck's view of intelligence in the exercises for Chapter 6.)

c   Compare this definition with the operational definition by Jensen in this chapter.

Learning refers to increased frequency or speed of response emission as a result of practice. It excludes changes in response tendency due to maturation or other 'internal' physiological changes such as those due to lesions or general atrophy of the nervous system.

a   Is this an acceptable definition of learning? Why or why not?

b   Given that we can learn a skill or response 'tendency' without overtly performing it, would this preclude the possibility of defining learning solely in *operational* terms?

2   Siegler et al (1972, p 104) criticise RD Laing's contention that 'schizophrenia' is not 'really' a disease. They state:

> First, Laing finds the practice of assigning diagnostic labels to patients unacceptable. He says: 'It is wrong to impute a hypothetical disease of unknown etiology and undiscovered pathology to someone unless he can prove otherwise' (R.D. Laing, *The politics of experience*, 1967, p 71). Laing is certainly entitled to believe that this is wrong, but it is only fair to note that the practice of medicine consists to a great extent of imputing hypothetical diseases of unknown etiology and undiscovered pathology to patients who are in no position to prove otherwise. *All diseases are hypothetical, all are labels*. There is no such thing as diabetes, there are only individuals who have certain experiences and physical symptoms which are said to have some relation to the hypothetical disease. Yet such a disease entity is an extremely powerful category, for all its philosophical inelegance [emphasis added].

a   What is the authors' reason for claiming that 'all diseases are hypothetical, all are labels'? What objections can be made to this claim?

b   How is the concept of *reification* relevant to both Laing's original statement (quoted) and to Siegler et al's objection?

3   (i)   Aggression is behaviour intended to harm (physically or psychologically) another living organism.

   (ii)   Aggression research deals with 'collective or individual fighting behaviour in man and animals and with all those emotional states which accompany it' (Maple and Matheson 1973, p 3).

   (iii) Aggression is a global concept which embraces behaviours deliberately or intentionally delivering noxious stimuli to other organisms.

   (iv)   Aggression refers to any type of energetic, highly aroused, potentially physically harmful behaviour.

Compare these definitions of aggression, and ask yourself the following questions:

a   Does each allow behaviour to be unambiguously labelled as aggressive or not? (For example, how, if at all, could each encompass the concept of 'unconscious' aggression, or ritualistic, 'instinctive' fighting in lower organisms?)

b   In the light of your answer to (a), can you suggest any 'operational' criteria for judging behaviour as aggressive?

4   There is a tendency among psychologists, as well as their students, to disregard theoretical issues concerning definitions of terms in the belief that these will disappear as more research findings accumulate. This may, of course, be quite justifiable. But it may perpetuate confusions.

   The following passages are taken from McClelland's famous paper, 'Some Social Consequences of Achievement Motivation' (1955). He states, 'Today we have begun to study motivation in its own right', and, later, 'It is becoming increasingly clear that we must pay attention to the type of motive we are measuring, its particular origins, and its particular consequences for human behaviour and society'. Yet, discussing the achievement motive, 'The human motive about which we know the most at the present time', he concedes:

> It will have to suffice here to say that we have developed what appears to be a promising method of measuring the achievement motive ... There are those who argue that what we are identifying ... are not really motives at all but something else, perhaps habits.
> I don't want to seem too light hearted about psychological theory, but I should hate to see too much energy expended in debating the point. If someone can plan and execute a better research by calling these measures habits, so much the better ...

> The fact of the matter is that we know too little about either motives or habits to get into a very useful discussion as to which is which. The important thing is that we accumulate data as rapidly and systematically as we can. Then I believe these theoretical issues will have a way of boiling them selves down to a meaningful level at which they can be settled. (McClelland, in King 1961, p 80)

a   Comment on the relationship between definition and data expressed here. Is McClelland consistent in his viewpoint in the sections quoted?

b   Are the explanatory (including predictive) consequences of an achievement motive similar to those implied by calling it a 'habit'? If not, can we avoid some attempt at precise definition?

5   By the term 'thinking' we mean a connected flow of ideas or mental actions directed towards some clear end or purpose. Such a definition distinguishes between true thinking on the one hand, and dreams and day-dreams on the other. In fantasy, for example, our thoughts wander, are often unconnected and are not consciously checked (Lovell 1968, p 21).

a   What type of definition is this?

b   What assumptions does it make?

c   Given this definition of thinking, what mental processes other than fantasy, dreams and day-dreams would be excluded?

d   '... (P)ersonality represents those characteristics of the person that account for consistent patterns of behaviour' (Pervin 1993, p 3).

Is this a useful definition, or is it theoretically 'loaded' and/or too narrow?

6   'Put most simply, gender identity is an individual's structured set of gendered personal identities' (Ashmore 1990, p 514).

a   This appears circular. What would need to be specified to avoid that criticism?

chapter 5

Interpreting psychological evidence

In scientific investigations it is permitted to invent any hypothesis, and if it explains various large and independent classes of facts it rises to the rank of a well-grounded theory.

Charles Darwin

INTRODUCTION

Psychology, one often hears, is just 'common sense'. If this were true this chapter would be unnecessary, for it deals with three aspects of the interpretation of evidence which, although very sensible, are not commonly understood by newcomers to the study of human behaviour. Each section emphasises the need for care in the interpretation of misleadingly simple evidence — the type of evidence that non-psychologists all too readily invoke to support their generalisations. We emphasise the difficulties involved in drawing inferences, generalisations and theoretical conclusions from observational evidence.

First, we consider the comparative nature of evidence — stressing the need for appropriate 'control' conditions, the problems of confounded variables, and demand characteristics in psychological research. Second, we analyse the concept of 'cause' and distinguish it from correlation. Emphasis is placed on the difficulty of making causal inferences, given the many types of psychological research evidence. Third, we critically consider evidence based on man–animal and man–machine analogies.

In considering claims about the results of experimental research, there is relatively little room for disagreement. The majority of statements describing the outcomes will be uncontroversial reports of what happened — either what we have called 'observation statements' or statements readily obtained from them, such as descriptions of average performance levels on some task. In contrast, the discussion section of a paper (see Chapter 11) will contain many more controversial statements, for it is here that authors interpret the evidence provided by their research. They draw conclusions from the data, attempting to give the findings wider significance. In short, the writer will offer some *explanation* of them. Indeed, *interpreting* evidence *is* offering an **explanation** of it.

To develop an adequate explanation, it is critical to look for, and to compare, *alternative explanations*. Generally, evidence that is to be interpreted will consist of observed phenomena, correlations, statistically based descriptions of group differences, inferred experimental effects, and so on, and the interpretation will consist of some hypothesis (or hypotheses) intended to explain these phenomena. The question that always arises is: *Is this particular hypothesis the best explanation?* As we saw in Chapter 3 on explanation, sometimes what purports to be an explanation cannot be independently tested and so is of little interest. Other possible hypotheses may be testable, but shown to be false and therefore unsatisfactory; and sometimes the preferred explanation, although not conclusively ruled out on such grounds, is not judged to be as good as another explanation. The alternative may be simpler, less *ad hoc*, of wider generality, and so on. (Recall the criteria mentioned in Chapter 3.) The ability to evaluate psychological evidence, to make reasoned comparisons, is demanded of students at all levels of study. So, let us turn to some important aspects of this task.

THE COMPARATIVE NATURE OF EVIDENCE

In everyday conversations, as well as in more formal psychological discussions, people often makes statements about the effects of some set of conditions on some form of behaviour. For instance, they may claim that antisocial behaviour results from the exposure of young children to violent television programs, or that female sex roles are imposed by the child's early family life. However, the evidence on which assertions about such factors are based is seldom made explicit or critically evaluated. Most people simply rely on their own informal observations of a limited number of examples to support these claims. For the psychologist, however, this is not good enough. The psychologist will frequently question the conclusion of another person's argument by examining the evidence (or lack of it) which relates to that conclusion. Saying what causes some type of behaviour can often go beyond what is justified by the available evidence. You usually cannot directly observe causes; they can only be inferred. Justifying particular causal inferences is, perhaps, the most common task of psychology, so let us look at what is at stake in some examples which have been the subject of debate in the academic literature as well as in popular discussion of psychological issues.

Our first example concerns the interpretation of many unusual, dramatic forms of behaviour as being caused by a 'state' called 'hypnosis'. Most people have seen stage or television hypnotists such as David Copperfield apparently wielding inexplicable power over helpless individuals. Such dramatic demonstrations may make the observer seek some explanation of this apparent 'power' either in the hypnotist or in the person being 'controlled'. It is not unusual for various abnormal psychic powers to be attributed to the hypnotist, for he (it is usually a man) is in control of the situation.

Hypnosis has long interested psychologists. Indeed, it has perplexed them for well over a century. Subjects 'under the influence' of hypnotic suggestion have exhibited dramatic, seemingly inexplicable actions, even under carefully controlled laboratory conditions. These actions range from apparently 're-living' early 'unremembered' childhood experiences, to committing dangerous acts (such as handling ostensibly dangerous snakes) or acts which apparently conflict with the subject's moral beliefs (such as stealing). Recently, the question of whether adults can, under hypnosis, recall 'repressed memories' of sexual abuse has become a matter of serious public concern. The evaluation and the status of such 'memories' are questions that raise anew many of the issues dealt with in the older psychological literature on hypnosis.

In the light of demonstrations of apparently involuntary behaviour, it was tempting for psychologists to attribute some causal role to the state of hypnotic trance, for the evidence on which this interpretation rested seemed unambiguous. However, since the 1970s it has been emphasised that the numerous examples of hypnotically induced behaviour are, *of themselves*, insufficient to allow one to attribute a causal role to the hypothetical hypnotic state. It has been pointed out that many of the dramatic forms of behaviour apparently elicited by hypnosis can also be produced in subjects who are instructed to *pretend* they are hypnotised. That is, the *comparison* of groups of 'hypnotised' and 'unhypnotised' subjects, given otherwise similar instructions, does not always show the dramatic *differences* that might be expected if hypnosis is a powerful causal state. Subjects told to pretend they are hypnotised will also frequently perform ostensibly dangerous acts. For example, TX Barber, in an article titled 'Who Believes in Hypnosis?' (Maas 1974), points out that a variety of phenomena which were long assumed to be unique to hypnotised subjects could be observed in non-hypnotised persons as well. Some of the things people did were like the very dramatic actions induced by stage hypnotists, and included making their bodies rigid enough to be stretched out like a plank, head on one chair, feet on another; the disappearance of warts; and apparent insensitivity to pain!

Without going into further details of this case, it is clear that the original interpretation of both the nature and importance of the hypnotic 'trance', and the dramatic power attributed to hypnosis, depended on inadequate evidence. It had been wrongly assumed that the various feats just mentioned could be performed *only* by hypnotised subjects. The failure to *compare* groups of subjects given instructions to simulate hypnotic behaviour with those actually hypnotised rendered the apparent effects of hypnosis more unusual than they might otherwise have appeared. In short, the moral of this example is that demonstrating a phenomenon, *in isolation*, may be quite misleading. Showing *differences between* groups, not just describing the particular characteristics of any one group, is necessary if you are to infer that you have isolated the cause of a particular phenomenon.

CONTROL GROUPS

The hypnosis example has highlighted the need for comparative evidence. Normally, comparison conditions are incorporated into experimental designs in the form of what are called 'control groups'. There may be one or more of these in a particular experiment. A **control group** usually consists of a number of subjects exposed to the same conditions as those of the experimental group or groups, *except for one variable* in which the experimenter is primarily interested. In most simple experiments, the control group or condition constitutes a 'base rate' comparison condition against which experimental effects can be gauged. Therefore, in studies of the effects of practice on learning, at least two groups are necessary: one group practises a task for a certain period and is then assessed; the other spends an equivalent period on some irrelevant task and is then assessed. Assuming the groups are comparable at the outset, different performances are taken to reflect the effects of the intervening practice.

To return to the hypnosis example, appropriate control or comparison conditions were not regarded as necessary by early researchers in the area. This was probably because the dramatic phenomenon of hypnosis appeared to be so obviously different from the normal range of human behaviour that the need for comparison groups was never even considered. In many non-experimental contexts, comparison conditions are either considered unnecessary or are not studied owing to practical difficulties. For example, samples of black children in the United States, on average, have frequently been shown to score lower on standard IQ tests than did 'comparable' white children. How these data are to be interpreted, however, is a matter of great controversy. It depends on whether you accept the validity of comparisons between the samples actually tested. The obvious question which you might immediately ask is: In what respects are the black and white samples comparable? What factors (for example, motivational, educational or nutritional) might distinguish the groups? Can you ever really isolate samples of children who are alike in all relevant respects except for skin colour (if this is the basis for classifying children as 'black' or 'white')? Obviously, these questions are crucial for the interpretation of what might otherwise appear to be unambiguous data.

A further example that demonstrates the need for carefully chosen comparison groups would be evaluating the effectiveness of various types of psychological therapy. In this context, statements like the following might be made:

1 *'Fifty-five per cent of patients diagnosed as neurotic who have been treated by method A for a period of ten one-hour therapy sessions have recovered to a certain criterion.'* Despite its superficial precision, and the use of quantitative terms, this statement is not really informative if considered in isolation. It becomes significantly more informative when we add statements about appropriate comparison groups. These might include:

2 *'Only 10 per cent of similarly diagnosed patients given equal exposure to treatment B recover to the same criterion'*; and/or

3 *'Only 10 per cent of similarly diagnosed patients given* no treatment *recover to the same criterion.'*

Statements about the *relative* benefit of various treatment procedures are now possible, at least within the range of methods actually discussed. But when statements (2) and (3) are not made, the possibility is left open that *more than 55 per cent* of patients would recover, even if they were given *no therapy*. Obviously, if this were the case, the apparent effectiveness of method A would be quite illusory. This is not a purely hypothetical example. Some authors have argued that the 'spontaneous remission' rate for neurosis is very high over a relatively short period. That is, many people get over their psychological problem without any treatment. These examples remind us of those clever advertising slogans which use words like 'more' or 'improved' without specifying any comparison for the claim being made: 'These tyres give 50 per cent more grip ...' 'More grip than what?' we might well ask. (Such slogans are referred to in advertising as 'dangling comparatives'.)

PLACEBO EFFECTS; DEMAND CHARACTERISTICS

The example of the relative effectiveness of various methods of psychotherapy leads us to a discussion of what are often called **placebo effects**. In medical and pharmacological research, it is usual to provide one experimental comparison or control group with no actual medication or effective drug. This group is administered a 'placebo' — say, a sugar or salt solution or tablet which subjects are led to believe is an effective medicinal agent. This group is then compared with those groups given quantities of the drug being evaluated. An effective drug needs to be shown to be more beneficial than the placebo, rather than being compared with the absence of any form of medication. Similarly, in research into psychotherapy or education, a number of control groups analogous to placebo treatments may be necessary.

An interesting illustration of this point concerns what is known as the 'self-fulfilling prophecy' discovered in educational research. There is considerable evidence that, when teachers are given false information that certain students are likely to improve noticeably in academic performance, such children do, in fact, improve when compared with students of initially equivalent ability about whom different, pessimistic expectations are provided (Rosenthal and Jacobson 1968). The former group of students improved when assessed by independent assessors on such indices as abstract reasoning ability. It is not simply that the students' own teachers judge them more favourably on purely subjective grounds. It seems that the teachers' expectations of success are the reason for the (quite arbitrary) predictions being fulfilled. This is similar to the effects of placebos in medical situations, except that the self-fulfilling prophecy affects a second person who interacts with the person whose expectations are artificially altered. If self-fulfilling prophecies are as ubiquitous as research suggests they may be, then there is clearly a need for carefully selected control groups analogous to those given placebos in medical research to allow informative comparisons in many psychological studies.

Expectancy effects are instances of what have come to be generally known as demand characteristics when they influence the outcome of psychological research. Specifically, **demand characteristics** are the entire array of cues and information (whether accurate or misleading) about the experiment which the subject may rely on to aid their comprehension of the experimental situation. This information may consist of cues from the experimenter (such as subtle, non-verbal feedback), inferences — even rumours — circulating on campus about the research project, or hunches based on the subjects' prior knowledge of what they think are similar studies. Because most experimental subjects are keen to 'do the right thing' in the interests of 'science', they may conform to the demands of the experimental situation (as they experience it) in very subtle ways. In doing so, they may influence the outcome of the experiment.

Cues that inadvertently facilitate such conformity may be unconsciously provided by the experimenter. As early as 1955, Greenspoon required subjects to produce as many different kinds of words as they could, reinforcing plural nouns with the response 'Uh huh'. This significantly increased the incidence of plural nouns relative to a control period when no such cues were provided, although subjects did not report any awareness of the reinforcement or its effect. In a similar way, experimenters themselves may be subject to the influence of demand characteristics. Their expectations may be covertly communicated to the experimental subject, even if the subject is non-human. Or they may interpret evidence or perceive the experimental phenomena in accordance with their own wishes, especially if the evidence consists of relatively ambiguous responses such as dream reports or stories elicited to reveal people's motives or desires.

The most famous instance of experimenter-provided cues of which the experimenter was himself unaware is the case of the horse known as Clever Hans (Rosenthal 1964). Hans could apparently add or multiply simple numbers, giving the answer by tapping his hoof the appropriate number of times. The experts of the day were baffled because, even when his owner was not present, Hans still solved the mathematical problems. But the horse was not as clever as a gentleman named Pfungst who demonstrated that whenever people proposed problems for the horse, they inadvertently gave the animal the answer by tilting their heads when the requisite number of taps had been given. The horse had learned to tap until that cue was provided, and it was reinforced for stopping at that point.

Rosenthal (1966, in Sampson 1971, p 81) also showed how experimenters (in this case, student-experimenters) were influenced by their expectations in determining the outcomes of experimental procedures. Half of the 'experimenters' were told that their subjects were inclined to view a series of photographs in terms of 'success', while half were led to expect subjects to see 'failure' in the photographs of faces which they judged. Naturally, subjects were assigned at random to the two groups of 'experimenters', yet their judgments conformed to the respective expectations in how they rated the photographs. Apparently, the 'experimenters' had communicated their expectations to the subjects in some subtle way.

Simply changing the conditions under which people worked, rather than making any particular, specific changes, was shown in the famous 'Hawthorne' study to improve workers' productivity (Roethlisberger and Dickson 1939). This is analogous to a placebo effect in that it seems to have been the fact that intervention occurred, not whether it was of any particular type, that improved the participants' output.

Rosnow and Rosenthal (1997) have reviewed the various 'artefacts' (or unintended factors) which may influence the outcome of psychological research. These include the biases introduced by using volunteer subjects (especially psychology undergraduates), experimenter expectations, and the 'demand characteristics' of the experimental situation (above). Their very readable book covers the problems in sophisticated detail and could profitably be read before designing or conducting research using human subjects.

CONFOUNDED VARIABLES

Demand characteristics cannot easily be disentangled from the experimental variables which are explicitly considered in a given research design. Insofar as they co-vary with the latter, they are examples of what are known as **confounded variables**. Such variables occur in research whenever potentially effective variables are not adequately separated but are 'overlaid' on some other, specified independent variable or variables. If this occurs, it is impossible to draw unambiguous conclusions from the evidence that the research provides. That is, competing, alternative explanations will not have been excluded by the research design. So, in this section, we consider some of the things that need to be borne in mind when interpreting experimental or other comparative studies in psychology.

Consider the following (fictitious, simplified) example: the hypothesis that a certain drug (which we will call 'panacea 007') has the effect of inhibiting aggression in children in direct proportion to their age. That is, the older the child, the more potent is the drug's inhibitory effect. To establish this would involve a very complex research design if the most patent types of confounding were to be eliminated. It would require much more than merely administering equal quantities of the drug to equal-sized random samples of, say, three-, five-, seven-, nine- and 11-year-olds. Assuming that some acceptable index of aggression (and hence its inhibition) is available which is reliable and generally accepted, there is a large number of independent variables that require control if confounding is to be minimised. To take just a few examples:

1   The body weights of subjects would vary (systematically) with age. Yet body weight, *as such*, is presumably not the variable responsible for the different effects of 'panacea 007'. Hence, some account of this variable must be taken.

2   Children's knowledge (or expectations) about the possible nature of the experiment (that is, demand characteristics) may vary with age, older subjects being more likely to understand the nature of the study and perhaps to act on their assumed knowledge. Thus, in the absence of subtle instructions or additional placebo groups, 'panacea 007' might be effective in direct proportion to the intellectual maturity of the persons to whom it is administered!

3   There may be a range of other, subtle factors, such as dietary variables, which are confounded with age. These may *interact* with the drug to give what appear to be trends due to age alone.

In fact, the list of variables that are possibly confounded with a very general variable, such as age, is indefinite.

As this fictitious example suggests, the essence of experimental design, and hence the interpretation of research generally, consists of *isolating* and *controlling* those variables which might otherwise be confounded with the variable or variables of primary interest. Although this can be achieved only imperfectly, that is no reason to ignore such an important practice. In effect, almost every time we criticise the conclusions drawn from research, we are pointing to the possibility of confounding: we show that some other explanation of the results is possible, because a variable not considered could have intervened.

When someone denies that the reason African-American children perform more poorly on particular IQ tests than whites is 'racial' (that is, genetic),[1] they are saying that other (environmental) factors are confounded with race. Of course, as this example illustrates, some variables

---

[1] In discussing the evidence for racial or other large population differences on some psychological dimension, the research data actually concern *samples* drawn from the respective populations. Obviously, all members of these populations are not tested.

   However, inferential statistics provide estimates of the probability that one's sample data can be 'safely' assumed to reflect population characteristics.

cannot be separately manipulated; by their natures they co-vary. In practice, it is not possible to vary 'racial' characteristics while holding the social effects of skin colour constant, for instance. In all but unrealistically 'ideal' circumstances, psychological variables are often inextricable. Hence, differences of opinion may exist concerning the one piece of evidence insofar as confounding leaves open a number of plausible, alternative explanations.

CASE STUDIES

Despite the impossibility of disentangling all the potentially confounded variables, some of the most suggestive and theoretically influential psychological evidence does not come from carefully controlled laboratory studies or large-scale research projects at all. Rather, it comes in the form of **case studies** of individual persons (for example, psychiatric patients), families, or social groups and institutions. In these cases there is, by definition, no possibility of precise comparisons between individuals or groups which differ in only one or a few specific respects. In view of our previous discussion, this would seem to preclude case studies from having much 'scientific' interest. In fact, however, they are widely cited and discussed. The reason for this is not hard to find. Case studies frequently exemplify complex forms of behaviour and extreme environmental situations that may not be replicable in an 'artificial' laboratory situation. For this reason alone, they may be invaluable. (The experience of severe trauma, physical or mental abuse, drug use, and so on, cannot be studied under controlled conditions where individual variables are isolated.)

The interpretation of case studies has become one of the most controversial areas of psychological debate, especially in the fields of psychopathology, the etiology (causation) of drug dependence and in social psychology. We will discuss case studies by referring to an historical example which illustrates very graphically the complexities of interpreting these important kinds of evidence: the 'political' versus the medical interpretation of schizophrenia. It centred on the case studies discussed by RD Laing and A Esterson in their book *Sanity, Madness and the Family* (1970). The authors discussed 11 families from each of which one member had been hospitalised owing to what was diagnosed as 'schizophrenia'. Each family was presented in terms of its internal dynamics — especially its patterns of interpersonal communication. After reading these cases, we begin to appreciate what it might be like to be enmeshed in such families. We begin to understand the experience of the family dynamics, although no attempt was made to 'explain' the phenomenon of schizophrenia in the sense that we have discussed 'explanation' in previous chapters. Still, it was clearly implied that the family dynamics caused or contributed to the pathological reaction which the authors called 'madness' or which other psychologists had usually labelled 'schizophrenia'.

To deny that detailed reports such as Laing's provide genuine and important psychological insight would seem to be unduly narrow-minded. How, therefore, can we reconcile the obvious methodological weaknesses of discussing isolated, selected examples with the requirement of comparison groups? This is a very important issue. Rachman (1973, pp 184–5), for example, criticised Laing and Esterson's family case studies on precisely the methodological grounds discussed in this chapter. He argued that their cases lack the necessary comparison or control groups and that the authors therefore may have confused correlated variables with causal variables due to their failure to distinguish factors which could have been confounded.

> Do the families described by Laing behave differently from those in which one member is a delinquent? Do they behave differently from those in which one member is brain-damaged or obsessional or asthmatic or just normal? Even if differences can be demonstrated, further research would be needed before concluding that the observed differences have a special significance in relation to schizophrenic behaviour ... The transcripts presented by Laing and Esterson provide evidence of disturbed behaviour and attitudes in most of the eleven families. Many other research groups have also shown that the families of schizophrenic patients display disturbed behaviour and attitudes. This could support the theory that schizophrenia is caused by the patient's family.[2] Four other possible interpretations are: the family disturbance is a result of the patient's serious disorder; the patient's disorder is caused by extra-familial factors, but is exacerbated by disturbance in the family; the family disturbance is initially caused by coping with the patient's disorder, but then exacerbates the disorder; the family disturbance is a visible sign of genetically determined disorders of behaviour in the relatives of a person who is genetically vulnerable, as seen by his schizophrenic disorder.

Clearly, Laing's case studies raise as many problems as they were considered to clarify. Certainly, Rachman has shown that they are inconclusive and, by themselves do not constitute methodologically rigorous evidence. For very similar reasons, many psychologists reject much of the theory of Freudian psychology on the grounds that no compelling evidence, only isolated case material, is offered in its support (at least in the theory's original formulation).

In addition, psychologists sceptical about the value of case studies frequently make the following points:

---

[2] The concepts of 'cause' and 'correlation' are considered in the following section of this chapter.

1 Case studies are subject to selective, biased or distorted reporting. For example, Freud wrote notes on cases after, not during, the actual interview period. Might he not have selectively recalled or emphasised those aspects most consistent with his preconceived ideas?

2 Case studies at best merely *exemplify* a range of phenomena. One, or even a number of apparently similar instances, does not indicate a general rule (the problem of **induction**). To take a Freudian illustration, the fact that one little boy, 'Little Hans', showed ambivalent emotions towards his mother and father at the time that he was discovering sexual gratification through masturbation, does not indicate that these conflicts and pleasures are universal, or even common, in male children.

3 The absence of relevant comparison phenomena means that there are no statistical procedures appropriate to evaluating case study evidence which would allow firm conclusions about the precise role of particular variables.

4 The interpretation of case material is **post hoc** — that is, it occurs 'after the event'. It is often possible to discover events in people's lives which may, in retrospect, appear to be related to subsequent behaviour, but which might not have been adequate to predict such behaviour in advance. Unless this information is used to make predictions about further cases, the 'evidence' is, at best, suggestive and at worst, misleading. This is because the precise conditions of a particular case are not **replicable**. It is a desirable feature of scientific method that the conditions of an experiment should be repeatable in detail to allow others to retest hypotheses. But, by definition, case studies fail to meet this requirement.

In answer to these criticisms, two points might be made. First, it must be admitted that biases are possible and need to be carefully guarded against. Tape-recordings, (especially video-tape-recordings) of interviews may overcome this problem, although there are often difficult ethical dilemmas involved in such practices.

Second, it must be admitted that case studies are suggestive, rather than conclusive. They need to be supplemented by more controlled, comparative observations in which particular variables are isolated. But these restrictions should not be taken to mean that case studies are of no value. After all, many scientific hypotheses began as hunches based on one or a few cases that may have been only accidentally observed.

CORRELATION AND CAUSE

Whether or not we are trained in psychology, our view of the world involves many generalisations about psychological causes and effects.

Few of us pause to examine the evidence on which such generalisations are based, although that evidence may be very weak support for our beliefs. Let us consider in detail a common correlational argument to clarify the difficulties involved in interpreting complex social phenomena in terms of psychological causes. This is the question of whether 'broken homes' (as they were once called) *cause* 'juvenile (teenage) delinquency'. (This example is presented in an abbreviated and somewhat simplified form to make clear the issues involved.)

Assuming that precise definitions of the terms 'broken home' and 'juvenile delinquency' have been agreed upon for the sake of argument, and accepting that there are data that show that significantly more juvenile delinquents come from broken homes than would be expected by chance, is this sufficient to justify the stated belief about the *cause* of delinquency? Or are other interpretations more plausible? To answer these questions, we must consider more fully the distinction between the concepts of **cause** and **correlation**.

First, it must be remembered that two factors may vary together in systematic ways without being causally related. That is, correlation is *not* causation. For instance, people's heights and weights are positively correlated. Yet, it would be quite unusual to say that a person's height was the cause of their weight. It is even more unlikely that we would interpret a person's weight as the cause of their height. Second, events which occur close together in time or space are not necessarily causally related, even if one invariably follows the other: night invariably follows day, but it is surely not 'caused by' day; neither is the red traffic light caused by the amber light which invariably precedes it. Such examples suggest that the use of the word 'cause' in the statement linking juvenile delinquency and broken homes may be quite unwarranted. In the example as presented, the only evidence relating the two was correlational: the two factors were statistically associated and no more. Hence, it is logically possible to interpret *either* factor as the/a cause (or a component of the cause) of the other. For instance, the statistics are quite consistent with the assertion that juvenile delinquency causes homes to break up! The meagre correlational evidence is also consistent with a third, perhaps more plausible, interpretation: it can be argued that delinquency and broken homes are correlated owing to some third factor or set of factors which has yet to be specified. A general social factor like poverty or unemployment might be cited. Thus, the evidence on which the original generalisation was based may be consistent with at least two other interpretations.

A more recent, equally contentious example is the assumed 'effects' of pornography on violent sexual assault:

> The argument that research does not show pornography to be harmful will no longer wash. There are now a substantial and

growing number of large-scale population studies showing clear connections between the availability of pornography and the level of sexual violence ...

In the US, the eight major men's magazines (Chic, Club, Genesis, Hustler, Oui, Playboy and Penthouse) have sales that are five times higher per capita in Alaska and Nevada than in other states such as North Dakota — and rape rates are six times higher per capita in Alaska and Nevada than North Dakota. Overall a fairly strong correlation was found between rape and circulation rates in the fifty states, even with controls for potentially confounding variables such as region, climate, propensity to report rape and police practices ...

However, an argument frequently presented in the face of such data is that correlation is not the same as cause: perhaps both these variables occur together because they are the result of some other factor ... However, if the argument were sustainable, then subsequent moves to restrict pornography in already open societies should have no demonstrable effects. Consider, then, the fact that in Hawaii in 1974, restrictions were placed on the sale of pornographic material. Rape figures fell for the following three years. The restrictions were then lifted and rape immediately increased. Again, in Oklahoma county 'adult' stores were closed in 1985, and a 25% decrease in rape occurred over the next five years ... [while] in the remainder of Oklahoma, there was no such law and no decrease in the rape rate. (Goldsmith 1996, pp 127–29)

Even though Goldsmith points out that correlation is not the same as cause, she still leaves open the question at issue in the way she presents the evidence. Most obviously, factors which lead to restrictions on pornography (increased community concern, surveillance, publicity, and so on) might themselves explain the correlation without postulating a direct causal relationship between the availability of pornography as such, and the prevalence of rape. (You might ask what other factors might explain the correlation cited.)

So, far from being obvious, causal relationships in many cases are difficult to determine. They can be reasonably *inferred* only after a careful examination of the evidence. Causes are *not* directly observed, although ordinary language does seem to give that impression. This apparently pedantic point has at least one important practical consequence. Because the causal relationship between two events or other phenomena is seldom obvious, psychologists employ the terms 'independent' and 'dependent' variable. Despite their names, these expressions are relatively neutral with respect to cause-and-effect assumptions. They refer to the manner in which variables are manipulated and studied rather than to their status as causes or effects. Briefly, we can define them as follows:

The independent variable is that which is manipulated (that is, systematically varied) by the experimenter. For example, we might study the short-term memory performance of subjects under various degrees of distraction by extraneous noise. The independent variable would be the level of distracting noise that is varied by the experimenter.

The dependent variable is that which is observed to see if it varies as a function of differences in the independent variable. In the above example, it would be short-term memory performance.

In this example, a cause–effect inference would be quite justified, but this is not always the case. The choice of which variable should be thought of as independent is somewhat arbitrary, or, at best, reflects the experimenter's expectations. In our juvenile delinquency example, we could conceptualise 'home environment' as either the dependent or independent variable, depending on the particular research hypothesis being investigated. Regardless of how we chose to name the variables, it would not determine the status of either as a 'cause' or 'effect'. Despite its name, 'dependent' need not be interpreted as meaning 'caused'; it is a more general term than that. So, where two factors or dimensions of behaviour are expected to be correlated, it is a procedural matter which is thought of as 'dependent'. But because the names seem to imply that one variable determines changes in the other, you need to be careful not to **beg the question** of the direction of possible relationships when you formulate questions and hypotheses.

Still, it is advisable for you to try to think in terms of these variables, despite their apparent artificiality. This will reduce the tendency to jump to conclusions about 'causes' and 'effects' just because some factors appear to co-vary. (Think of all the psychological generalisations made about the causes(?) of different behaviour between males and females, for example, which are based only on correlations between vaguely defined personality variables.)

Having illustrated the difficulties of inferring causal relationships from correlational data, we have not yet said anything positive about the concept of 'cause'. What does the word mean, and when is its use justified in psychology? Before trying to answer these questions, it should be emphasised that the analysis of the concept of cause is quite a difficult and controversial philosophical problem. There are some philosophers (indeed, some psychologists as well) who would dispense with the word altogether. We cannot enter into this argument here, so what follows is a brief discussion intended to facilitate the interpretation of typical psychological evidence. However, we need to discuss the notion of cause in more detail if we are to develop the ability to be critically analytical about psychological evidence.

One way to analyse the meaning of a word is to substitute an alternative in various contexts. Therefore, let us try to replace the word 'cause' by some other phrases. This can be achieved by means of simple examples. Some events are impossible without the occurrence of certain other events or the presence of certain conditions. There cannot be fire without oxygen, for instance. Another way of putting this is to say that the presence of oxygen is a **necessary condition** for the occurrence of fire. There are, of course, a number of other conditions necessary for this event. But we would not normally say that any one of these 'caused' the fire, although we might acknowledge that each was 'part of the cause', or 'one of a set of causal factors'.

On the other hand, some events always give rise to certain other events — they are said to be *sufficient* for their occurrence. These conditions, although sufficient, may not be necessary for the event. For example, barring exceptional circumstances, being shot in the heart is a sufficient condition for dying, but it is obviously not a necessary condition — there are many other conditions sufficient for death to occur (that is, other ways of dying).

Using this terminology, we might argue that the word 'cause', as used in the sciences, refers to **sufficient conditions** for the occurrence of a certain event. Necessary conditions are not what is usually meant by the word 'cause'. But that does not mean that the isolation of necessary conditions is of no interest to psychology or any other science. This may be an important task in its own right. For instance, if an animal is to speak English, a necessary condition may be that the animal is a member of the species *homo sapiens*. This would be an important hypothesis, although it does not specify sufficient conditions for speaking a particular natural language, like English. Such a causal account would require the specification of additional factors, such as whether the person had been exposed to examples of the language for a certain duration, at certain ages, and so on.

The main task involved in the interpretation of psychological evidence might therefore be seen as deciding whether you have isolated necessary and/or sufficient conditions in your research. This is seldom a simple matter. To return to our previous example concerning broken homes (*A*) and delinquency (*B*), it can be seen that the following types of questions may be formulated:

1 Is *A* a sufficient condition for *B*?

   (Translated, this would read: Is the break-up of a family a sufficient condition for the occurrence of juvenile delinquency in one or more of the family's members?)

2 Is *B* a sufficient condition for *A*?

   (Is the presence of a delinquent enough to break up a home?)

3 Is *A* a necessary condition for *B*?

(Is a broken home a necessary condition for juvenile delinquency?; or Can a juvenile delinquent not come from a broken home?)

4   Is *B* a necessary condition for *A*?

(Is it possible for a broken home not to include one or more juvenile delinquents as members?)

Without delving into the logic of these situations, it is clear that questions (1) and (4), and questions (2) and (3) are closely related. For if *A* is a sufficient condition for *B*, then *B* is a necessary condition for *A*. A simple example showing this is the relationship between a class of objects and a wholly contained class. Being an apple is sufficient for being a piece of fruit, but it is not a *necessary* condition. Being a piece of fruit is a necessary condition for being an apple, but it is not *sufficient*. In this example, it should be noted, it would be unusual to use the word 'cause', despite the use of 'necessary and sufficient conditions'. This raises some interesting questions about the concept of causality, and its relationship to the logic of classification. We cannot pursue the matter further in this elementary discussion, however. Instead, let us return to the immediate implications of our digression into these logical questions for our discussion of the interpretation of evidence.

The point we wish to emphasise is that it is frequently not unambiguously clear if you have isolated conditions which you could term sufficient for the occurrence of some phenomenon. At the risk of sounding ultra-cautious, it is probably fair to conclude that you are typically justified only in asserting that significant relationships between specific variables have been established. You might then go on to make tentative interpretations concerning cause and effect. Of course, the confidence with which you do this depends on the individual case, but you will find authors cautious in using the word 'cause' in psychological literature. What you do often find are conclusions which might be translated to read, '*A* (the independent variable studied) is one of a set of conditions which are jointly sufficient for the occurrence of *B* (the so-called dependent variable studied).'

In our example, you could expect to find research indicating that (certain types of) broken homes, in conjunction with certain other interacting factors, are sufficient to produce delinquency. Such a conclusion would leave many other questions unanswered, and would not be the only possible answer you could give to the question, 'What causes juvenile delinquency?' This raises another point: the question 'what causes juvenile delinquency?' is really very simplistic, and is impossible to answer by means of one single statement. It is like asking a psychologist 'what causes crime?' or 'why do people go mad?'. Anyone prepared to give what they thought was an adequate answer to such general questions would either be very naive or in possession of evidence that is unknown to psychology. Unfortunately, many students undertake the study of psychology with just such unanswerable questions in mind. This is hardly surprising. Our culture and media frequently highlight research into complex causality as finding *the* cause for syndromes of behaviour as varied and culturally relative as, say, 'homosexuality'.

Popular media reports of psychological research usually jump to causal conclusions by choosing unsubtle and undefined words to express relationships between variables, even when the reports are ironically sceptical. *The Sydney Morning Herald*, on the same day (7 July 1993), printed the following two items:

> **Born gay**: it's all in the genes ('... scientists believe they will eventually be able to isolate a "gay gene" which men inherit from their mothers', the report claimed);
> **Genes get credit for the way we vote** ('... and it might be genes — rather than upbringing or environment — which also determine one's attitude to Medicare, the death penalty, religion and trade unions', it reported, citing twin studies as evidence).

Note that the words 'cause' and 'sufficient condition' are not used in the newspaper, but it is clearly causes that are being postulated. Without examining the proposed evidence, you might be able to spell out, using the terminology we have introduced above, just what causal relationships are being asserted between which variables.

Within philosophy and statistics there has been considerable recent discussion of the circumstances in which causal inferences may or may not be warranted. One major contributor has been Clark Glymour. We finish this section by selecting from his list of some of the difficulties he identifies as involved in making an inference from observed correlations to causation. Some of these overlap with those we have discussed.

Glymour (1998a) considers correlational data from samples. He points to the following possible difficulties:

1 Little may actually be known beforehand about the causal relations, or absence of causal relations, among the variables. In typical social studies, time order often provides the only reliable information — negative information at that — about cause and effect (effects cannot precede their causes).

2 Observed associations may be due to unmeasured or unrecorded common causes (as in our delinquency case above).

3 A vast number of alternative possible hypotheses — the larger the number of measured variables and observed positive correlations,

the more astronomical the set of possible causal structures. When latent variables are allowed, the number of possible causal structures is literally infinite.

4   Several (or even a great many) hypothetical structures may equally account for the same correlations, no matter how large the sample, and in finite samples a great many models may fit the data quite well.

5   A sample may be unrepresentative of a larger population because membership in the sample is influenced by some of the very features whose causal relations are the object of study. (Think of correlations between 'race', so called, and IQ.)

6   A sample may be unrepresentative by chance.

7   Values for sundry variables may be unrecorded for some units in the sample.

8   Relations among variables may be complicated by feedback, as between education and IQ where expectations based on IQ might affect educational environment. (Adapted from pp 18–19.)

This list can serve as a useful check in your critical assessment of arguments from correlational premisses to causal conclusions.

Glymour adds the following comments warning of some of the remaining difficulties in the generally more secure area of arguing to causal conclusions using evidence obtained from experiments.

> Many of the same difficulties beset causal inference in experimental contexts, even though experimental design aims to remove the possibility of confounding common causes of treatment and to maximize prior knowledge of the causal structure of the experimental system. Psychological experiments often concern unobserved and uncontrolled features; clinical experiments sometimes try to investigate multiple treatments and multiple outcomes simultaneously, with entirely parallel problems about confounding and feedback, especially in longitudinal studies. Sample selection and attrition in experiments, especially experiments with humans, can create selection bias as in (5) and can result in missing values. The distribution of treatments in experiments is controlled by the experimenter but the distribution of outcomes, which may conform to no familiar pattern, is not. (p 19)

In the light of these kinds of examples, it is no surprise that some psychologists have tried to replace all cause–effect language by other expressions. They may therefore speak of 'functional relationships' between particular variables, leaving the question of cause and effect deliberately quite open. Whether this is ultimately a satisfactory method of avoiding the problems we have mentioned does not matter at this point. What is important is that students should carefully consider all the possible interpretations of psychological evidence. You should then attempt to *justify* (that is, argue in favour of) the particular interpretation which you support. If no particular interpretation (causal or other) seems more reasonable than others, it is obviously best to leave the causal inference open. The evidence may not be definitive, and any attempt to impose an interpretation may misrepresent the evidence, suggesting causes where none has been found, as the journalistic examples (above) clearly suggest.

FICTITIOUS CAUSES

Psychology is particularly prone to the postulation of all manner of 'internal', 'mental' causes which are inferred solely on the basis of people's behaviour. In everyday situations these generally pass unnoticed. In more formal discussions, however, they are frequently quite misleading or may prove virtually meaningless when closely analysed. Hence, the title of this section refers to verbal labels that purport to indicate specific psychological causes but, in fact, do not. They are **fictitious causes**.

For example, if it is known that a certain person is good at mathematics, the 'cause' of this skill may be sought 'inside the person's head', so to speak. Of course, what is inside a person's head is related to how well they can do mathematics. That is not the issue. But to 'explain' the behaviour by saying, for example, that the person in question has a high level of mathematical ability or a 'well-developed faculty for dealing with mathematical concepts' is not particularly informative. It is not very different from simply asserting that someone is good at mathematics because they are good at mathematics! In other words, the hypothesised ability might be said merely to 'shift the problem, not solve it' — that is the behaviour is reinterpreted in terms of a mental predisposition which *itself* still requires explanation. Another way of putting this criticism is to say that the proposal 'makes the problem into a postulate'. In our example, the behaviour still needs to be explained, despite the hypothetical 'faculty' or skill which is said to 'underlie' or cause it.

It is important to be aware of the ease with which this type of hypothetical 'cause' can be invoked. Remember that behaviour does not explain itself: describing actions as aggressive, intelligent, gregarious, and so on, is quite legitimate. But postulating inner causes for such actions by merely naming some ill-defined mental faculty or instinct to correspond to the observed behaviour is not, by itself, explanatory. Having made this point, however, the case against such postulates should not be overstated. Should the hypothesised faculty or instinct be supported by **independent evidence**, then its status may be quite different. That is, should its existence explain a number of otherwise unexplained facts, it may not be a circular postulate. In our earlier discussion of explanation, the notion of independent evidence was introduced. Briefly, it was argued that explanation requires evidence for postulated causes which is independent of (or additional to) the behaviour being explained. That is to say, there is nothing vacuous about proposing (to continue our example) an instinct for gregariousness, *provided that* there are reasons for postulating it *apart from* the particular gregarious behaviour it is intended to explain.

Some recent work addresses the problem of independent evidence for hypothesised intervening causal factors. Elliott Sober (1998) puts the problem quite generally as one of considering a system initially as a 'black box' — of unknown internal structure. The system will be subject to various causal inputs which lead to certain effects or outputs. The question in this context becomes: under what circumstances would the postulation of inner causal factors ('intervening variables' in his terminology) make a difference in the observed relation between the input causes and the output effects? We cannot pursue the technicalities here, but Sober argues that, subject to reasonable background assumptions, a 'predictive difference between an intervening variable model and a no-intervening variable model obtains *no matter how many causes there are, as long as there are at least two effects*' (p 478). We will comment on an application of this view in Chapter 7.

To conclude, although psychologists generally assume that every event has a cause (a view known as **determinism**), it does not follow that every time causes are attributed to mental faculties, forces (dispositions) or capacities, genuine information has been provided. The verbal label 'cause' is not, in itself, an indication that a real causal factor has been isolated.

EVIDENCE FROM ANALOGIES

The interpretation of psychological evidence is further complicated by the prevalence of *analogical arguments*. An *analogy* is an argument based on assumed or demonstrable similarities or parallels between two objects, processes or events. What is known about one set of phenomena is employed in an attempt to explain the other. Analogies seek to relate unfamiliar (or unexplained) phenomena to familiar, explicable phenomena, by asserting that the two are alike in relevant respects. In psychology, analogies generally fall into two classes: those that assert similarities between the behaviour of humans and other animal species, and those that seek models for human behaviour, or cognitive processes, in the functions of machines — especially electronic computers. Thus defined, analogies include a number of quite 'weak' or tenuous assertions of similarities, as well as 'stronger', more rigorous attempts to 'model' psychological processes. It is, therefore, necessary to evaluate each proposed analogy on its merits: analogies *as such* cannot be excluded from psychology; but nor is every proposed analogy of scientific interest.

ANTHROPOMORPHIC METAPHORS

Let us look briefly at some relatively 'weak' analogies, before discussing ways of judging more rigorous instances. Weak analogies are essentially metaphorical interpretations of psychological phenomena, frequently reflecting figures of speech that are ingrained in colloquial language. For example, the behaviour of animals is sometimes interpreted as being metaphorically similar to that of humans: we speak of humans displaying 'pecking orders' (status or dominance hierarchies), or of their being part of a 'rat race' (being unduly competitive), and so on. The assumption underlying these figures of speech appears to be that humans are like animals in respect of these characteristics, presumably for similar (biological) reasons. However, in these cases there is little attempt at detailed explanation. The metaphor merely labels (and/or passes judgment on) the behaviour in a manner that is of literary rather than of psychological significance. (Recall the requirement of independent evidence, above. It is clearly not met in these cases.)

Similarly, human motives or intentions are often attributed to animals: we say that dogs are 'brave' or 'loyal', or that lemmings 'commit suicide', describing these animals as though their behaviour were consciously intended or were motivated by human values. This practice is termed **anthropomorphism**. It is frequently found in discussions of animal behaviour by writers of popular books on controversial topics (for example, Robert Ardrey's entertaining, although suspect, analysis of the origins and nature of human territorial behaviour in *The Territorial Imperative* (1969), or more recently, Wrangham and Peterson's *Demonic Males* (1997)). The tendency to anthropomorphise is very great if apparently inexplicable biological phenomena appear to be like those of human society. Hence the widely held interpretation of the mass migration of lemmings which culminates in their death as an act of 'suicide' — an interpretation which a moment's reflection will show to be very difficult to sustain. For example, does each lemming (a small rodent) consciously 'decide' that its life is not worth living? Clearly these considerations are quite inappropriate for understanding the behaviour of rodents. In fact, there is no evidence that the mass deaths *are* analogous to human suicide in any way. As Dubos (in Proshansky et al. 1970, p 204) has pointed out (unfortunately, adopting the anthropomorphic term 'mass psychosis' himself):

Although the nature of the initial stimulus that prompts the lemmings to migrate is not understood, crowding is almost certainly one of its aspects. As the rodents become more and more crowded they fall victims to a kind of mass psychosis. The result is a wild scrambling about that, contrary to legend, is not necessarily a march toward the sea but merely random movement. The animals die, not by drowning, but by metabolic derangements associated with stress; lesions are commonly found in the brains and the adrenals.

The metaphorical interpretation of human suicide as lemming-like, and — its converse — of lemmings committing mass suicide, are therefore quite unjustified. But like many anthropomorphic metaphors, because it is part of our language, it is difficult for students new to psychology to avoid. The principal argument against such figures of speech is that they are seldom of genuine explanatory value: describing animals as though they were humans makes their behaviour *more*, not less, difficult to explain because it introduces additional factors into the description of the explanandum. In the lemmings example, we have to explain not only why the rodents migrate periodically, but also why they (consciously?) seek to end their lives.

If these examples of metaphorical language seem relatively innocuous, it must be stressed that there are many important 'models' of human behaviour that are essentially extended analogies. With recent advances in the biological study of animal behaviour, and with the rapidly accelerating sophistication of electronic computing devices, psychological literature is replete with animal and machine analogies. The fertilisation of psychology by the disciplines of ethology (studying instinctive animal behaviour) and automata theory (formal discussions of computation and computers) has made it essential for students to be aware of the advantages and limitations of advanced forms of analogical argument. It could reasonably be claimed that many of the significant psychological questions currently being debated rely very heavily on this type of argument. To begin discussing the issues raised by such analogies, let us return to a distinction we made in Chapter 3.

DESCRIPTION VERSUS EXPLANATION

You will recall that our discussion of the problems of explanation considered the issue of analytic 'explanations' which we argued were inadequate because they simply reflected an author's choice of definitions. We pointed out that merely stipulating a new term as a replacement for some other descriptive expression was not, by itself, explanatory. Similarly, in considering analogies, the similarities asserted between the two sets of phenomena, and their inclusion under the one general descriptive term, will require detailed justification. It is, at best, a preliminary step to assert that two events or objects are *similar in certain respects* and to label them with the one term. For example, if it is observed that humans, as well as some species of birds, adopt status-defining hierarchies around which much of their respective social organisation revolves, it is tempting to speak of each species exhibiting 'pecking orders'. The common name reflects the observed (or inferred) similarities. The difficulties with extended analogical argument begin at the next step. Here, we attempt not only to describe the respective behaviours as similar, but to use this putative similarity as the basis for explanation.

Thus, having described both avian and human 'pecking orders', we may then seek to assert that both have the same cause (or type of cause). Hence, if it is known that avian pecking orders are 'instinctive', it is tempting to argue that a similar cause operates in humans: that human status hierarchies are also instinctive. Clearly, this is an *inference* which may or may not be justified, as the following example illustrates. Discussing human territorial behaviour, Ardrey (1969, p 16) states:

> The parallel between human marriage and animal pairing requires no lecturer with a long pointed wand. The parallel between human desire for a place that is one's own and animal instincts to stake out such a private domain requires even less demonstration ... Are we then, confronted by parallels of such a conspicuous order, to dismiss the possibility that man is a territorial species and that evolution, with its territorial imperative has perfected an innate behavioural mechanism commanding precisely the morality we seek?

This passage points to two parallels between animal and human behaviour. It then suggests, by means of a rhetorical question, that in both cases ('marriage' and 'territoriality') there are biological causes in animals and man alike. This is, in effect, an analogical jump from the description of similar behaviour in different species to the inference of its common instinctive cause. But merely interpreting animal pair formation and territorial behaviour as similar to human marriage and home ownership (to exaggerate a little!) does not, *by itself*, justify such an inference. It does not follow that because two phenomena are described in similar terms (however appropriate that description may seem), their causes are similar or identical.

Lest we be thought to have used only examples from non-psychologists, the famous British psychologis, Hans Eysenck shows that authors may assume anthropomorphic analogies even as they deny that humans are different from other species, with amusing results:

> German shepherds are very law-abiding. They are easily conditioned and are well known to animal fanciers and shepherds for

> this property. Basenjis, however, are natural psychopaths, difficult
> or almost impossible to condition, disobedient and antisocial.
> (Eysenck 1983, p 61)

The trouble with analogies is that, although they are easy to find, they are difficult to justify. If analogies are to be of theoretical interest, it is necessary for their proponent to do the following:

1   Show that the two species or phenomena being compared are alike in more than name only — that is, that the choice of a similar descriptive term is not an arbitrary one which suits the proponent's preconceptions (cf Eysenck's use of 'law-abiding' and 'psychotic' applied to dogs).

2   To avoid this, detailed specification is needed of *how* the two phenomena are alike — that is, an (operational) objectively testable formulation of what *dimensions of behaviour* are hypothetically similar.

3   Some predictions are necessary concerning *independent evidence* which would support (or possibly refute) the inferred causal account of the phenomenon being explained. These criteria are like those discussed previously for evaluating other forms of explanation.

Let us now consider them in relation to more detailed animal and machine analogies.

ANIMAL ANALOGIES

The principal difficulty with animal–man analogies is that there are literally thousands of animal, bird and insect species. Each has some peculiar behavioural characteristics: some birds mate for life; some are 'territorial'; some hoard objects; some eat the young of their own species under some conditions; others make ritualised, stereotyped mating displays, and so on. Amongst mammals, even amongst primates, some of these behaviours can also be found. Therefore, anyone wishing to assert an analogy between human monogamy, territoriality, hoarding, cannibalism or mating practices, and the activities of some other animal species, will probably be able to do so if they select their examples carefully. But this is quite a facile, purely *arbitrary* use of analogy, which fails to satisfy any of the three criteria proposed above. The example we discuss below epitomises the process, although the proponent was a famous name in the field. Discussing maternal love, Harlow (1971, p 6) stated:

> Girls will respond to babies — all babies — long before they
> approach adolescence. Attitude differences that are apparently

inherent were demonstrated in the responses of preadolescent female and male macaque monkeys to rhesus monkey babies (Chamove et al., 1967). Since the preadolescent macaques had never seen infants younger than themselves and had not been raised by real monkey mothers who could have imparted their own attitudes towards babies, we may assume that the differences in response pattern were primarily innately determined. When they were confronted with a baby monkey, almost all the responses made by the female monkeys were positive and pleasant, including contact, caressing and cuddling. These maternal-type baby responses were conspicuously absent in the males.

He went on:

Some years ago a photograph (which showed a baby monkey wrapped in a white blanket, eyes wide open and lips pursed) ... was projected on a screen at a women's college in Virginia. All 500 girls in the audience gave simultaneous gasps of ecstasy. The same test has since been conducted with many college audiences. Not only are all males completely unresponsive but the presence of males in co-educational audiences inhibits the feminine ecstasy response. Evidently nature has not only constructed women to pro-duce babies, but has also prepared them from the outset to be mothers.

This argument invites criticism on several grounds. As an instance of analogy, it fails to meet the three criteria presented above:

1 It is essentially a very selective use of one primate species.
2 It fails to specify how the macaque and human maternal responses and ecstasy response are comparable (that is, in what ways these are similar, or are part of more general sets of analogous behaviour).
3 There is no evidence advanced, independent of the response itself, to show that the human 'ecstasy response' is innate.

To put the problem of analogies in other terms, one could say that they frequently allow their proponent to 'have it both ways' — that is, to accept what is really inconsistent evidence while maintaining the original hypothesis. Not surprisingly, feminist critiques of arguments like Harlow's quickly followed. These included Weisstein (in Brown 1973, p 412), who pointed out at the time when such analogies were very common that:

One strategy that has been used is to extrapolate from primate behaviour to 'innate' human preference by noticing certain trends in primate behaviour as one moves phylogenetically closer to humans. But there are great difficulties with this approach. When behaviours of lower primates are directly opposite to those of higher primates, or to those one expects of humans, they can be dismissed on evolutionary grounds — higher primates and/or humans grew out of that old stuff. On the other hand, if the behaviour of higher primates is counter to the behaviour considered natural for humans, while the behaviour of some lower primate is considered the natural one for humans, the higher primate behaviour can be dismissed also, on the grounds that it has diverged from an older, prototypical pattern. So either way, one can select those behaviours one wants to prove as innate for humans.

What Weisstein objects to in this passage is the post hoc interpretation of evidence to suit a given theory. It follows that one important method of overcoming the arbitrariness of these interpretations is to require that analogical arguments be evaluated by their *predictive* power, just as other explanations are usually judged. This requirement is particularly important if it is asserted that similar phenomena (in different species) have a similar cause (as Harlow asserts regarding the 'ecstasy' response in female macaques and female Virginians). What is required to substantiate Harlow's claim is evidence (employing appropriate controls and comparison conditions) that the human response is unlearned, as it is in macaques. In other words, as with all viable explanations, analogies require the support of what we previously called independent evidence (Chapter 3) concerning hypothesised causes of behaviour. If we are to argue that the female ecstasy response to babies is instinctive, we need to provide more evidence than that it occurs in humans and is instinctive in some other species.

But let us not unduly stress the negative aspects of animal analogies. There are many examples of quite precise and heuristically important analogical arguments in psychology. Some of Harlow's own work on social deprivation in monkeys might fall into this category, if cautiously interpreted (see Harlow and Harlow 1962; Harlow 1971). Harlow deprived infant monkeys of various types of social, physical or maternal stimulation during the first two years of life. The onset and duration of deprivation were varied. The results suggested the need for certain social experiences within critical periods if the monkeys were to develop into 'normal' mature members of the species. Without infant social play, for instance, the monkeys were unable to groom, mate or care for their own offspring in the manner typical of their species. If results such as these are extrapolated to humans, they suggest that until about four years of age the child is particularly vulnerable to social deprivation that may have long-term detrimental effects. (This takes into account the different rates of physical development of the two species.) Although the resulting hypotheses may not be confirmed in all details when tested for the human case, the example does, at least, illustrate the way an analogy guides the formulation of quite detailed hypotheses for testing.

Moreover, the animal case indicates *possible* mechanisms for a particular type of behaviour. It is circumstantial evidence for the existence of such mechanisms in humans. Observations of primates help to show what range of behaviour exists in nature, and therefore to *suggest* causes for human behaviour. If one primate species exhibits certain well-defined behaviour, the causes of which are known for that species, this, at least, leaves open the possibility that similar human behaviour *may* have similar causes.

So, although we have warned against the arbitrary adoption of analogies, it is important to realise that they may be quite useful if carefully formulated. Analogies are a legitimate aspect of psychological argument insofar as they generate hypotheses capable of empirical evaluation.

MACHINE ANALOGIES

As well as making comparisons across species of animals, psychologists have also sought to understand human cognition through knowledge of the structure and/or function of human-made machines. As machine technology has developed, so has the detail of the analogy changed. In a general sense, the human body and nervous system are 'mechanical', although not in the way that this might be said of an internal combustion engine or a hydraulic lift. In a more precise sense, however, some analogy might be asserted between the structure of an artificial device and that of a natural system.[3] It might be hypothesised that there is a one-to-one correspondence between the physical components (and hence their respective functions) in the two systems. For instance, the gross anatomy of the human eye is often compared to the structure of a simple camera, each component of the former (cornea, lens, retina) being analogous to a component of the latter (lens filter, lens, film). But, in those examples of **machine analogies** of interest to psychologists, such structural equivalences are seldom postulated. More frequently, comparisons are aimed at elucidating or exemplifying certain aspects of 'thought' or brain *function*.

Clearly, the structure and function of any system are interdependent, as the camera example readily testifies. However, it is possible to study the functions of a system in relative isolation from its precise physical structure. Hence, psychologists are usually less concerned

---

[3] Strictly speaking, it is usual to call such structural correspondences *homologous* rather than using the term *analogous*.

about the physical components of a system chosen to model human functions (for example, problem-solving or pattern recognition) than they are about the functional equivalences between the behaviour of the former system (for example, a computer) and that of the human being. Machine–human analogies are not necessarily intended to imply an identical physical cause for the functions of the two systems in question.

During the last 20 years, the concepts and vocabulary of 'information processing' and 'control' devices such as electronic computers and self-regulating machines have infiltrated much of the territory of traditional psychology. By adopting the terminology of information processing and storage technology, 'cognitive' psychologists have attempted to 'model' human thought along lines exhibited by artificial devices. Because this has sometimes been interpreted as suggesting that psychologists uncritically accept an almost complete analogy between computers and people, we need to examine the value of such models.

Electronic computation devices are relevant to psychology in two general ways. First, they are studied in order to answer questions about the nature and limitations of particular descriptions of complex 'thought'. Here psychologists are interested in what has come to be known as *artificial intelligence* — that is, in whether the machine can solve problems of a type usually regarded as peculiar to humans, such as playing chess, translating colloquial French into English or composing a fugue. Artificial intelligence research is directed at *what* machines can do, with little emphasis on *how* they operate, and, consequently, shows little interest in whether the machine 'models' human 'thought' in precise detail.

Second, and of more direct relevance, is research referred to as *computer simulation* of human cognitive processes. In this research the emphasis is on programming the machine to display, in as much detail as possible, the processes by which humans hypothetically solve a particular type of problem. The researcher deliberately 'models' (reflects the structure and sequence of) human cognition in the processes performed by the machine. Clearly, this procedure assumes that a *precise* description (or hypothetical account) of the human processes is available on which to 'model' each step in the computer program. The psychologist's interest in the machine (or, more accurately, in its program) is to ask if the initial psychological description is a viable or *realistic* (in programming terms) account of the processes in question.

Perhaps the most famous pioneering attempt to simulate the problem-solving behaviour of humans was the work of Newell, Shaw and Simon (1960). They called their program the General Problem Solver (GPS):

> GPS grew out of an earlier computer program ... which discovered
> proofs to theorems in the sentential calculus of Whitehead and
> Russell ... The effectiveness of the Logic Theorist led to revised pro-
> grams aimed at simulating in detail the problem-solving behaviour
> of humans in the psychological laboratory. The human data were
> obtained by asking college sophomores to solve problems in sym-
> bolic logic, 'thinking aloud' as much as possible while they worked.
> GPS is the program constructed to describe as closely as possible
> the behaviour of the laboratory subjects as revealed in their oral
> comments and the steps they wrote down in working the problem.
> (pp 257–58)

A successful simulation such as GPS, effected for a number of problem solutions, demonstrates at the very least that certain information-
processing strategies are *sufficient* to solve the respective problems.
This does *not* show that humans *necessarily* adopt such strategies, but
it is consistent with that hypothesis (especially if the computer program
derives from human protocols). The description on which the program
is based is therefore 'testable' by means of the simulation — at least in
the sense that failure to simulate would suggest the inadequacy of the
original description.

However, we need to interpret computer analogies cautiously,
whether these purport to be examples of 'artificial intelligence' or sim-
ulations. Just as the arbitrary, ad hoc adoption of animal analogies may
lead to trivial, purely descriptive accounts of behaviour, it is also possible to employ computer metaphors in a vague, relatively uninformative
manner. It is all too easy simply to replace words like 'problem-solving'
by 'goal-directed information processing', or 'perception of cues' by
expressions such as 'analysis of stimulus features'; or to refer to abstract
(often ill-defined) concepts like 'thinking' as 'information transformation'. But this jargon, by *itself*, may not generate valid insights into the
nature of the processes involved. A computer simulation is a detailed
attempt to model (realise in some other medium) some aspect of human
'thought'; it is not just a metaphorical word-game. After all, both birds
and helicopters 'fly', but the latter are not very useful 'models' of the
former, despite our use of the one word for the behaviour of both.

It should also be remembered that the use of analogies is a continuing two-way process. The model used for comparison with the
explanandum is itself constantly being redescribed or even discarded in
the light of new information about both itself and the explanandum.
As new computer 'languages' develop, for example, models such as
GPS have been superseded; new information about human thought
will affect the detailed model also. It is therefore best to regard analogies, especially computer analogies, as tentative 'heuristic' aids to psychological inquiry: their value lies in suggesting hypotheses by
explicating the details of psychological phenomena.

Strictly speaking, all analogies or models are *incomplete*. Nobody would assert that the eye was like a camera in all respects. However, even allowing for this, it may be most illuminating to know exactly how the two differ — especially if they have been *assumed* to function in similar ways. When an analogy is shown unexpectedly to break down, a new conception of the phenomenon being modelled may arise. That is, negative evidence may be very important by showing how a possible model (which may have been widely assumed to be valid) is not a detailed analogue of a particular phenomenon. (For example, people, because of memory and time limitations, do not play chess as implied in some of the early computer programs.)

To reiterate, our language is replete with metaphorical expressions which assume that behaviour or thought is analogous to phenomena that are more fully understood (for example, 'simple' animals or machines). But analogies require detailed specification of the dimensions of such assumed similarities if they are to be of potential explanatory value. The requirements of *predictive* power and of *independent evidence* apply to analogies as to other forms of proposed explanation. Failure to meet these criteria may result in arbitrary, ad hoc interpretations that merely replace one unexplained phenomenon by another.

REIFICATION OF ANALOGY: AN EXAMPLE

Confusion of a metaphor or 'model' with the reality to which it is hypothetically analogous is one form of **reification.** This concept, introduced in Chapter 4, was defined as the process of interpreting abstractions as concrete realities, of 'confusing words with things'. Not only have particular words (like 'intelligence', or 'creativity') frequently been subject to reification, but also complex sets of interrelated assumptions have sometimes been interpreted in this way because analogues or models of psychological processes have been accepted as 'real': the 'as if' quality of analogies has been overlooked. A controversial, yet quite instructive example of this process is the so-called medical model in abnormal psychology and psychiatry.

For a variety of historical and sociological reasons, psychiatry has adopted many non-psychological concepts to categorise and explain 'abnormal' behaviour. Hence, people who are 'anxious', 'depressed', 'confused', 'unable to cope with life's demands', 'suicidal' or 'criminal' have, at different times, been labelled 'mentally ill'. Once they are so diagnosed, it follows that mental hospitals and physical or psychological therapy are assumed to be appropriate solutions to their problems: that just as people who are *physically* ill require medical treatment to recover normal functioning, so do people who are *mentally* ill.

In the eyes of critics of this approach, medical jargon and the assumptions which this embodies (that is, the 'medical model') have been given the status of *descriptions* of psychological phenomena rather than being merely an elaborate *analogy* which exhibits limited similarities with those psychological phenomena. That is, the metaphor has been mistaken for reality. Instead of saying that a person is acting *as though* he were (physically) ill, we say she *is* ill — although we deem this illness 'mental'. So, although there may be no evidence of physical *disease* in many psychological disturbances such as 'neuroses' or what used to unashamedly be called 'perversions', such as homosexuality, the medical model designated them as *illnesses*. The whole terminology of 'abnormal' psychology is pseudo-medical, although, as many recent authors have emphasised, this vocabulary is not the only one possible. The medical model may not be essential for the description (nor, therefore, for the explanation) of some or all of the behaviour which society regards as 'strange', maladaptive or 'sick'.

A pertinent example that illustrates this is homosexuality. It is possible to discuss homosexual behaviour without regarding it as a 'symptom' of some 'illness' which a person 'suffers from' or 'carries around inside himself or herself' (like diabetes, tuberculosis or cancer) requiring cure by appropriate treatment. We could argue that homosexuality is no more a 'disease' which is responsible for particular 'symptoms' (that is, behaviour) than are heterosexuality, maturity, femininity or masculinity, for example. To assume that there is a disease entity underlying homosexuality is to follow the (reified) medical model. It is instructive to recall that not very long ago, some abnormal behaviour was regarded as 'sin' and taken to have metaphysical causes. Replacing the 'religious model' by the 'medical model' involved many social, as well as scientific, changes. Exorcising the demonological jargon from psychology has been achieved, but have we replaced one ghostly cause by another, merely through employing a medical approach to behaviour that the community deems 'sick' in a metaphorical sense?

SUMMARY

The most informative evidence in psychology is comparative, involving control groups or comparisons between conditions that differ on one independent variable only. For this reason, placebo effects and other experimental pseudo-effects (resulting from uncontrolled or extraneous variables, including 'demand characteristics' in research situations) need to be carefully considered.

Cause is not to be confused with correlation. Causal inference involves identifying conditions which are sufficient (not just necessary) for a particular phenomenon. However, most evidence is 'messy', and involves co-varying (correlated) variables that require careful disentangling and evaluation, as in the example of 'delinquency' correlated with 'broken homes'.

Merely labelling behaviour or measures of performance (for example, mathematical test scores) as a faculty is not the same as providing a non-circular, causal explanation.

Drawing analogies between humans and other animals and between humans and computers is a frequent source of potential explanation in psychology. Criteria of independent evidence and predictive power need to be met when proposing analogies as explanations. Superficial metaphors need to be avoided. In the case of 'models' of, say, 'abnormal' behaviour, or other general patterns of cognition or personality, it is important to examine the precise claims being made about the actual causes of the behaviours in question and not to accept the analogical label uncritically.

Psychological evidence is only sufficient for causal explanations when it is comparative, precise and suggests new, testable predictions.

KEYWORDS

EXPLANATION • CONTROL GROUP • PLACEBO EFFECTS • EXPECTANCY EFFECTS • DEMAND CHARACTERISTICS • CONFOUNDED VARIABLES • CASE STUDIES • INDUCTION • POST HOC EXPLANATION • CAUSE • CORRELATION • (IN)DEPENDENT VARIABLE • BEG THE QUESTION • NECESSARY CONDITION • SUFFICIENT CONDITION • FICTITIOUS CAUSES • INDEPENDENT EVIDENCE • DETERMINISM • ANTHROPOMORPHISM • MACHINE (COMPUTER) ANALOGIES • REIFICATION

EXERCISES

1   It is quite clear that one of the effects of living under crowded conditions is that the likelihood of suicide is greatly increased. There is evidence that the rate of suicide is significantly greater in those urban areas that have been developed for high-density living. What more evidence could be required?

a   In what other ways could the evidence (as presented) be interpreted? What are some competing explanations of it?

b   What type of evidence would be required to support convincingly the conclusion asserted in the argument?

c   In view of your answers to (a) and (b), is the causal relationship postulated in the quoted passage justified?

2   Consider the following passages. In each case, rewrite by adding premisses which would yield the conclusion more convincing support. (Recall our discussion of the comparative nature of evidence and of correlation versus cause.)

a   Sixty-five per cent of all prostitutes come from families from which one parent has been absent since the child's infancy, so prostitution is probably caused by parental neglect.

b   The evidence shows that marijuana smoking leads to other forms of drug taking which may be of an addictive nature. Virtually all drug addicts report having smoked marijuana before taking up other, 'harder' drugs.

c   There is little doubt that aspirin is an effective agent for the relief of headaches. People who take aspirin almost invariably report a reduction or cessation of pain.

3   The following data might be used to argue that attendance at a privately conducted secondary school caused students to perform better than they would have if they had attended 'public' schools.

	Public schools	*Private schools*
% Students matriculating	38	86
% Students not matriculating	62	14

(These results are statistically significant.)

Do these data alone offer strong support for the original contention? If not, what additional evidence would be necessary to enable you to accept that conclusion? (Think of possible confounded variables — that is, possible alternative explanations for statistics like these.)

4   Evaluate the following critical argument by Clark Glymour (1998b, pp 39–40):

> The abstract of David Shanks' recent Experimental Psychology Society Prize Lecture (1995) contains a hidden puzzle:
>
> We can predict and control events in the world via associative learning. Such learning is rational if we come to believe that an associative relationship exists between a pair of events only when it truly does.
>
> Leaving aside the particulars of Shanks' theory, his answer — we learn about causes by observing associations — is I believe correct. The puzzle is how it could possibly be the correct answer.
>
> I am sure that, like everyone else, Shanks learned that correlation is not causation, but his second sentence collapses the distinction and confounds learning associations with learning how to predict and control. Knowing only the associations between A and B doesn't usually enable us to control either A or B.

5   The argument presented below exhibits so many of the fallacies which we have discussed as to constitute an excellent example for sharpening your critical skills. Indeed, Alan C Elms mounts a strong attack on arguments from analogy in social psychology in his book *Social Psychology and Social Relevance* (1972), which cites this example:

> Prostitution (the offering of sexual favours in return for material benefits) exists in the animal world among primates. Since man is a primate, we must therefore recognise that prostitution is a part of our over-all inheritance from our furry ancestors. As such it can never be discarded as long as our species survives, no matter how much wishful thinking we indulge in. When a modern girl marries for wealth and/or status … she is simply obeying a powerful female instinct shared by our cousins the gibbons and monkeys and baboons for many millions of years. We can no more suppress prostitution than we can any of our other inherited instincts. (R Ardrey, letter to Playboy, March 1967)

a   What logical errors are obvious in Ardrey's argument?

b   If one allows that prostitution is 'part of our over-all inheritance from our furry ancestors' on the basis of Ardrey's arguments, what other forms of social behaviour would need to be called 'instinctive'? What does this suggest about the original argument?

6 The rhetoric may be different, the language more formal, but what similarities are there between Kenrick's analogising (below) and Ardrey's (above)?

> The Ugandan Kob, an antelope found on the plains of Africa, demonstrates, in exaggerated form, some of the differences between mammalian males and females ... Courtship is brief, and the female cares for the young with no help from the male. Males will mate with any female who enters their stamping ground. In sum, males are more dominance-oriented, and are correspondingly larger and more aggressive. Females care for offspring and are more selective in choosing a mate. Consistent with the Ugandan Kob, (human) females seem to be more selective in taking advantage of a casual mating opportunity, and thus only high-status males have multiple wives ...
>
> Male flirtation gestures are similar in humans and chimpanzees. Interestingly, these are gestures that are also used in dominance interactions, such as direct staring and 'dominance swaggering'. On the other hand, female microgestures suggest 'coyness'. (Kenrick 1987, pp 19, 22)

chapter 6

Some common weaknesses in psychological argument

A man who has committed a mistake and does not correct it is committing another mistake.

Confucius

The discussion of psychological issues is complicated by a number of subtle (and not-so-subtle) fallacies of which students need to be aware. Many of these are difficult to classify, for they are not necessarily logical errors in the narrow sense defined in Chapters 1 and 2. They are more general inadequacies which involve inconsistencies, over-simplifications and conceptual confusions of various kinds. As such, each of the five considered in this chapter involves some abuse or omission of the canons of good argument. Specifically, they concern:

- the use of illegitimate appeals to 'win' arguments;
- the tendency to force opposing explanations into over-simplifying, mutually exclusive categories;
- the confusion of 'relative' with absolute terms in psychological discourse;
- arguments in which there is insufficient detail to relate precisely the proposed explanation to what it is meant to explain; and, finally,
- the failure to distinguish between matters of fact and matters of evaluation.

ILLEGITIMATE APPEALS AND ASSERTIONS

In Chapter 2 we highlighted the importance of argument and its superiority to unsupported assertion. We saw that arguments do not merely state their conclusions; they also give reasons in support of them. They show ways in which their respective conclusions can be evaluated. We noted that in many arguments (even extended ones), some of the supporting statements are not made explicit, but are left unstated. However, if the argument is to be useful, its premises should initially be less controversial than the conclusion. (If this is not so, the argument, in a sense, does not progress — its premises will be disputed, regardless of the conclusion they are advanced to support.)

We also distinguished two main types of relatively uncontroversial statements — the class of **analytic statements** and the class of **observation statements**. We saw how useful these statements could be in refuting scientific theories by means of the argument form *modus tollens*. Indeed, *modus tollens* is an argument form which often involves an analytic statement ('If p then q') and an observation statement ('Not q') which together imply the falsity of an (otherwise more controversial) statement (represented here as p). In these cases, an appeal to observational and analytic truths is made to evaluate a theoretical statement.

In contrast to this paradigm, there are two commonly used, but less legitimate, appeals that are assumed to justify the acceptance of a particular statement. These are perhaps best described as ways of *persuading* rather than of *showing* others that a statement should be judged true. One of them is a type of argument; the other is not really an argument at all. Both involve some kind of appeal to authority, but make the appeal in different ways. We shall call the first 'argument from authority', and the second 'appeals to fact' and examine them in turn.

ARGUMENT FROM AUTHORITY

If you seek to support your viewpoint simply by invoking the prestige or authority of some well-known expert, you may be arguing or seeking to persuade without regard for the merits of the evidence. To put this more formally, to **argue from authority** is to propose the statement that a particular 'expert' holds a certain view, as sufficient or significant support for that view. It may even be supposed that an argument is better insofar as more experts can be cited who agree with the conclusion. Sometimes, the argument includes premises that purport to justify the expert's claim to relevant expertise. This type of argument is apparent in the following rather blatant examples:

1 The general consensus among the *experts* who have studied this question as *objectively* and *scientifically* as possible is that there is no proof of innate racial differences in intellectual ability. (This is a close paraphrase of a statement in Klineberg 1964; each of the italicised words appeared in the original.)

On the other hand, prior to arguing that there is considerable evidence to support the proposition that such innate racial differences *do* exist, Eysenck (1971, p 15) stated:

2 'I would be prepared to assert that experts (real experts that is) would agree with at least 90% of what I am going to say ...'

It is tempting to try to settle which of the authors is correct by trying to ascertain which is more 'expert'. But this really has nothing to do with the value of the arguments which each advances or the truth of the conclusions they reach. As Eysenck himself has commented, 'experts' abound in psychology whenever public interest in controversial issues is high. But arguments are not valid, nor statements true, because they are presented by experts (whether 'real' or not). It is the arguments and statements themselves, not their proponents, that must be evaluated; appeals to expertise or status are often merely 'window dressing' — rhetorical techniques aimed at achieving *uncritical* support for the point of view advanced. Criticism of a person, rather than of their arguments, is known as an **argument ad hominem** and is to be avoided for the same reasons as arguing from authority. It is therefore quite irrelevant to refute or confirm the status or credentials of a proponent of a particular conclusion in the hope of discrediting or supporting their argument. This may be acceptable (or at least accepted) in political debate, but it has no place in academic discussion.

To persuade their readers, authors sometimes imply the inexpertness or even the immorality of a supporter of a view that they wish to criticise. A variation of this consists of labelling a statement, argument or its proponent with an expression that carries negative connotations in order to denigrate that statement, argument or person. Generally, however, authors assert a consensus in support of their viewpoint, rather than attacking their real or imagined opponents. For example:

> In the main, contemporary practising psychologists do not believe that there is a particular window that provides an undistorted view of psychological reality ... most therapists are comfortable with the diversity of theories, treating them as models and metaphors. (Polkinghorne 1992, p 158)

Or, more assertively:

> In the view of practically everyone, a transducer is a function from usually external physical events to cognitive events ... Now, as many investigators have recognised, there is no such thing as a neutral description of a physical event; there is no innocent eye, no disinterested observation language. (Pylyshyn 1984, p 168)

Note how the claims made here seek to convey a consensus supporting the author's point of view.

Appeals to an assumed consensus or convention may reflect what has recently been labelled 'political correctness'. Although fashions change in this regard, we may often hear arguments dismissed as 'racist', 'sexist', 'behaviouristic' or 'Freudian', without any attempt at refutation. Such pejorative labels are irrelevant to the evaluation of the arguments to which they are gratuitously attached. Clearly, the important point is that, in general, someone's stating that something is the case is no guarantee that it is the case.

Despite this, however, we do rely to a great extent on what others claim — we trust that their statements are true. Of course, the degree of trust will depend on the particular context in which the statement is advanced.

The varying deference given to authority can be seen from the different general approaches to the 'results' section and the 'discussion' section when we critically evaluate a psychological paper or article. The usual practice is to take the 'results' as read, while being more critical or evaluative of the 'discussion' section. Usually, the 'results' section contains either simple observation statements or statements readily obtained from them, like statistical summaries, percentages, standard deviations, means, and so on. Most authors of papers are taken to be 'authorities' on these matters. If they write that there was a certain outcome to the experiment, then most readers accept that as true. In contrast, authors are not viewed as authorities when readers consider possible explanations and interpretations of the results in the 'discussion' section of a paper. As a result, they need to *argue*, as opposed to merely *state*, their position. Then you, their reader can critically assess their reasoning, and try to think of alternative explanations and results that confirm or conflict with those explanations.

Of course, although it is not always done, you should also be critical of the 'results' section of the paper. It is not uncommon for authors uncritically to assume that one observation guarantees that another holds, and to report only the latter. For example, an author may report 'None of the subjects surveyed had read *Playboy*', when a more accurate report would have been 'None of the subjects surveyed admitted having read *Playboy*'. To accept the first report could be to uncritically accept a false statement (perhaps through misplaced reliance on another's authority).

Hence, the question is not whether we are to accept statements made by authorities or experts, but whether we are prepared to accept a statement, even a theoretically controversial one, simply because it has authoritative support.

APPEALS TO 'FACT'

Psychology is frequently condemned for its lack of factual information. Despite this, there is a tendency for authors to claim that the evidence supporting their viewpoint is 'established' or 'widely accepted' fact. This may be no more than a rhetorical device, similar to appeals to the authority or the status of a source of information. Whenever psychologists claim to be simply presenting the facts, it is advisable to read what they say with care. This is not because there are no 'facts' in psychology, but because the presentation and interpretation of what are claimed to be facts may be questionable.

The error of **appealing to 'the facts'** is the error of simply asserting a statement, instead of presenting an argument of which it is the conclusion. People use phrases such as 'It is obvious that ...' and 'The simple fact is that ...' when they are not going to present an argument but simply assert a statement. As we mentioned earlier, in every argument some statements must be left without argued support (that is, the initial premises), so there will always be some statements that are simply stated, not argued. (Ideally, these should be less controversial than the conclusion they support.) The mistake of appealing to the 'facts' occurs when a *controversial* statement is simply asserted. To *claim* that a statement presents a 'fact' does not alter its truth or falsity.

Statements must be either true or false, but there are often many ways of expressing the same statement which involve different words or phrases. Hence, what appears to be a 'fact' to one author may not be accepted as a fact by another author because it is couched in the language of a controversial theory.

To illustrate this, consider the observation that people sometimes attack others when frustrated by people who are themselves relatively immune to attack. This can be described in a number of slightly different ways, each of which is in some sense consistent with the fact expressed here in informal language. However, close examination of each possible description reveals that the words adopted give the 'fact' a rather different status in each theoretical context. First, it might be said that it is a fact that 'humans displace their aggression on to others'. Second, someone could merely claim that 'humans seek scapegoats for their frustrated aggressive tendencies'. A third formulation might be 'in humans, the stimuli associated with interference to ongoing goal-directed behaviour increase the probability of vigorous physical reactions to all subsequent stimuli'. (Doubtless there are other possible descriptions.) Let us consider the sense in which these statements are factual.

The first (which is a rather Freudian) and the last (which is a very behaviouristic) interpretation may each be judged true. Each may be a 'fact'. But it must also be emphasised that each sentence uses words having quite different meanings within their usual theoretical context — the terms of the respective statements are not theoretically 'neutral'. (Recall our discussion of theoretical contexts in Chapter 4.) Indeed, their theoretical backgrounds may be incompatible in many respects. Certainly the word 'displacement' would not be accepted without redefinition by behaviourists. They might question whether the phenomenon of 'displacement' ever occurred in the sense specified by strictly Freudian theory. 'Displacement' is a *theory-laden* term in that it assumes that there exists some 'energy' or 'drive' which is capable of being 'released' and 'redirected' if 'blocked'. So, one psychologist's fact may be another's fiction, even though both theorists may claim to be describing the same phenomenon. The appeal to 'fact' may be rhetorical strategy aimed at encouraging uncritical acceptance of a particular (covertly theoretical) argument.

MISLEADING DICHOTOMIES

In psychological debates, the participants frequently resort to over-simplified contradictory alternatives, what we shall call **misleading dichotomies**. By this we mean that alternative arguments are seen as reflecting either one set of factors or an alternative, incompatible set, even when these alternatives may be seen to be compatible with one another if analysed more carefully. This tendency to see psychological explanations as black or white (not as black and white, or shades of grey) is exemplified by the numerous controversies concerning the hypothesised effects of hereditary and environmental factors on many psychological phenomena, the most controversial being, perhaps, intelligence and sex roles (gender). New students of psychology seem to carry very strong prejudices about the role of nature and nurture. Perhaps students are reluctant to accept that people are genetically programmed, because this seems to deny our apparent human autonomy (an issue considered in Chapter 7).

While the distinction between nature and nurture, or 'innate' and 'learned' characteristics, may be useful in many contexts, it may also create a misleadingly crude dichotomy that encourages the over-simplification of important psychological issues. This result is particularly likely if a further tendency is present — namely, the practice of searching for single, clearly distinguishable causes of a phenomenon when a complex set of causal factors may be operative. For instance, laypeople, if not psychologists, often speak of 'the cause of schizophrenia' or 'the cause of stuttering' in a manner which suggests that only one factor is responsible for each of the respective phenomena. Of course, there are many alternatives to this. For example, it is possible that the complex patterns of behaviour labelled 'schizophrenia' result from a genetically determined biochemical abnormality alone; or from one of a number of such abnormalities; or from one or more of these in the presence of certain traumatic life experiences; or from a complex series of life experiences regardless of any biochemical abnormality. Indeed, each of these alternatives has been proposed at various times in the history of research into schizophrenia.

To illustrate the ease with which you may propose questions (and also interpret explanations) in terms of over-simplifying dichotomies and single causal factors, we shall discuss an example from a discipline other than psychology. This case sheds considerable light on some major psychological issues, however. It concerns the factors responsible for the height to which humans grow. Let us first consider this in the light of the 'genetic' versus 'environmental' factors dichotomy, for this is an instance where common sense suggests that the dichotomy is quite valid.

We usually assume that we inherit either our stature or, at least, the potential to develop a certain stature. Informal observation shows that tall parents tend to have tall offspring and shorter parents children of smaller stature. From this it is generally concluded that a person's height is genetically determined. However, height is not determined *solely* by genetic factors; nor is the relationship between genetic factors and non-genetic factors (for example, nutritional intake) at all simple in respect of their relative or interacting contributions to stature. For example, quite rapid increases in the average height of a population may occur when dietary habits are altered, even though it had previously been assumed that the population was of short stature as a result of genetic factors. The most dramatic illustration of this is the Japanese population, whose height has increased noticeably since the Second World War, possibly, in part, as a result of increased amounts of red meat in its diet and/or changed exercise patterns (perhaps due to American influence).

As Hunt pointed out three decades ago, however, Europeans, and Americans themselves, may have undergone a similar transformation over the past few hundred years. Discussing the possibility of greatly increased intellectual development through new forms of early education, he stated:

> In connection with this possibility of a general increase in intelligence, we should consider also what has happened to the stature of human beings. It appears to have increased by nearly a foot without benefit of selective breeding or natural selection. While visiting Festival Port in Jamestown, Virginia recently, we examined the reproduction of the ships which brought the settlers from England. They were astoundingly small. The guide reported that the average height of those immigrants was less than 5 feet, and that the still famous Captain John Smith was considered to be unusually tall at 5 feet 2 inches. The guide's 'instruction book' puts the authority for these statements in the Sween Library at William and Mary. I have been unable to check the evidence, but scrutiny of the armour on display in various museums in England implies that the stature of the aristocrats who wore it must typically have been about the reported size of those immigrants to Jamestown.
>
> Also, the guide for the U.S. Constitution includes in his spiel the statement that the headroom between decks needed to be no more than 5 feet and 6 inches because the average stature of sailors in the War of 1812 was about 5 feet and 2 inches. This increase in height can occur within a single generation ... such evidence of an increase in the average height for human beings, the reasons for which are still a matter largely of conjecture, should have some force in increasing the credibility for the genetic potentiality for a general increase in intelligence. (1969, pp 144–45)

The example of human stature (and its possible analogy with intelligence) indicates the dangers of assuming a simple dichotomy between hereditary and environmental factors, even in the case of a well-defined biological trait.

Yet, psychologists and their students continue to make assertions about causal factors which all too frequently presume a rigid dichotomy between such factors. In addition to the debate about the determinants of intelligence, another perennially controversial issue is the origins of sex roles in young children and therefore of gender identity in adulthood. In this case, what begins as a difference of emphasis between proponents of the views that sex roles are substantially biologically 'given', and that they are learned, can too easily be reduced to a debate couched in dogmatically held dichotomies. But in a debate concerning such complex interacting factors as those responsible for sexual/gender identity and role development, no exclusive concentration on innate or environmental factors is likely to do justice to the range of phenomena to be explained. The subtlety and complexity of this topic can readily be appreciated by reference to one of the pioneering works in the field. Money and Ehrhardt concluded:

> The most likely explanation of the origins of homosexuality, bisexuality, and heterosexuality of gender identity is that certain sexually dimorphic traits or dispositions are laid down in the brain before birth which may facilitate the establishment of either of the three conditions but are too strongly bivalent to be exclusive and invariant determinants of either homo- or heterosexuality, or of their shared bisexual state. The primary origins of the three conditions lie in the developmental period of a child's life after birth, particularly during the years of late infancy and early childhood, when gender identity is being established. The state of knowledge as of the present does not permit any hypotheses (many psychodynamic claims to the contrary) that will predict with certainty which biographical conditions will ensure that an anatomically normal boy or girl will become erotically homosexual, bisexual, or heterosexual. Once the pattern is established in the early development years, however, it is remarkably tenacious. The hormones of puberty bring it into full expression. (1972, p 235)

Clearly, any causal account of such complex behaviour must be carefully formulated if it is not to imply an over-simplified dichotomisation of alternatives. This conclusion requires some qualification, however. Frequently, to claim that sex roles are learned, not determined biologically, is not intended to deny entirely the relevance of biological factors. Rather, it is meant to suggest that, even given the range of biological predispositions, environmental factors may be sufficient to override these in the determination of relevant behaviour.

This claim does not rely so crudely on the nature–nurture dichotomy, although it also needs to be stated very carefully if it is to avoid that over-simplifying tendency.

RELATIVE TERMS

We have discussed in Chapter 4 some of the problems involved in defining psychological concepts. Here we shall consider some further subtleties of terms that are frequently sources of confusion. We emphasise that many psychological terms are capable of definition only in a **relative**, rather than an **absolute**, way, although this is not to say that such concepts are totally arbitrary. This seems an important issue, because it is often argued that words such as 'intelligent', 'normal', 'introverted' and 'masculine' (and their respective opposites) are incapable of precise definition owing to their being 'purely relative' (although what this means is seldom explicated). Such alleged relativity is then held to imply that each is totally or largely 'arbitrary' — that is, that each is capable of no systematic justification.

Asserting that a term is relative may be merely a rhetorical tactic, unless it is specified *how* it is relative. This point requires emphasis because, in a sense, practically every adjective applicable to behaviour might be said to be relative. Ordinary terms like 'quick', 'slow', 'complex', 'simple', and so on, can be precisely understood only if a certain context is assumed. Their interpretation is *relative to their context* in much the same way as the terms we shall consider in detail in this section. Therefore, let us first consider some possible interpretations of saying that a psychological predicate is 'relative'. We shall use the examples of 'intelligent' and 'masculine', both of which can be argued to be so in at least three respects. We shall then ask whether these terms are necessarily 'arbitrary' in any significant sense. First, let us clarify a possible confusion. Rather than speaking of a term or concept as being 'relative', it might be more accurate to say that the *use* of a term, or the *criteria* for applying a term or concept, are 'relative' — not the concept itself. However, it is conventional to use the short expression and we shall follow this practice.

'INTELLIGENT'

The adjective 'intelligent' is a relative term in three important respects. First, the concept refers to (or, more accurately, *evaluates*) dimensions of behaviour along an assumed **continuum.** It is a graded notion. Persons are not simply classified as either intelligent *or* unintelligent, but as relatively so — that is, relative to the range of behaviour of the population with whom they are compared. Although the conventional distinction between 'intelligent' and 'unintelligent' behaviour (or persons) seems to imply a *dichotomy* rather than a *continuum*, the potential range of judgments concerning human intelligence is not restricted to two or any other finite number.

Clearly, there can be no single, precise demarcation of intelligent from unintelligent behaviour. One practical result of this is the difficulty of classifying degrees of mental subnormality — the criteria adopted being subject to considerable debate. For instance, the differences between persons with measured IQs of 65 and 75 (which were once given the names 'mentally subnormal' and 'borderline', respectively) may be rather difficult to specify unequivocally. Still greater uncertainty pertains when one person has an IQ of 69 and another a score of 71. Here the resulting difference in psychiatric classification might be seen more as a matter of rigid adherence to a numerical criterion than as a reflection of significant psychological characteristics. In such circumstances, it would be fair to call the classification (or its decision point: IQ = 70) an *arbitrary* one, although that is not to suggest that it is either meaningless or easily avoided.

The second sense in which 'intelligent' is relative is rather more subtle. It concerns the fact that the continuum of behaviour considered to exemplify degrees of intelligence is based on a *culturally relative* judgment. Although it need not be argued that 'intelligent' changes its meaning when applied to different cultures,[1] the criteria for judging behaviour as intelligent are themselves relative to specific cultural norms and values, at least to some extent. There are different criteria to which judgments of intelligence relate in different cultures. Although it would seem fair to claim, for example, that one ethnic group lived longer on average than another, without spelling out the criteria for this judgment (these being uncontroversial), this would not be so when judgments were made about the comparative intelligence of two ethnic groups. In this case, criteria to which the comparisons relate may well be controversial. In particular, it is likely to be argued that they would be different from one culture to another and hence quite unlike those on which judgments about relative longevity are based. If this point is accepted, it may be concluded that judgments about the relative intelligence of different cultural groups may be difficult, if not impossible, to make.

Third, 'intelligent' is a relative term in a somewhat more technical sense. When psychologists assess people's IQs, they assign numerical values on which are based qualitative description ('superior intellect', 'educationally subnormal' and so on) by comparing an individual against the range of scores obtained from a normative population (called the standardisation population). Hence, if a seven-year-old

---

[1] See 'Definitions and criteria for the use of theoretical terms' in Chapter 4.

English child has an IQ of 105 points, this is meaningful data only in the light of the standardisation group with which they are most appropriately comparable; in this case a statistically adequate, representative sample of English seven-year-olds. Statements about a person's IQ implicitly compare that person to a set of statistical norms.

Furthermore, to be of maximum value, these quantitative statements also need to specify the exact type of psychological test on which the assessment is based. Quantitative IQ values as absolute scores are not as meaningful as their numerical precision might suggest. For instance, it is possible that an IQ of 115 on one test (relative to specified norms) may be equivalent to an IQ of 110 or 120 on another test, owing to peculiarities of standardisation. Although conventional psychometric practice attempts to minimise such anomalies, they are possible, given the nature of concepts like intelligence and their methods of assessment.[2] (Chapter 8 discusses more of the difficulties encountered when making psychological statements using numbers.)

'MASCULINE'

Although psychologists are less concerned to measure and assign numbers to people's 'masculinity' (to yield, perhaps, an MQ?), the predicates 'masculine' and 'feminine' are common in everyday discussion of psychological topics. The layperson's lack of knowledge about the scientific validity of the *assumed* dimension or dimensions of behaviour labelled as being 'masculine', to various degrees, has not reduced the tendency to judge a diverse range of behaviour according to this concept. Despite this, both the nonspecialist and the expert generally fail to analyse what 'masculine' means, ignoring that, like 'intelligent', the adjective is 'relative' in a number of subtle respects.

At the risk of quoting an extreme example, we can illustrate the conceptual (and ideological) absurdity of rigidly dichotomous discussion of such issues when an author ignores the relativities we have outlined. Anthony Storr, a writer on popular psychology, cited Jung in a 1968 book on aggression.

> As Jung used to point out, it is characteristic that the woman who appears in the unrelated man and the man who manifests himself in the unrelated woman are of inferior quality (to the 'related' woman and man). The man whose *feminine* side does not find itself projected upon a woman will be subject to unpredictable moods and an inferior emotionalism which can be pejoratively termed effeminate. The woman whose *masculine* aspect is not contained in the lover or husband becomes opinionated and

---

[2] The one test may itself be re-normed over time, as is mentioned in Exercise 1, Chapter 2.

dogmatic, and shows that insecure assertiveness which men find
tiresome when they have to work for female executives. (p 94, italics added)

We do not need to be radical feminists to find much to question in this
very dated set of unsubstantiated assertions. But the example is instructive in the present context. So, let us concentrate on the author's use
of the predicates which we have italicised.

The first thing to notice is that Storr both accepts and denies that
the masculinity–femininity dichotomy is an over-simplification which
fails to appreciate the continuous range and continuing variability of
behaviour to which the adjectives might be said to apply. He assumes
(with Jung) that all people have a masculine and a feminine 'side' (that
is, that everyone is, to some degree, *both* masculine and feminine).
However, at the same time, acceptance of both aspects of one's self is
claimed to produce an inferior man or woman. That is, Storr argues that
a man is normal only when he 'projects' his feminine qualities. (Does
this really mean when he *rejects* those qualities?) Similarly, a woman
must allow her so-called masculine aspects to be 'contained' in a lover
or husband. But this seems a peculiar way to speak about the concepts
of masculinity–femininity. What Storr effectively does is to *reify* the
concepts by ignoring the *relative* nature of the masculinity–femininity
continuum (if there is such a continuum). Although he had stated that
'... we all have within us potentialities of being both masculine and feminine', his use of the concrete expressions 'feminine side' and 'masculine
aspect' suggests that these potentialities are discrete, biological entities,
or at least biologically based characteristics which each person possesses. Storr confirms this impression when he later speaks of the male's
'fully masculine role' (which, incidentally, involves 'dominance' of
women!) and of females being (potentially at least) 'fully feminine'. In
other words, there are *absolute* criteria for calling a person, or their role,
fully (completely) masculine or feminine, despite the fact that we are all
both to some extent.

To see more clearly how Storr is committed to an inconsistent or
absurd interpretation of masculinity, you could ask what sense can be
made of his notion of complete masculinity (or its opposite) by returning to the example of intelligence. It would surely be peculiar to assert
that some people are fully (completely or totally) intelligent, for the
same reason that it would be so to say that someone was, for example,
tall or heavy in any absolute degree. Clearly, everyone is intelligent to
some degree; there is no absolute zero point on such dimensions and
no absolute upper limit. Yet, Storr would have us believe that some
people are fully masculine, although he never really defines this term.
(This is reminiscent of old advertisements which claimed that the

smoker of a particular brand of cigarettes was 'all man'. It seems fair to conclude that some apparently expert argument can be as conceptually crude as such sexist advertising.)

But surely, it will be objected, the word 'masculine' is not meaningless, even if people like Storr have used it rather thoughtlessly. Let us therefore discuss how, as a relative concept, it can be employed in technically more sophisticated contexts, provided that it is carefully qualified. As indicated above, the predicate is relative in much the same way as the term 'intelligent'. First, if it is accepted that there is a *continuum* of behaviour ranging from what *a particular culture specifies* as extremely feminine to extremely masculine, then there is no *absolute* criterion for assigning the word to any specific, invariant type of behaviour. As the italicised qualification emphasises, the term 'masculine' applies only within the framework of culturally defined criteria. What 21st-century Westerners call masculine is not what would be judged in, say, a traditional New Guinea Highland, or Australian Aboriginal, society. It is well known that within certain cultures, biological males are typically passive, even 'maternal' (to Western eyes). To say that these men are not truly masculine is to impose the values of our own culture on another culture and to *judge*, rather than describe, that culture. This type of reasoning entirely ignores the cultural relativity of the criteria. Yet this, incidentally, is what Storr did, confusing biological inevitability with cultural determination by equating masculinity with what males generally do in his own society.

'MISSING LINKS'

We have illustrated the tendency for psychological debates to rely on potentially over-simplifying dichotomies — especially when single causal factors are assumed. Another common weakness to which psychological argument is especially prone consists of outlining in only the most general terms the causal factors which are hypothetically responsible for a particular type of behaviour, without providing any details of how such factors might operate to produce the relevant effects. In other words, there are 'gaps' or 'missing links' between the explanandum and the generalisation that purports to explain it. There are many examples of this, because, to some extent, it is inevitable that not all the mediating steps in causal accounts of complex phenomena will be known or spelt out at any particular time.

Nevertheless, some putative explanations lack so many details as to be of very limited value. The most instructive examples of such inadequacies are to be found where generalisations are proposed to explain a range of phenomena but in which neither the generalisation nor the phenomena being explained are described in precise terms. The vagueness of both the explanans and explanandum then serves to camouflage the insufficient (or non-existent) mediating factors. For example:

> The general growth in permissiveness in homes, schools, and courts has led to a significant reduction in the number of conditioning contingencies to which children are exposed. It would follow as a direct consequence that they would grow up with a much weaker conscience, and consequently that many more children would be led to engage in criminal and antisocial activities. (Eysenck, in Laaufer and Day 1983, p 65)

This kind of generalisation relates two very vague factors: permissiveness and antisocial activities, without suggesting mechanisms that could account for their empirical relationship. Let us illustrate the way in which explanatory arguments may involve this weakness by discussing a similar 'common-sense' generalisation: that inadequate maternal care leads to psychological maladjustment, and by developing this generalisation into more sophisticated versions of the hypothesised relationship between the two factors.

We will argue that there are two main inadequacies in examples such as this. We call these:

- insufficient distinctions in terminology; and
- inadequate accounts of factors mediating between explanans and explandandum.

You will see that these are closely related in that the former makes the latter virtually unavoidable. In the present case, if we do not attempt to distinguish various types of 'inadequate maternal care', and some precise forms of 'psychological maladjustment', then it will be impossible to advance beyond very vague generalisations. Let us, therefore, turn to a detailed discussion of this example.

In the 1960s and 1970s, a controversy concerning the nature and duration of the effects of 'maternal deprivation' centred on the theoretical writings of John Bowlby (for example, Bowlby 1969, 1973) and research findings from both non-human primates and human infants. It was a controversy that still has direct relevance to a variety of social welfare policies, to arguments about the 'liberation' of women and to the changing nature of the Western nuclear family. Unfortunately, popular discussion of the issue has frequently polarised into support for, or opposition to, generalisations which assert a simple causal relationship between 'maternal deprivation' (variously defined) and a variety of psychological 'abnormalities' (given names like 'delinquency' or 'psychopathy'). Such a polarisation glosses over the complexities of this area of psychological research in a way that illustrates only too clearly the lack of detailed analysis behind many psychological generalisations — especially those concerning the causes of 'deviant' behaviour ('antisocial', above) or psychopathology.

Without discussing the details of research findings in this area, let us attempt to clarify the questions which fall under the topic of the generalisation, and itemise some of the possible links in the hypothesised causal chain between a child's maternal environment and its adolescent or adult personality. To facilitate this discussion, we shall refer to the monograph by Michael Rutter (1972) entitled *Maternal Deprivation Reassessed*, which approached the issue by attempting to detail precise questions subsidiary to the generalisation we are considering. Very sensibly, Rutter makes relatively subtle terminological distinctions and, in the light of these, searches for possible mechanisms through which various types of deprivation might affect human development. Without outlining all these distinctions and possible mechanisms, we shall concentrate on the way Rutter attempted to fill in the missing links in the argument concerning only the long-term consequences of maternal deprivation (that is, not the immediate short-term 'protest' and 'despair' that babies exhibit when separated from mothers and/or when placed in strange environments under certain conditions).

Rutter pointed to the need to specify (a) what types of 'maladjustment' are (hypothetically) produced; and (b) what precise aspects of the child's social, physical or maternal environment are associated with each. In relation to (a), at least five possible forms of maladjustment are distinguished: mental retardation, dwarfism, delinquency, 'affectionless psychopathy' and possibly 'depression' (p 79). Hence, any argument concerning the relationship between 'maternal deprivation' and 'maladjustment' must be judged on its ability to specify the (presumably different) factors involved in each of these outcomes. The issues then become quite complex. There are many psychological processes that need to be distinguished under the general heading of 'maternal deprivation' if the possible causal mechanisms are to be described in any detail. Indeed, Rutter distinguished over 10 possible factors which might be (sometimes inappropriately) included under the general heading of 'maternal deprivation'. Associated with each possible factor is a different conception of the manner by which the maladjustment(s) is(are) produced. In fact, some of the relevant factors may not involve deprivation of maternal care as such, at all! This is possible because the child's maternal environment may have been confused (that is, confounded) with other aspects of the social and physical environment by various authors writing on the subject. Rutter therefore distinguished the following questions (among others). You will notice how subtle some of the alternative interpretations of the nature of 'maternal deprivation' may be. Is the critical factor essentially the lack of maternal care as such, or is it one or more of the following?

1 The disruption of existing (social) bonds or the failure to form bonds with others generally.

2 The change of environment which might accompany that disruption (for example, sudden hospitalisation).

3 Sensory privation or general social privation (reduced physical stimulation, lack of social interactions involving speech, smiling, and so on).

4 Nutritional privation.

5 Failure to form bonds, specifically with the mother.

6 Distorted relationships generally or with the mother in particular.

7 Imitation of 'faulty models' (that is, parents). Or perhaps faulty imitation of models.

8 Some combination of these and/or other factors (for example, specific, genetically determined predispositions).

To relate adequately the independent and dependent variables in the generalisation, we would need to consider how each or some combination of these could produce each or some combination of the five 'maladjustments' referred to previously. We have, therefore, moved a long way from the original generalisation. The benefit of this type of analysis, however, cannot be over-estimated. Without making the types of distinctions Rutter makes, and without analysing all the possible causal connections between different types of 'deprivation' and different types of 'maladjustment', it would not be possible to propose any coherent argument on topics as complex as the one we are discussing. It is, therefore, essential to try to provide details as to how hypothetical causes actually function to produce their (assumed) effects. Even given the above analysis of the possible role of various types of environmental stress which were indiscriminately lumped together under the one term in the original generalisation, the precise biological and psychological processes by which these affect later behaviour have still to be detailed.

However, leaving this aside, our example illustrates the importance of going beyond vague generalisations, even those couched in what appear to be 'technical' terms (such as 'maternal deprivation'). It illustrates the value of asking precisely how the variables are causally related, thus allowing us to fill in the 'missing links' between the variables in the original generalisation.

'IS' AND 'OUGHT'

The last decade has seen renewed controversy about the social responsibility and the environmental impact of the physical sciences and resulting technological advances. It has become clear that questions of cultural value intrude into the study of even the most 'objective' science. Similar, and in some respects more important, questions of value and social responsibility and the issue of ethical controls arise in the behavioural and medical fields. The question which confronts physical scientists — whether their discoveries are potentially dangerous to humanity or the environment — is one which is becoming increasingly difficult to separate from the more routine, physical questions studied. Similarly, psychological knowledge may be used or abused by social agencies. Furthermore, those questions regarded as warranting scientific study will be so judged depending on the cultural ethos and personal values of the individual scientist, be they physicist or psychologist. The result of this may be that psychological knowledge frequently reflects specific *value-orientations* through what it *assumes* as much as through its explicit formulation.

When psychological expertise is cited as support for social practices, such orientations may be obvious only with the advantage of hindsight. (For example, many feminists have pointed out the sexist biases inherent in much of the literature on personality.) At other times, however, the question of values is more explicit — especially when theories are to be 'applied' to alter an individual person's behaviour. Here the question of what *is* the case, and what *should* be the case, or what behaviour ought to be exhibited by an individual, is clearly controversial.

For instance, the techniques of behaviour therapy (or 'modification') based on the principles of classical and operant conditioning have at times been applied to the control of excessive drinking, to trying to change the sexual preferences and practices of gay men, and to reducing the expression of aggression. Such psychological techniques raise (or at least highlight) some important issues. Among these are the following: What is the relevance of psychological knowledge and technology to social practice? What is 'deviant' or 'antisocial' behaviour? Should such behaviour be subject to psychological 'therapy'?

These issues are extremely complex, and can neither be summarily answered nor quickly dismissed. But this much can be said: they are not questions to which psychological theory can, by itself, provide answers. Indeed, it can be argued that such questions are essentially 'political', 'social' or 'moral', rather than psychological. Let us expand on this assertion in order to clarify the nature of the relationship between *facts* and *values*, *knowledge* and *action*, *empirical statements* and *moral statements*.

Briefly, moral statements either involve *evaluative* terms or else are *imperative* in form. They employ expressions like 'good' or 'should' (or their opposites). They may, of course, involve 'disguised' or implicit moral concepts. For example, it might be said that '*Democratic* child-rearing practices promote psychologically *healthier* children than do *authoritarian* practices', or that 'Behaviour therapy *dehumanises* the persons on whom it is practised'. In these cases, it could be argued that the concepts of 'health', 'dehumanisation' (and, indeed, of 'democratic' and 'authoritarian' practices) have an evaluative as well as a descriptive meaning. By labelling them as evaluative, we imply that their conventional use expresses either a positive or a negative value judgment concerning the phenomena to which they apply. To take a clear example of this contrast, compare 'Jones killed Smith' with 'Jones murdered Smith'. Although these two statements may describe the same event, the second goes beyond the first in conventionally expressing the judgment that Jones was wrong to kill Smith. Frequently, of course, there is less unanimity about whether the terms express positive or negative value judgments. For the term 'murder' the situation is clear, but for many terms we need to know details of the speaker's values or those of his audience in order to determine what type of judgment (if any) is being offered.

A phrase like 'Fred is obedient' or 'Bill is ambitious' will involve a positive value judgment when used by some speakers, but will be used by others to express a negative judgment. Depending on who used the terms, 'development', 'artistic', even 'scientific' may imply differing value judgments of the phenomena to which they are taken to apply. We could say of such terms that they are '*theory-laden*' (or theory-dependent) in an even stronger sense than those to which the term was applied in Chapter 4. Their theoretical bias extends beyond any particular psychological assumptions and encompasses moral values.

Some philosophers concerned with the analysis of moral concepts have long held that arguments which attempt to derive evaluative or imperative conclusions from purely 'factual' premisses must be invalid. They claim that there can be no logical implication between factual premisses and imperative or prescriptive conclusions. This is usually expressed by saying that *an 'is' can not imply an 'ought'*. Any argument with a conclusion involving 'ought', 'good' or similar expression is, according to this view, invalid *unless its* premisses include similar evaluative or imperative expressions. Supporters of this view might cite the following example:

> Social deprivation retards both the cognitive and emotional development of young children. ***Therefore***, children ***should*** be provided with intense social stimulation.

Although, at first glance, this might look like a valid argument, it is not — at least not in the form in which it is presented here. Either the argument is incomplete or it is invalid. The conclusion does not follow from the premiss. If, instead of judging the argument invalid, we take it to be an **enthymeme** (incomplete), the missing premiss would seem to be linked with some judgment concerning the desirability of certain outcomes. A more complete form of the argument might therefore read:

> Social deprivation retards both the cognitive and emotional development of young children. It is desirable that children (should) develop these capacities as much as possible. Therefore, children should be provided with intense social stimulation.

Now, the evaluative premiss, involving the concept of desirability, seems to make the argument valid. Unlike the first premiss, the additional statement explicitly expresses a value judgment, although it may be a judgment that others find questionable.

But even when we thus augment the argument, it remains invalid. It may be that social deprivation retards both the cognitive and emotional development of young children, and it may be considered desirable that children develop these capacities as much as possible, but it need not follow that children should be provided with intense social stimulation. For it may be possible that providing intense social stimulation adequate for the benefits outlined will also produce such deleterious side-effects that it should be objected that it cannot be done. There may be such overwhelming reasons against providing social stimulation sufficiently intense to develop children cognitively and emotionally that the reasons cited in the premiss for this course of action are overridden. Hence, to improve the argument, it would need to be further augmented. For example, we could interpret the meaning of 'should' in the conclusion to mean, narrowly, 'should, for these reasons', or we could add a premiss to the effect that there are no undesirable side-effects of the recommended policy. (Yet, even with these additions, it would still be strictly invalid. Why?)

This example suggests that one useful way of interpreting *'is/ought' arguments* is to regard them as incomplete. They may be seen as implicitly asserting conditional propositions — that is, as being of the form *'If* situation X is desirable, good, etc., then facts A, B, C imply that conditions L, M, N should be implemented'. On this interpretation, the only psychological content in an evaluative or prescriptive argument is in the second part of the conditional statement. But if there is no consensus about the evaluative clause of the conditional, then there may be no agreement about what the conclusion means with respect to desirable actions, no matter how voluminous is the psychological evidence that supports the factual premisses.

One of the main dangers of using evaluative terms is that they *seem* to bridge the gap between factual statements and the policy statements that may be wrongly thought to follow from them. To return to our previous examples, no one is likely to be misled about the evaluative term 'murder', but words such as 'retard' and 'development', taken from psychological literature, are usually stipulated to have only a descriptive meaning. However, there may be a shift back to the evaluative assumptions that are implicit in the non-stipulated everyday use of the same terms when they are employed in examples such as that quoted earlier. It is therefore important to avoid covertly changing from 'descriptive' to 'evaluative' meanings and also to make explicit any evaluative assumptions that may be implicit in the use of the terms you choose.

This point is at the foundation of some very important psychological controversies and needs to be recognised. It can be illustrated by returning to an example discussed previously. Let us again assume, for the sake of argument, that African-Americans, on the average, perform below European-Americans on standard tests of intelligence. Let us further assume that the evidence favours the argument that this difference is largely genetically determined and not entirely due to environmental influences. It is natural to ask what relation this 'fact' would bear to moral questions. For example, racial discrimination is frequently justified (at least by its proponents) by such arguments as the 'biological inferiority' of black-skinned people.

Obviously, that people ought to practise racial discrimination is not *implied* by the presence of supposed racial differences in ability. To argue from these assumed differences to certain courses of action — either prejudice against, or increased facilities for, African-Americans, requires an additional premiss. This concerns desirable social outcomes, and acceptance of it may differ from one person (including one psychologist) to another. Social values are not *determined* or changed by psychological research alone.

Hence, it is possible to accept evidence concerning 'racial' differences in ability, but also to believe that either (a) African-American children require segregation from the general population from which they differ as a group; or (b) they should be integrated and treated identically with other children; or to believe neither of these. It is not *irrational* to believe that there are innate racial differences in measured intelligence, yet to be quite 'liberal' politically. Similarly, prejudice is possible without the support of the 'evidence' of the inferiority of the rejected group. Although prejudiced people seek out (and frequently distort) evidence concerning the 'inferiority' of the groups they wish to reject, this 'justification' for their prejudice does not logically validate their position. (It is not rationally based.)

Perhaps a good example which highlights the relationships between 'facts', prejudice and actions is the following: identical twins, as a group, have been shown to score sightly below the average of the general population on intelligence tests (Mittler 1971). Yet, no one would seriously suggest that this evidence implies that twins *as a group* should be treated in special ways or denied privileges. Identical twins are not given special educational attention; they have never been segregated into their own schools. The 'is' of evidence does not imply the 'ought' of action! (This example is not intended to offend twins. One of the authors is a member of this group.)

Therefore, value judgments and imperatives to action might be seen as examples of **rhetorical argument** and criticised as such where appropriate. But students of psychology seldom accept this point, as the following quotations from their essays indicate:

- Discussing the role of the mass media in encouraging violent behaviour, one student comments: 'The chief *offender* to the contribution of violent acts … is the television set'.

- Discussing whether there is evidence for innate racial differences in intelligence, one student ended his essay with the essentially irrelevant comment: 'Many less intelligent people are warm and friendly and therefore make for a *much better world* than a person who feels insecure unless he knows he is better than someone else.'

- Another example would be: 'The practice of aversive conditioning applied to homosexual behaviour is *reprehensible* because it makes the victim "sexless" rather than heterosexual'. Here, although not fully specified, the evidence does not really imply that the practice of aversive therapy *ought* to be eliminated, unless we accept (as we might) a further unstated premiss which places the value of active sexuality (including homosexuality) above that of inert sexuality. So, the evidence could be used to support other points of view. It might be argued (by puritans, perhaps) that aversive therapy is good, precisely because it has such a negative effect!

So, you need to be aware of the distinction between 'facts' and 'values' and sensitive to the subtle ways in which these are confused in psychological debate. This is because a counter-argument aimed at another person's political or moral assumptions, rather than at the substance of their argument, may be quite irrelevant in an academic context. On the other hand, it is sometimes possible to reject the alleged basis of various proposals for social action or prejudiced attitudes by pointing to this same distinction. As we have seen, if someone attempts to justify, say, racial segregation on the basis of the 'fact' that there are racial differences in intelligence, then a critic can point out that there is no logical relationship (no implication) between the evidence cited and the practice advocated. Indeed, the critic need not even refute the evidence.

SUMMARY

Let us summarise the various concerns of this chapter: proposing valid arguments and persuasive explanations in psychology is not to be confused with merely trying to convince by appealing to the authority of a source, either by claiming that it is a 'factual' or an authoritative basis for your claim. To make these appeals is to overlook the need to evaluate critically the evidence or theoretical propositions at issue. Similarly, arguing against the person proposing a point of view, rather than their actual arguments, is illegitimate. (This is called argument ad hominem.)

The discussion of psychological issues is complicated by a number of subtle (and not-so-subtle) fallacies of which students need to be aware. Many of these are difficult to classify, for they are not necessarily logical errors in the narrow sense defined in Chapters 1 and 2. They are more general inadequacies which involve inconsistencies, over-simplifications and conceptual confusions of various kinds. As such, each of the problems considered in this chapter involves some abuse or omission of the canons of good argument. Specifically, they concern:

- the use of illegitimate appeals to 'win' arguments;
- the tendency to force opposing explanations into over-simplifying, mutually exclusive categories;
- arguments in which there is insufficient detail to relate precisely the proposed explanans to the explanandum; and, finally,
- the failure to distinguish between matters of fact and matters of evaluation.

You should also guard against proposing explanations in terms of simplistic, incompatible factors such as 'heredity' or 'environment', and try to avoid using concepts like 'masculine' versus 'feminine' as though these labels were clearly dichotomous. Such concepts may be thought of as *relative* in several respects: they are culturally relative; they may only be meaningful relative to a continuum of behaviours which need to be explicitly defined; and they may involve relative (measurement-based) judgments and comparisons (as with 'intelligence').

Generalisations which sound like psychological explanations (we cited lack of maternal care leading to stress and maladjustment) are unlikely to be adequate in formal psychological contexts unless what we called 'missing links' are specified. These show the precise mechanisms that could explain the phenomena which are claimed to be related.

There is no *logical* relationship between factual claims and moral prescriptions. So, the issue of what should be done to remedy some psychological problem may need to be argued for on other than a factual basis. You need to guard against confusing factual claims with evaluative or judgmental assertions.

KEYWORDS

ANALYTIC STATEMENT • OBSERVATION STATEMENT • ARGUMENT FROM AUTHORITY • ARGUMENT AD HOMINEM • APPEALS TO 'FACT' • MISLEADING DICHOTOMIES • RELATIVE CONCEPTS • ABSOLUTE CONCEPTS • CONTINUUM • IS/OUGHT • ENTHYMEME • RHETORICAL ARGUMENT

EXERCISES

1   The hypothesis that women, if only given the opportunity and encouragement, would equal or surpass the creative achievements of men is hardly defensible: and it is only those who exalt intellectual creativity above all else who are concerned to demonstrate that women can compete with men in this respect.

It is a sad reflection upon our civilisation that we should ever be concerned with such a problem, for its existence demonstrates our alienation from our instinctive roots ... Women have no need to compete with men, for what they alone can do is the more essential. Love, the bearing of children and the making of a home are creative activities without which we would perish; and only a civilisation in which basic values have become distorted would make these sterile comparisons. (Storr 1968, pp 88–89)

a   What rhetorical strategies does Storr employ in this passage?

b   How does the passage rely on implicit and explicit value judgments to argue its case?

c   What assumptions (of a 'factual' nature) does the passage make?

d   What assumed dichotomies underlie the author's discussion of women's 'roles'?

2   The myth of early man's aggressiveness belongs in the same class as the myth of 'the beast', that is, the belief that most, if not all wild animals are ferocious killers ... These myths represent the projection of our acquired deplorabilities (sic) upon the screen of 'Nature'. What we are unwilling to acknowledge as essentially of our own making, the consequence of our own disordering in the man-made environment, we saddle upon 'Nature', upon 'phylogenetically programmed' or 'innate' factors. It is very comforting, and if, somehow, one can correct it all with findings on greylag goslings, studied for their 'releaser mechanisms', and relate the findings on fish, birds and other animals to man, it makes everything all the easier to understand and to accept.

What, in fact, such writers do in addition to perpetrating their wholly erroneous view of human nature, is to divert attention from the real sources of man's aggression and destructiveness, namely, the many false and contradictory values by which, in an overcrowded, highly competitive, threatening world, he so desperately attempts to live. It is not man's nature, but his nurture, in such a world, that requires our attention. (Montagu 1968, p l6) a   What rhetorical devices does Montagu employ in this passage?

b   Is his nature–nurture dichotomy sufficiently subtle to allow rejection of the 'biological' arguments he attacks? Why or why not?

c   By adopting explicitly *evaluative* terminology, does Montagu strengthen or weaken his argument?

3   The following example is of more than historical interest. It shows that psychologists sometimes claim knowledge of great social significance. You may be able to think of more recent examples of similar claims about 'ethnic' or 'racial' differences in scholastic performance or ability (say, in relation to matriculation scores of different groups of Australians).

> ... just as there is not one physics for Aryans, and another for Jews, so there is not one intelligence for whites, another quite different type for blacks. The ability to reason, to abstract, to educe relations and correlates, is fundamental to intelligent activity, to educational progress and to professional competence; the colour of a man's skin has nothing to do with the truth or otherwise of these statements. I.Q. tests, imperfect as they undoubtedly still are, are a first step towards a better understanding, and a proper measurement, of these important aspects of human nature. (Eysenck 1971, p 79)

a   Is this passage consistent with the arguments advanced in Chapter 5 for the *relative* nature of the concept of intelligence? Why or why not?

b   Is the analogy between 'Aryan physics' and 'black intelligence' an appropriate one to support Eysenck's views?

c   What might be meant by the 'proper' measurement of intelligence?

d   Compare this passage with that from earlier in Eysenck's book quoted in Chapter 4, Exercise 1. Is the approach to definition in both consistent?

4   Obviously homosexuals are 'born' not 'made'. This must be the case because frequently only one member of a family exhibits homosexuality even though his/her siblings have been raised in the same (or very similar) home environment. If homosexuality were the result of one's interpersonal environment, it would not be expected that such diversity should exist in the same family. If, on the other hand, sexual role and preference are like the colours of one's hair and eyes, genetically determined, such diversity is easily accounted for.

a   What alternatives to being *either* 'born as', or 'made into', a homosexual, could be postulated?

b   Is it possible to consider environments as *similar*, in the absence of information about the person who is exposed to them — that is, might not the one (objectively defined) environment be psychologically different for different people? How relevant is this point to the quoted argument?

5 Seigler et al (in Boyers and Orrill 1972, p 105) criticise RD Laing's opinions about the medical profession and 'medical model' of psychiatry in the following terms:

> On the whole, people feel that the advantages of the medical model are such that it is worth preserving the social fiction which is required to sustain it. But not everyone is of this opinion; some people, for example Christian Scientists, feel that other values take precedence. As an individual, Laing is free to put forth any view on these matters that he chooses but as a physician he is not free to put forth the view that the social fiction called medicine is more harmful than helpful.

a   Is this an argument?

b   What persuasive techniques does the passage employ? Is it evaluative or does it use argument ad hominem?

6 You express astonishment at the fact that it is so easy to make men enthusiastic about a war and add your suspicions that there is something at work in them — an instinct for hatred and destruction — which goes halfway to meet the efforts of the warmongers …
   I can only express my entire agreement. We believe in the existence of an instinct for hatred and destruction … According to our hypothesis human instincts are of only two kinds: Those which seek to preserve and unite which we call 'erotic' … and those which seek to destroy and kill and which we group together as the aggressive or destructive instinct … Neither of these instincts is any less essential than the other … it seems as though an instinct of the one sort can scarcely ever operate in isolation; it is always accompanied — or, as we say alloyed — with a certain quota from the other side, which modifies its aims, or is, in some cases, what enables it to achieve that aim … The difficulty of isolating the two classes of instinct in their actual manifestations is indeed what has so long prevented us from recognising them. (Freud, writing to Einstein, 1932, quoted in Maple and Matheson 1973, pp 21–22)

a   By dichotomising instincts into two apparently discrete, opposed classes, Freud seeks to explain human wars. In the light of previous discussion of misleading dichotomies and 'missing links', what criticisms can be made of his argument?

b   How could one isolate, by 'their actual manifestations', the roles of such instincts?

chapter 7

Levels of explanation

Explaining metaphysics to the nation —
I wish he would explain his explanation.

Lord Byron (of Samuel Taylor Coleridge)

INTRODUCTION

Psychology[1] is a very diverse science with many sub-areas and branches — physiological psychology, learning theory, the psychology of perception, ecological psychology, developmental psychology and evolutionary psychology, among many others. While there is much general agreement, specialists within differing areas can disagree strongly over the way their science is practised — for example, what counts as data and what kinds of explanations are permissible. Some researchers in physiological psychology may have a poor view of the explanations on offer in cognitive science, rejecting the whole framework and disparaging them as 'brainless' (to use a term from one critic).

In this chapter we consider several kinds of explanation that either did not fit into our discussion of explanation in Chapter 3 or were treated too briefly there.

Among the many pleasures of studying any science is the discovery of new facts — information one did not have and the satisfactions of enhanced understanding — of making sense of things. The satisfactions of enhanced understanding come from providing explanations. We have already discussed general kinds of explanation in Chapter 3. In this chapter we consider aspects of other kinds of explanation — other ways of achieving understanding.

It is generally agreed that the sciences, in all their diversity, are about one 'world', although they each focus on different parts and aspects of it. It is also notable that different sciences use different terminology and concepts: they classify and relate things to each other in different ways, even when they may be talking about the same things. They have different 'takes' on this world. Even within one discipline, there can be different branches each employing different terms and concepts.

One aim of this chapter is to consider the place of psychology and some of its branches within this unity and diversity. What, for example, is the relation of psychology to physics or to physiology?

Most students come to the study of psychology having had some experience learning other sciences at high school — perhaps biology, physics or chemistry. No student starts psychology without a common-sense view of what makes people work. For example, as young children we legitimately expect parents to be angry when they find that something they value has been broken. We are all social creatures, and if we are in any position to study anything we must have already found our

---

[1] This chapter ranges widely over a number of topics, some of them requiring quite close study. Beginning students, if reading through the book, might be advised to read the rest of the book first and dip back into this chapter selectively afterwards.

way through a variety of interactions with other people and we will have taken advantage of judgments about what they think and want. We will have been using this common-sense knowledge of how people work in our day-to-day lives. So, one aim of this chapter is to consider what relation psychology has to some of the practical pre-scientific views we have about people. Is the assumption that people act on the basis of their beliefs to achieve their goals of the same kind as the view that the sun goes around the earth?

A unifying theme in this chapter is that despite the diversity of the sciences and branches of science, the differing disciplines and branches can be valuable sources of information for each other.

In order to examine the relationships amongst different fields of explanation relevant to mental and behavioural phenomena, we will distinguish and label various kinds of potential explanation. The question of 'levels' of explanation revolves around these relationships. For example, are evolutionary or genetic explanations more 'fundamental' or more 'basic' (because more physical/biological) than are social or folk psychological accounts? We will need to be quite self-conscious and analytical about what type of explanation is being discussed if we are to think clearly about these 'levels' and the interrelationships between them.

There are many ways of classifying explanations. Ernest Nagel began a major work (1961) with the following division: *deductive*, *probabilistic*, *functional* (or *teleological*) and *genetic*. Some classifications attempt to unify all kinds of explanation and take explanations from particular sciences as their model. (Indeed, we discuss this in Chapter 3.)

In this chapter, we will consider, if rather too briefly in most cases, several kinds of explanation that have been taken to be important in the social and behavioural sciences. We label these: *reductionist, folk psychological, dispositional, information processing or representational, componential, connectionist, functional* and *evolutionary* explanations. The list is not exhaustive and the kinds of explanation in the list sometimes overlap, but it does include most of the kinds of explanation psychology students will meet that were not covered or do not readily fit into the discussion in Chapter 3. We give a brief outline of each of these before looking at them in greater detail.

Reductionist explanations attempt to connect different (branches of) sciences. The idea is that phenomena identified and possibly explained by one science (say, psychology) can be given an explanation in a more 'fundamental' science (say, physics). Such explanations may both come from the same area of science but postulate different levels of causation: an effect noted in cognitive psychology may be explained within cognitive neuroscience.

Folk psychological explanations are the ones we use in our daily lives; they explain behaviour in terms of beliefs, desires and intentions. Reason-giving explanations and purposive explanations are part of this familiar, if prescientific, kind of explanation. When this kind of explanation is applied to non-humans, it is sometimes called an *anthropomorphising* explanation.

Dispositional explanations are also a familiar part of our everyday repertoire of explanations. They attribute a disposition or tendency to something in explaining what happens to it. 'Fragility' is a dispositional concept. We explain why something has broken by referring to its fragility and the fact that it received a blow. A psychological example would be 'irritability'. Someone's overreaction may be explained by their irritability and by an experience of a negative kind.

Related to folk psychological explanations are **information processing or representational explanations**. Explanations of this kind take much of their detailed inspiration from human experience with computers — concepts needed to understand computer operation are applied to people.

Componential explanations are an analytic kind of explanation that explains the capacity of properties of a system in terms of two factors: the properties and capacities of the parts of the system (its components); and their organisation in relation to each other. This is a very general kind of explanation widely used in understanding complex (psychological) systems and incorporates many information processing explanations.

Connectionist explanations are at a lower level than many in formal psychology and work in a more abstract way. Strictly, connectionists do not offer psychological explanations — they do not claim to explain human behaviour or properties. Instead, they give what could be called explanatory accounts or sketches of the behaviour and capacities of artificial systems (neural nets) of idealised but neuron-like units. But there has been, and there remains, potential for considerable transfer to the psychological arena of many of the concepts used in explaining these systems.

Functional explanations have as their focus what something *does* rather than what it *is*. Many of the concepts used not only in our unadorned conceptual schemes, but also in science, identify things by their causal role or profile — how they are affected by other things and what effects they have. Below we distinguish two senses of function, one closely associated with componential explanation and the other relevant to evolutionary explanations.

Evolutionary explanations are the final kind we consider. These are one kind of genetic explanation. Genetic explanations place things in time and are concerned with change. They connect present states with their origins, or at least prior states. In developmental terms, once object constancy is achieved (very early) the question arises for things — where were they before? When object 'inconstancy' develops — this is the same object as before, but it has changed — the question arises, what were they like before and how did they come to be the way they are now? Historical explanations are a special kind of genetic explanation (also so-called narrative explanations).

Two main sources of genetic explanations within psychology are developmental psychology and evolutionary psychology (of which more below). It is worth noting that evolutionary psychology and developmental psychology interact strongly with other branches of psychology — if one branch of psychology proposes that things are thus and so, but an advanced developmental psychology provides reason to think that they could not have developed in that way or if evolutionary psychology suggests there seems to be no way that *homo sapiens* could have evolved to be like that, then there will be tension between these branches.

More specifically, the final type of explanation we consider is that provided by **evolutionary psychology**. As noted, this is a particular kind of genetic explanation. Evolutionary psychology offers an account of how present-day humans may have acquired their characteristics and capacities through the process of (Darwinian) evolution.

REDUCTIONIST EXPLANATIONS

What relations hold between psychology and other social, biological or physical sciences? One view is that some sciences are more 'fundamental' than others. This view asserts that physics is the most fundamental, with chemistry between physics and, say, biology and psychology less fundamental again.

These relations can be pictured in the following hierarchy:

psychology
biology
physics

corresponding, loosely speaking, in reverse order to the study of all matter (physics), living matter (biology) and living 'minded' matter (psychology).

A more detailed picture might include other sciences and subdivide psychology thus:

social psychology
individual psychology
biology

biochemistry
chemistry
physics

In this hierarchical view, it is not clear what is meant by the expression 'more fundamental'. One possibility is that the more fundamental science deals with things that are *parts* of the less fundamental science. For example, to oversimplify, groups of people consist of people who consist of cells which consist of organic molecules consisting of atoms which in turn consist of fundamental particles (cf physics).

Among many others, one important science left out of this hierarchy is what is currently called 'neuroscience'. People may consist mostly of cells, but they are not exclusively neurons. So it does not fit the simple hierarchy, although a knowledge of the nervous system is particularly important because of its causal role as part of the various *control* systems within people.[2]

With this hierarchical view in mind, some are tempted to argue that all 'psychological' accounts of behaviour (including both mentalistic and more behaviouristic formulations) can be replaced ultimately by explanations in the *physical* sciences. The promise of this program is twofold: not only would the inconsistencies and questionable assumptions of colloquial language be avoided, the whole range of mentalistic concepts in psychology would also be precisely and unambiguously redefined. Often the proposed reduction does not go all the way down to physics. It is then a call to replace 'the mind' and 'behaviour' by neurophysiological or biochemical concepts. Churchland (1988) exemplifies the appeal of this program:

> If materialism,[3] in the end, is true, then it is the conceptual framework of a completed neuroscience that will embody the essential wisdom about our inner nature ...
>
> Suppose we trained our native mechanisms to make a new and more detailed set of discriminations, a set that corresponded not to the primitive psychological taxonomy of ordinary language, but to some more penetrating taxonomy of states drawn from a 'completed' neuroscience. And suppose we trained ourselves to respond to that reconfigured activity with judgements that were framed, as a matter of habit, in the appropriate concepts from neuroscience ...
>
> Glucose consumption in the forebrain, dopamine levels in the thalamus, the coding vectors in neural pathways, resonances in the

---

[2] There are many other possible hierarchies we could present, and none of them stand up to detailed scrutiny. We should note that similar issues arise *within* the branches of psychology as well.

[3] Sometimes identified as the view that the world is composed entirely of matter.

*n*th level of the peristriatal cortex, and countless other neurophysiological niceties could be moved into the objective focus of our
introspective discrimination and conceptual recognition, just as G
min chords and A+9 chords are moved into the objective focus of
trained musicians' auditory discrimination and conceptual recognition [emphasis added]. (pp 179–80)

This radical proposal is known as **reductionism**. In its most popular
form, it asserts that all scientific information will (or could) ultimately
form a unified body of knowledge encoded in a self-contained language
of the physical sciences. Therefore, psychology is but a transitory discipline which will be 'reduced to' physiology (especially neurophysiology)
and biochemistry. These two disciplines will eventually be subsumed
under the laws of microphysics, as is already apparent in some fields of
chemistry. Thus, there is a hierarchy of sciences, all resting ultimately on
physics, and all capable of being replaced by its concepts and laws — at
least at some time in the future. At present, psychology appears to be far
removed from physics, but, according to this view, it will be redefined
within the conceptual domain of this fundamental science. Indeed, it
could be claimed that intermediate stages in this reductionist program
are already evident. For example, both behaviourism and some of the
findings of contemporary neurophysiology seem to provide adequate
explanations of some phenomena without recourse to traditional psychological (or at least mentalistic) concepts.

Using the physical sciences as a model, many argue that the process
of 'reduction' is continuously occurring. To support this point of view,
the example of successful reduction of a concept of one science to the
domain of a 'more general' or 'more basic' discipline, which is frequently cited, is that of 'temperature'. Long before detailed knowledge
of molecular theory and thermodynamics, regularities ('laws') involving temperature changes in gases had been formulated by Boyle and
Charles. With the development of micro-physical theory, it became evident that the expression 'temperature of gas X could be taken to refer
to the mean kinetic energy of the particles of that gas'. That is, the
expressions 'temperature' and 'mean kinetic energy' were accepted as
contingently identical — they referred to the same phenomenon
despite their initially different meanings.

Or to put this point in the language of Chapter 4, the two expressions, although of different 'intension', were shown to have identical
'extensions'. New theories and more sophisticated measurement procedures allowed what was previously a useful, well-defined concept to
be subsumed under physical laws having a range of application which
is far broader than the phenomena to which the concept was originally relevant. Although Boyle and Charles were not aware of the actual
details of what nowadays temperature is taken to be, their laws were

both empirically supported and theoretically viable within the context for which they were devised. The laws were nonetheless reducible to instances of more general micro-physical regularities.

It is not surprising that this example is frequently cited to suggest that psychological concepts will ultimately be reinterpreted in a similar manner as referring to physico-chemical processes.[4] This is despite the fact that these psychological concepts may appear quite adequate within their current range of application.

For example, Moss (1965) provides a vague suggestion concerning the possible reduction of 'hypnosis' to physiological variables when he asserts (p 50):

> It would be comforting if evidence were available concerning the physiological concomitants of hypnosis. *Because all behavior must be ultimately reducible to biological processes (and eventually to Physics and Chemistry)* identification of neurophysiological mechanisms involved could constitute a long stride towards alleviating the array of competing interpretations now in existence on the molar level of behavioral description. However it must be acknowledged that reduction of hypnotic behavior to physiological events at the present state in our knowledge would constitute little more than a substitution of one set of terms for another [emphasis added].

Although there is much that could be objected to in this statement, it illustrates the tendency to assume that reductionism is both possible and desirable without offering any detailed justification for this view. Similar unsupported assertions can also be found which *deny* the possibility (and/or desirability) of reductionism.

The issue of reductionism is important in elementary psychology for precisely this reason. Students all too often *assume* either that mentalistic concepts are appropriate and/or essential to psychology (that is, irreducible) or, on the contrary, that no explanation which is not behaviouristic or physiological can be regarded as adequate. In either case, the student may easily overlook important aspects of the explanatory adequacy of alternative theories or the value of other concepts.

Therefore, in the following brief discussion we shall attempt to spell out some of the difficulties involved in maintaining a consistent conceptual framework in one's approach to psychological argument in the face of assumptions concerning the possibility or impossibility of reductionism.

---

[4] This reduction within physics is frequently cited. It is worth noting however, that studies in the philosophy of science indicate that other reductions or attempted reductions in physics and in other branches of science do not fit one simple pattern — they are very diverse.

It is helpful here to draw a number of distinctions and to tease out what is plausible in the temptation to reductionism. The idea that the sciences, although different, concern a single world and that physics is in some way fundamental can be expressed using the concept of **supervenience**. A class M of properties — for example, psychological properties — supervenes on another class P of properties — for example, physical properties — if no two things can differ in which M properties apply to them without differing in their P properties. If the M properties supervene on the P properties, then no one thing can change in any of its M properties without changing in at least one P property. It is widely accepted that psychological properties supervene in this sense on physical properties. If you change your psychological properties — say, from thinking about Byron to thinking about Shakespeare — then some of your physical properties will be different. Notice, though, that given our present ignorance we have no detailed idea what these may be.

It is important to point out, however, that if one science is supervenient on another, it does not follow that the first can necessarily be reduced to the second. One reason for this is that the concepts used in the first science may not be identifiable with any (combination of) concepts in the second. To use our Byron example, given, among other differences, the extraordinarily detailed diversity of brains, there may be no common set of physical properties possessed by every person, past present and future, when they are 'thinking of Byron'. Such properties or concepts used in one science are said to be *multiply realisable* in the other. A simple example of a multiply realised concept is the everyday notion of a calculator — there need be no particular physical properties shared exclusively by every calculator. Every calculator is a physical object. But although all will be physical, some will be electrical, some mechanical, some might be chemical — such as DNA devices. Others will be quantum devices, and so on. No particular combination of physical properties as such will identify the class of calculators.

But as well, part of the important work done in any science is to classify and group various entities (sometimes called natural kinds) and then to find out what properties they have and what relations they may have to other classes of entities. These relations may be expressed, for example, in the form of simple general statements of the kind 'all Fs are Gs'. Thus, 'all mammals are warm-blooded' claims that a particular grouping of living creatures has a property — warm-bloodedness. Progress occurs when classifications can be found in terms of which useful explanatory and predictive general statements can be made. Thus, despite their superficial similarity to fish, whales turn out to be better classed as mammals in these respects. Often as a science progresses, reclassifications occur, and of course different sciences typically classify different things and in different ways. There is no guarantee that, where it is possible to translate these generalisations into a reducing theory, the resulting generalisations will be useful and explanatory.

Behaviourism is one form of reductionism that confronts students very early in their careers.[5] As a form of reductionism it seeks to redefine phenomena treated by a variety of theoretical perspectives into physical, more directly observable, concepts limited to stimuli and responses. It might be regarded as an intermediate or transitional stage in the ultimate rejection of traditional mentalistic concepts in psychology.

Although all psychologists study 'behaviour' (broadly defined), there are great differences between them on the issue of reductionism. Consider, for the sake of argument, the rather vague concept 'anxiety'. In both informal and psycho-analytic language, the word refers to mental states involving fear, tension or apprehension. Psychoanalysis even allows 'unconscious' anxiety. Indeed, unconscious anxiety concerning sexual and aggressive wishes is hypothesised by Freud to be of great significance in personality development. Therefore, in psychoanalytic literature, anxiety is indicated by a variety of indirect manifestations — in the 'symptoms' of neurosis, the thematic content of dreams and fantasies, defensive personal reactions, and so on. Reductionists could assert that anxiety consists only of particular behavioural reactions. Or they may say that the term actually refers to physico-chemical processes such as cardiovascular, respiratory or muscular conditions associated with the activity of the sympathetic nervous system. They might further argue that knowledge of such processes is both necessary and sufficient to explain the more 'mentalistic' aspects of anxiety. By this they mean that anxiety is *nothing more than* a set of physiological reactions. Hence, when our knowledge of physiology is more fully developed, the reduction of anxiety to some set of physiological reactions will be successfully effected.

This example is superficially analogous to the case of 'temperature' which we mentioned previously. Temperature was once indicated only by changes in the mercury volume of a thermometer and/or by its subjective psychological effects (whether the substance being measured felt hot or cold, and so on). But without knowing more precisely 'what temperature was', it was nevertheless possible for scientists to discuss it informally (as it is now for people who know nothing about microphysics) and also to incorporate the concept into a precise and heuristically

---

[5] Two schools of behaviourism are sometimes distinguished:

(a) *methodological behaviourism*, which does not deny the existence of 'mental' phenomena, but asserts that these are inherently 'private' and, therefore, cannot be scientifically studied;

(b) *philosophical or metaphysical behaviourism*, which denies the existence of mental phenomena as distinct from physical processes, and therefore focuses on observable 'behaviour' (because 'that is all there is!').

valuable set of 'laws'. Similarly, not knowing what anxiety 'really is', we can still employ the concept quite fruitfully in psychology or in our day-to-day affairs. You don't need to be a neuro-physiologist to understand what it means to be anxious about your examinations, for instance. Ultimately, however, psychologists may need to reinterpret the expression in the light of information from the biological or physical sciences. Just as we now take 'water' to refer to H_2O molecules (within a certain temperature range), and 'temperature' applied to gases, to refer to the mean kinetic energy of the particles of a substance, so we may ultimately take 'anxiety' to refer to specific physiological reactions and to nothing over and above such reactions.

It comes as no surprise to find many arguments being advanced against both behaviourist and other reductionist programs. However, because these are usually directed at the materialist or physicalist foundations of reductionism, they raise questions of philosophical analysis beyond our present scope. Consequently, we will leave this issue open and proceed to make a number of general, yet important, points which have direct practical implications for psychological argument. These should help you to avoid some common conceptual confusions associated with this issue.

FACILE OR TRIVIAL REDUCTIONS

Reductionism offers deceptively simple solutions to some very complex problems. It is tempting to try to avoid virtually all explanations phrased in conventional psychological terms by replacing these with other more 'basic' explanatory terms from physiology, for example.

In previous discussion (Chapter 4) of circularly defined concepts used to explain behaviour (for example, 'instinct', various 'mental faculties', and so on), we saw how easy it was to propose *trivial* (non-informative) 'explanations' of complex behaviour. Reductionist accounts of behaviour are also open to this abuse: what appears to be a reductionist claim may, in fact, be merely a convenient, arbitrary or *post hoc* postulate having little or no *independent evidence* in its support. That is, apart from the behaviour being explained, there may be no evidence for the particular explanation offered. This is sometimes referred to as 'transforming a problem into a postulate'. By this it is meant that the problem (for example, what is 'hypnosis'?) is gratuitously converted into an 'explanation' (for example, 'Hypnosis is a physiological state which causes people to behave in certain specified ways'). The explanandum is used to explain itself with the help of an unsupported reductionist assumption. In informal discourse, examples of this are easy to find. One case is the frequent assertion that being a criminal or a homosexual, say, is 'in one's blood' in such a way that all further discussion of possible causes is superfluous. Such accounts are not informative unless some specific hypothesis about the genetic bases for the relevant behaviours can be advanced on *grounds other than the occurrence of the behaviours in question (criminality, homosexuality)*.

Genuine reductionist arguments seek to subsume a 'secondary' science (for example, psychology) within the more generally applicable concepts and laws of a 'primary' science. They are not merely facile claims that there *must be* a physiological cause for all behaviour. It is the details of the reductionist explanation which are crucial in any particular case.

The important point to emphasise from this discussion is that precise, informative explanations are preferable to vague or circular postulates whether or not the latter appear to be reductionist and therefore 'fundamental' or 'basic'. Because all explanations are proposed within particular contexts, as answers to specific questions, it may be impossible to decide which of two explanations is the more 'fundamental'. Certainly, the primary consideration should not be whether or not a putative explanation is reductionist.

INCONSISTENT TERMINOLOGY

'Psychoneurobiochemeducation' is the title of a paper by Krech (1971). This facetious title suggests that psychology is not an isolated discipline but is constantly interacting with many other branches of science. This view generates the enthusiasm that many psychologists show for reductionist arguments. But the title also suggests the danger of indiscriminately adopting parts of the vocabulary of diverse disciplines for describing the one set of phenomena. This practice may create considerable confusion, whether or not a reductionist argument is, in fact, appropriate to the phenomena being discussed.

For example, although Krech is speaking only in very general terms, he sometimes gives the impression that psychological words such as 'memory' are likely to be replaced by physico-chemical expressions. He says, ' ... for every separate memory in the mind we will eventually find a differentiated chemical in the brain — "chemical memory pellets" as it were' (Krech 1971, p 94). Such futuristic speculations are often quite justifiable and need not raise any serious conceptual issues. However, they do not really demonstrate, in detail, how the reductionist program is to be effected. For instance, it might be asked how 'separate memories' could be defined in a manner that would equate them with Krech's 'memory pellets'. (Would such a 'pellet' correspond to 'thinking of Bryon', to use our example?) Given that there is dispute about the best description of 'what is learned' or what aspects of information are stored in memory, and how they are structured, the assumption that 'separate memories' will correspond to distinct physical structures in a manner analogous to pellets is naive, to say the least. Like all pseudo-reductionist speculations, its simplicity is superficially appealing. But the cost of thinking in such simple terms may be confusion between psychological descriptions of memory (concerning information encoding, storage and retrieval) and physiological hypotheses which, although concerned with the same phenomena, do not necessarily relate to what is known of memory in the psychological literature.

Other examples also show that serious conceptual confusions may result from the premature assumption of reductionism. This is particularly apparent in students' written work, where the vocabulary of one discipline is employed indiscriminately to explain phenomena more usually described in a different theoretical language. Lacking any detailed procedures for relating the two sets of concepts, it is all too easy for authors to create complex theoretical anomalies in their written arguments. These are generally indicated when authors vacillate between theoretical terms from different scientific disciplines, shifting the argument from one level of explanation to another quite arbitrarily.

In the example of premature or pseudo-reductionist explanation to be considered below, criticism is primarily made on the grounds of explanatory inadequacy rather than pointing to reductionism per se. We point out that it is not sufficient categorically to reject explanations simply because they are reductionist, but it is legitimate to evaluate their explanatory force in the light of the general criteria for adequate explanation which were outlined in Chapter 3 — especially those concerning circularity.

Most students of elementary psychology are familiar with the observations and 'laws' of perceptual organisation proposed by Gestalt theorists such as Wertheimer and Kohler. The major tenets of Gestalt theory might be stated very briefly as:

1   An emphasis on the structured 'wholeness' of perception. Visual experience consists of organised 'wholes' rather than discrete, disjoint components. The whole is greater than (or more accurately, qualitatively different from) the sum of its parts.

2   A number of 'laws' of perceptual organisation are proposed. These state that properties such as the similarity, proximity and closure of elements lead to their perceptual organisation.

3   But such organisation is not intrinsic to the perceived stimuli; it is 'imposed on' them by the perceiver.

4   Therefore, a principle of *psychoneural isomorphism* is proposed to account for these organisational properties. This asserts a one-to-one correspondence between 'brain fields' and the perceived

organisation of stimulus configurations. That is, the structural properties of the brain bear a precise relationship to the aspects of perceptual experience emphasised in the laws of organisation.[6]

The Gestaltists are somewhat ambiguous concerning whether this is a *causal* relationship between two distinct phenomena, or whether logical and psychological regularities are two aspects of the same reality. In either case, the principle is essentially reductionist, for the physiological process would be regarded as 'basic' on both interpretations. Prentice, calling the concept of *isomorphism* a hypothesis, states: '[I]t comes nearest, perhaps, to what has sometimes been called the "double aspect" theory, the view that cortical events and phenomenal facts are merely two ways of looking at the same natural phenomenon, two faces of the same coin, as it were'. (Prentice, in Koch 1959, p 435)

Granted that isomorphism is a hypothesis, it is, nevertheless, possible to employ the language of the hypothetical physiology of perception to 'explain' psychological phenomena in a deceptively simple manner. The result is a mixture of inconsistent concepts and expressions. For example, Gestalt effects like 'closure' can be spoken of as 'field effects' in the sensory projection areas of the cortex. These field effects (which are hypothetical, at best) may be described as 'forces', 'valences', and so on, in pseudo-physical terminology. Hence, it becomes difficult to distinguish between 'field' or 'force' as applied to some (possible) cortical event and the metaphorical description of psychological (mental) phenomena in similar terms. Rather than being 'reductionist', such accounts may not be essentially explanatory at all and may merely generate considerable confusion due to the vacillation between 'physical' and 'psychological' levels of description.

Recall that reductions are effected by establishing the *contingent identity* (that is, the identical extension or denotation) of two or more expressions. However, the arbitrary equation of perceptual effects and brain-field properties *asserts*, rather than *demonstrates*, such an identity. In fairness to Gestalt theorists, the lack of independent evidence for such cortical properties has long been acknowledged and the claim of reductionism is seldom explicitly argued. Nevertheless, the frequent confusion between the description of perceptual experience and (hypothetical) neurological states renders the theory difficult to evaluate. It provides the shadow, rather than the substance, of a reductionist explanation — not because it is not reductionist, but because it is not adequately explanatory.

---

[6] Prentice (1959) provides a detailed, basically sympathetic account of Gestalt theory (as a theory).

FOLK PSYCHOLOGICAL EXPLANATIONS

We are all 'folk psychologists', proposing explanations with or without any explicit tuition in the academic field of psychology. Explanations of this kind are used in our day-to-day dealings with each other, predominantly in explaining behaviour but in other applications as well. A familiar kind of common-sense explanation, they have come to be called **folk psychological explanations**. Typically, in these kinds of explanation of a person's behaviour, we attribute beliefs and desires to them and take them to be acting rationally — that is, acting on the basis of their beliefs to satisfy their desires. Why did Mary swerve her car? She saw (and hence believed there was) a large truck heading towards her and acted as she did because she wanted to avoid a collision. Why are there people in this lecture theatre right now? They intend to hear Professor X and believe she will be speaking here very soon.

Many familiar expressions in natural language are used to express explanations of this kind. We speak of the *reason* someone had for acting, what their *purpose* was, what they *intended*, and so on. As we have seen for explanations generally, when other parts of a full explanation can be taken for granted we only mention the salient parts. For example, in explaining someone's action we may only refer to what they wanted to achieve (desire), because it is taken for granted that they believe doing what they did would achieve that result. Similarly, we can explain someone's taking a back route home by saying they thought it would be quicker (belief), taking the relevant desire(s) for granted.

It is worth reminding ourselves how effective explanations like this can be and what a powerful tool this account of people's behaviour is, 'pre-scientific' though it may be. To adapt an example from Jerry Fodor: Professor X (from the paragraph before last) may have agreed to give her talk three months ago, from across the country. After her acceptance, her name was included in the list of speakers and two weeks before the event a return air ticket arrived in the mail. Now, having adjusted her behaviour in myriad ways — to mention only two — packing her bag the night before and cutting short a conversation with a colleague that otherwise would have led to her missing the plane, there she is only five minutes' walk from the lecture theatre. Viewing her body merely as a lump of matter buffeted by *physical* forces is no way to predict its presence on this side of the country so close to this venue at this time. Her presence is obviously to be explained in *psychological* ways.

Psychologists commonly view folk psychological explanations like this as unsatisfactory from a scientific point of view. Sometimes the source of this view is scruples about the quality of the evidence justifying the attributions of belief and desire in particular cases. For practical purposes, however, it seems clear there is no doing without them in understanding our fellows. Some writers, however, have suggested that the need for explanations of this kind merely reflects the undeveloped stage of our science. In the quote earlier in this chapter, Churchland refers to the 'primitive psychological taxonomy of ordinary language'. He has, in fact, advocated eliminating this kind of explanation entirely and replacing it with a more scientific kind — for example, as provided by neuroscience. The view he expressed is not that both kinds of explanation have their place; rather, the neuroscientific kind should supplant the folk psychological. This is clearly a radical position that is sometimes given the clumsy label '*eliminativism*', although it is a version of what we have called reductionism.

Before leaving the topic of folk psychology, we should note that social psychology frequently supplies a very different content for everyday explanations, related instead to concepts such as 'dispositions'. Von Eckardt (1997, p 31) points out that:

> Social psychologists have been studying folk psychology for nearly 50 years under the labels 'self-perception', 'person perception', (or 'social perception') and, more recently, 'social cognition'.

People routinely explain behaviour by attributing traits or psychological dispositions to each other (for example, 'greediness'), and then identify related triggering circumstances (for example, the perceived availability of food). These have been called **trait-trigger** explanations. Explanations of these kinds clearly fit into the category of **dispositional** explanations, but like intentional and reason-giving explanations are part of our common-sense repertoire. In assessing such explanations our standard question about the quality and *independence* of the evidence for the claimed trait or disposition remains important. (Recall the discussion in Chapter 3.)

INFORMATION PROCESSING/REPRESENTATIONAL EXPLANATIONS

One of the major influences on information processing explanations in psychology has been the invention of the computer. The computer has been an extraordinarily valuable tool for use in the sciences, but the body of theory and expertise developed in constructing, operating and understanding them has also been seen as a valuable model for psychological theorising. This is sometimes expressed in the very strong view that the mind is a computer. A weaker view is that thinking is a *form of computation*.

What this claim comes to will depend on what we take a computer to be. Everyone reading this book is almost certainly familiar with some kind of computer, probably a personal computer, and will have used one for word-processing, graphics or game playing. Yet, if this is what a computer is, it seems far-fetched to claim that the mind is like such a machine in significant respects. We need to know how to think about or how to analyse computers if the claim is to be at all plausible.

Remarkably, in the history of ideas, there was a quite precise theoretical account of computation before there were any general-purpose computers operating. In the mid-1930s the British mathematician Alan Turing developed the idea of a device with only a finite number of internal states that could read and write discrete symbols on to a tape. He was able to show that these devices could perform many symbol manipulation tasks. For example, if (sequences of) the symbols were systematically interpreted as representing pairs of numbers, a device could be specified to read any pair of the symbols and write strings of symbols interpretable as their sum; or another device could deliver their product or the value of the first number raised to the power of the second, and so on. These examples are numerical but need not be. More remarkably still, he was able to show that a single machine of the same general kind of design, now called a Universal Turing Machine, could do everything that any of the special-purpose devices could do. He had developed the idea of a general-purpose programmable computer. A device which, although clearly physical — a kind of machine — had extraordinary flexibility and plasticity.

Many possible definitions of computation have been advanced. Brian Cantwell Smith considers no fewer than six in *The Age of Significance*, (Smith, forthcoming, vol 1), noting that no pair of definitions is equivalent and no single definition is adequate. A succinct one for our purposes is that computers are information processors — computation is a special case of information processing. In the growing subfield of cognitive science (which crosses the disciplinary boundaries amongst mathematics, psychology, neuroscience and computer sciences), a more informative widely used one is that *computers process information by manipulating symbols.* Symbols are in turn defined as the physical representations of information. This view is sometimes taken to characterise them as formal symbol manipulators — devices that manipulate symbols or representations solely on the basis of the physical characteristics of the symbols — independently of what, in normal contexts, would be called the meanings of the symbols.[7]

This is the kind of view of computation that has captured the imagination of psychological theorists. The great attraction is that these flexible devices could be programmed to manipulate representations in a way that reflected their meanings — much the way, as we noted

---

[7] Smith (forthcoming), in vol 2, argues (against this view) that computers do not in many cases manipulate symbols *independently* of their 'meanings'.

above, pairs of strings of symbols interpretable as standing for numbers could be manipulated by a computer to produce a string of symbols standing for their product. Under the appropriate interpretation, formal symbol manipulation could be seen as multiplication. A key application for cognitive psychologists was that these devices could be programmed to take pairs of strings of symbols representing, for example, two *premises* — two pieces of information — and manipulate them to produce a string of symbols that represented a *conclusion* which in fact followed from those premises. Under this interpretation, the symbol manipulation could be seen as logical deduction. Interpreted in the right way, symbol manipulation delivers the same result as logical thought — an important cognitive capacity.

The information processing approach takes the mind to be a computer, or more specifically, various cognitive processes are taken to be kinds of computation. Since there are many kinds of computers and computational processes, the question that arises in explaining cognitive capacities is what kind of computational processes underlie human cognitive processing. If 'thinking' is only formal symbol manipulation, what are the symbols and what are the basic processes of symbol manipulation? It is well known from computer science that many different computations are input–output equivalent. Although they achieve the result in different ways, they pair the same inputs and outputs. On this view, it is a matter of some importance if a process of computation is proposed to generate the correct pairings that there be *independent evidence* to support the claim that this *particular* computational process is the one people *actually* use. Unfortunately, the available evidence frequently fails to rule out many possible processes, so that arguments for specific proposals as to how the processing occurs frequently remain inconclusive.

Below, in the section on componential explanation, we provide a general framework into which information processing explanations fit.

THREE LEVELS OF EXPLANATION OF COMPLEX SYSTEMS

We have just briefly considered two kinds of explanation — folk psychological and information processing. A number of authors have made these the 'top' two levels in a framework of three levels of explanation argued to be especially appropriate for cognitive psychology. They have taken this framework from an influential general analysis by David Marr (1982) of levels of explanation for complex systems which was proposed in his work on a computational theory of vision. He distinguished three levels, which he called: the *computational*, the *algorithmic* and the *physical*.

The 'computational' level, rather misleadingly named, describes the task the system carries out in terms of its end-points — on a simple input–output view, the pairings of output with input. Notice that output need not be thought of as behaviour. Marr himself took the output end-point of the visual system to be an interpretation of the world as coloured three-dimensional objects. This level identifies *what* is done and perhaps (see below) should not be counted as explanatory at all.

The algorithmic level specifies in terms of computational procedures *how* the system produces the pairings specified at the above level. This is an information processing level.

The physical or implementational level shows *how* the system works in terms of the physical mechanism of the brain or the computer hardware, for example.

Some thinkers have adapted this framework to systematise understanding the behaviour of all complex systems by locating folk psychological and information processing explanations in relation to lower-level explanations in Marr's scheme.

Starting at the top, folk psychological explanations are taken to belong to a level of explanation (or organisation, when it is attributed to the system being explained) which has been called the *knowledge level* (Newell et al 1989, p 96), the *semantic level* (Pylyshyn 1989, p 57) and the *intentional stance* (Dennett 1998, p 253). This top level is the one with the poorest fit to Marr's hierarchy.

Dennett's hierarchy is a hierarchy of stances we can take in explaining or predicting the behaviour of complex systems. At the top is the **intentional stance** — here we explain/predict the behaviour of a system by attributing beliefs and desires and assuming it will act rationally. Any system susceptible to explanation by the intentional stance is called an intentional system. As we have observed, it is part of our everyday experience to use this stance in our dealings with fellow humans, but its proponents argue that it can usefully be applied much more widely through the animal (and even the plant) kingdom as well as to artefacts like computers.

Within the intentional stance, Dennett distinguishes further levels as certain special cases. He identifies classes of intentional stances in which the attributed beliefs and desires can be complex — for example, a second-order intentional stance attributes beliefs or desires *about* other simple beliefs or desires. Contrast attributing to Jo the belief that it is raining with attributing to her the belief that Chris thinks (or believes) it is late. In the first case, a simple belief is attributed. In the latter case, a second-order belief — a belief about a belief — is attributed. Creatures characterised as having second-order beliefs or desires are said to have a *theory of mind*. Some researchers claim that this distinction marks the difference between humans and other animals — only humans warrant treatment as *second*-order intentional systems.[8]

---

[8] See the discussion of Sober, below.

The second level is the **design stance**. Here we take the system to be designed to work in a certain way and predict its behaviour on the basis that it will work as designed. We assume it will not malfunction. Many of us, for example, find it most natural to adopt this stance in our dealings with alarm clocks. But more significantly, this can be seen as the level at which information processing psychology supplies explanations. Dennett has also called this the algorithmic level (1998, p 253), while Pylyshyn and Newell have called a special case of this level the *symbol level*. Their name for this level reflects an extra commitment on their part to the claim that the information processing at this level is carried out by formal symbol manipulation.

The third level is the **physical stance**, most frequently adopted in the physical sciences. Here we appeal to our knowledge of the initial physical state of the system and laws of nature to predict its behaviour. For example, think of predicting an eclipse of the sun, based on the positions of the sun, earth and moon and the laws of their motions. Pylyshyn calls this the physical or biological level. Unfortunately, for practical purposes when explaining the behaviour of *complex* systems (like computers or brains), our ignorance, among other things, of the needed details of the (initial) physical state typically precludes taking this stance (which, of course, is what is at stake in reductionism).

Having identified three levels at which explanations can be given, we need to ask how the levels are related to each other. What bearing should explanations at the intentional or knowledge level (for example, folk psychological explanations) have on those of researchers proposing information processing models of cognition at the design or algorithmic level? Dennett suggests the relation is similar to that between arithmetic and hand calculators — the intentional stance constrains the design stance by providing a normative theory that the design should match as well as possible. We have already distinguished *what* is done from *how* it is done. The contrast being drawn here is between what *ought* to be done and what *is* done. Dennett says the intentional stance 'reminds the designer or design-interpreter of *what the system is supposed to do*' (Dennett 1998, p 316).

Some psychologists reject all explanations from the top level as inadequate. A necessary condition for the upper level of explanation to be appropriate has recently been explored by Elliott Sober (1998), which we mentioned briefly in Chapter 5. His idea is that if experimental work does not justify inferring an intervening variable or causal factor, then it cannot support hypotheses about such things as intentional states taken as beliefs and desires, for these are just special kinds of intervening variables. He looks at some experimental work done with chimpanzees designed to test the hypothesis that they have a theory of mind — that they think other chimps think, and asks: Does this experiment even justify the claim that there is an intervening causal factor or variable of any kind operating? He finds that the answer is 'no', and so no case has been made for attributing a theory of mind.

Sober concludes:

> There is more to mentalistic hypotheses than the postulation of intervening variables. Attributions of beliefs and desires not only claim that intervening variables exist, but assign them a semantic content ... There presently exists a very large gap in our understanding of how attributions of mental states should be evaluated. Nonetheless the argument of the present paper suggests a kind of baseline: *if an intervening variable model cannot be justified, it is questionable whether one should spend time arguing about exactly what semantic content those supposed intervening variables possess*. (pp 494–95).

COMPONENTIAL EXPLANATIONS

In this section we present a useful framework that incorporates each of the preceding three levels of explanation while focusing on the second — variously called, as we have seen, the algorithmic level, the information processing level, the symbol level, and the level at which one adopts the design stance.

By way of easy introduction, consider how one can explain one specific cognitive ability: the ability to perform the following mental arithmetic task: *Multiply together two numbers expressed as roman numerals and give the answer as a roman numeral. For example, multiply together XXV and XL to get M.* A combination of familiar abilities or capacities can explain this. The ability to convert roman numerals to the familiar decimal arabic numerals, combined with the ability to multiply numbers expressed in that notation and then to convert back from arabic to roman numerals, could be the explanation of this ability for many people.[9]

Not all explanation consists of explanation of changes, showing how some effect is caused, or explaining why a system changed from one state to another — an area where the D-N model (of Chapter 3) is readily applied. Explaining the *properties* or *capacities* of *systems* is another important explanatory achievement of science. It has been called **componential explanation** (by Clark 1997), and more *generally property explanation* or *explanation by analysis* by Robert Cummins

---

[9] We have used this example because it is a particularly clear case. Powerful evidence is readily available that the explanation is correct. Compare the difficult investigative task of explaining the remarkable calculating abilities of an inarticulate idiot savant or something as mundane (but difficult to explain) as the human ability to recognise faces, even after they have changed with age.

(1983). It is a kind of explanation directed to showing what it is about a system that gives it certain properties, characteristics or capacities. An example from the physical sciences would be the explanation of a substance's flexibility in terms of its chemical structure.

The general idea is that we can explain how a system has certain properties or capacities by showing how these emerge from the properties or capacities of its parts (or components) and their organisation. In chemistry, the atomic theory of matter provides a nice example. Here, various properties and capacities of substances are explained in terms of the properties of their components and their organisation (or structure). Where the system's property or capacity is something it exhibits as the result of some process through time, the explanation can be thought of as explaining *how* a particular result is achieved.

Of course, a logically prior notion to how a result is achieved is *what* is done. Without some idea of what is done, there will in general be no way to check proposals as to how it is done. But as Cummins (1983, pp 141–42) says,

> [C]apacities are not explained by specifying them, be it oh-so-carefully-and-mathematically. They are explained by analysing them and ultimately by exhibiting their instantiations in the systems that have them. Specification of a capacity can be a fascinating and challenging scientific problem, but it is not explanation.

The explanation of a capacity will have three steps:

1 *Specification:* identifying what the capacity achieves.
2 *Analysis:* breaking it into its parts.
3 *Instantiation:* showing how it is realised physically.

Note the close parallel of these three steps to the three levels identified in the preceding section.

We have just considered specification (step 1). The process of identifying the components of a system and their relationship to each other is called *system analysis* (step 2). Artefacts are a good example where it can be relatively easy to identify components and their organisation. An illustration is an electrical circuit diagram showing how capacitors, resistors, and so on, are connected to each other. Sometimes, however, the capacity of a system to do something is analysed not in terms of the its components, but via the organised cooperation of a number of more basic capacities. Where the capacity itself is analysed into other capacities, this is called *functional analysis.* These may not even be capacities of specific components of the system, but capacities of the system as a whole. In the example above, a person's capacity to multiply together two numbers represented by roman numerals and give the product in roman numerals may be analysed into: the capacity to convert them into decimal notation; their capacity to multiply two decimally represented numbers together; and their capacity to convert back from decimal to roman numerals. In a case like this, the more basic capacities still seem to be capacities of the whole system.

As Cummins (1983, p 30) points out:

> The explanatory interest of functional analysis is roughly proportional to (i) the extent to which the analysing capacities are less sophisticated than the analysed capacities, (ii) the extent to which the analysing capacities are different in kind from the analysed capacities, and (iii) the relative sophistication of the program appealed to — i.e. the relative complexity of the organisation of the component parts/processes that is attributed to the system. (iii) is correlative with (i) and (ii): the greater the gap in sophistication and kind between analysing capacities and the analysed capacity, the more sophisticated the program must be to close the gap.

The third step, then, is to show how the capacity is instantiated in a particular system (or kind of system). Sometimes, as in much cognitive psychology, there is no obvious association of functions with components of the system. Yet, without some such association, we will not have shown how the capacity we have analysed is instantiated in the particular system which exhibits it. This part of the explanation will typically be guided by constraints from other sciences, such as biology or neuroscience. But, of course, it will frequently be the case that possible instantiations are very speculative indeed.

Many psychological capacities studied in cognitive psychology are specified in terms of some logical or semantic relationship between the input to the system and its output. A capacity to do mental arithmetic, say simple addition, can be specified as taking representations of two numbers as input and producing a representation of their sum as output. Here, the capacity is specified by interpreting its input and output as symbols representing numbers. A system that can have some of its physical states so interpreted can be viewed as an information processing system and we call its analysis *interpretive analysis*.

An important class of capacities for cognitive psychology are those specified (under interpretation) by some kind of inferential relation between their inputs and outputs. The output can be inferred from the inputs. Inputs and outputs can be treated as sentence-like and interpreted as propositions expressed by those structures. An obvious example, which we have already remarked on, is a human's capacity to draw a conclusion from a pair of premises. We call a capacity that can be specified in this way an *inferentially characterisable capacity*. The explanatory task will be to show how a system manages to get the right output.

As in this example, inputs and outputs can sometimes be taken to be strings of symbols — or sentence-like structures. An expert system in artificial intelligence is a non-biological system that can be inferentially characterised. Given strings of symbols (interpreted as) describing some situation (perhaps medical symptoms), it can combine these with symbols stored in a 'knowledge base' and output a string of symbols which can be interpreted as expressing the proposition that the patient has a particular disease.

We will use an example of Cummins where a visual illusion is to be explained. If an after-image is seen as being a spot on a reasonably close wall, then when the subject moves towards the wall the spot appears to shrink. This capacity to shrink after-images is explained informally by Cummins (1983, p 83) as follows:

> If there were a real spot on the wall, its image on the retina would expand on approach, unless the spot were itself shrinking. A real spot, shrinking at the right rate (i.e. as the square of the distance to the retina) would produce a retinal image of constant size. Since the retinal '(after-) image' remains constant in size the subject sees a shrinking spot on approach.

As Cummins notes, this capacity to shrink after-images is an inferentially characterised capacity — the conclusion that the spot is shrinking is inferred from the premises that the retinal image is not shrinking and the distance to the spot is decreasing. This inference is not a conscious inference, because the subject knows there is actually no spot there. The suggestion is that the subject's visual system treats the spot as though it were on the wall despite considerable evidence the subject has to the contrary. In doing so, the shrinking capacity is then taken to be normal functioning.

Cummins sees the explanation as requiring two phases, but our interest is only in phase one, which involves inferential characterisation. In this phase the visual system delivers the information that the after-image is shrinking.

Here is a flow-chart diagram of the explanation of the capacity to shrink after-images.

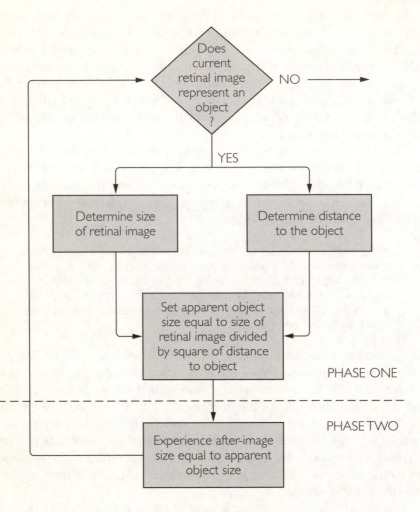

The 'pay-off' for distinguishing different types and different levels of analysis and explanation is to empower the student to criticise and evaluate the kinds of explanations found in the psychological literature. How are you to evaluate analytic or componential explanations?

A crucial part of explanation by analysis is the claim that anything with the identified components organised as they are will have the property being analysed. It is therefore important, when possible, to show that this is so *on the basis of properties of the components* (and their organisation) and to show that the analysing properties are obtainable from the properties of the components of the system.

A related requirement is that there should be *independent evidence* for the sub-capacities of the system or the properties and organisation of the components. If the claim is that the system has a particular property in virtue of being analysable in a certain way, then we don't want the claimed analysis to be the only source of evidence that the sub-capacities exist, or that the components have the properties claimed, or that they are organised in the specified way. Sometimes we can see that if the property had a certain analysis, then everything would work nicely and this can tempt us to think it must have that analysis (failing any other account). But this requirement demands independent evidence for the detailed account to be acceptable.

A final requirement is that the analysis not be circular — that the property being analysed should not appear illegitimately among the analysing properties. This is clearly desirable for non-graded properties. Where the property to be analysed is a graded[10] one (as intelligence, for example, is often taken to be), a consequence of this requirement is, at least, that any components that do have this property should have it to a lesser degree.

This last requirement is very important if we are to avoid explanations that commit the **homunculus fallacy**. This is the mistake of appealing (possibly covertly) in our explanation of a certain ability or capacity to the very ability we are trying to explain. We would make this mistake in giving a symbol-manipulation account of language comprehension if we postulated an agent that was required to 'understand' the symbols it was processing. The name refers to the picture of a little man, or homunculus — often taken to be an intelligent agent — 'inside the head' exercising the very ability he is called on to explain. The problem is one of a *potentially infinite regress* (that is, inside the homunculus would be another, and inside him another, and so on infinitely). Must the homunculus himself have his own homunculus, and so on?

It can be very tempting to use a kind of communicational model in cognitive psychology, and mistakenly to treat internal symbols or representations as we might the external symbols we use for communication. My ability to follow a recipe (external symbols), for example, may be a legitimate explanation of my cake-making ability. I read, understand and obey the instructions, and the cake is made. But if someone appeals to internal representations (symbols) to explain some cognitive ability, we should be wary that they are not illegitimately requiring that, for example, they be understood.

---

[10] Graded properties, unlike perfection, come in degrees.

CONNECTIONISM

In this section we look at explanatory models that operate closer to the physical or biological level than do many of the psychological explanations we have just been considering. What sorts of capacities and behaviour are possible with networks of idealised neuron-like units? And what of psychological interest can be learned from them?

Connectionist systems, also called *neural nets* and *parallel distributed processors*, consist of interconnected processing units, or nodes. Some of these are distinguished as input units and some as output units. Any remaining ones are called 'hidden' units. Units are typically arranged in layers, so that units in the same layer are not directly connected to each other. A common configuration would consist of an input layer, zero or more hidden layers, and an output layer. The following diagram shows a simple 'feed-forward' neural net with one hidden layer.

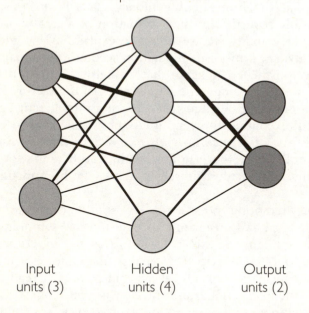

Simple Neural Net

| Input | Hidden | Output |
| units (3) | units (4) | units (2) |

The individual connections between units are uni-directional: output from one unit is (part of) the input to any unit it is connected to.

Each connection carries a weight or strength which reflects the degree and kind of influence the unit whose output it is connected to can have on the unit it leads to. What is affected in this way is called the *state of activation* of the unit. A connection can have an excitatory or an inhibitory effect on the level of activation of the unit it feeds into, and the magnitude of this effect is determined in part by the weight or strength of the connection. In the above diagram, the differing thicknesses of the connection lines reflect their differing weights. Units adjust their state of activation depending on their total inputs, and their current state according to an activation rule. The overall input to a unit is the weighted sum of all its inputs — that is, the sum for each of its inputs of the product of the strength of that connection and the magnitude of that input, the latter being typically identical to the output of the unit from which it is sent. Activation rules can be quite diverse, but an example of a simple rule would be one which determines that the new activation of the unit is, say, 1 if the net input exceeds a certain threshold and 0 otherwise. Notice that in this particularly simple case, the prior level of activation of the unit plays no part in determining its new level.

This new state of activation determines the new output along each of the connections leading from it. In simple cases, the new output might just be equal to the state of activation.

So, there are two main kinds of components to a neural net — the units, which can be of three kinds (input, hidden and output), and the connections. The units are characterised by two features — their thresholds and their level of activation. The connections are characterised by their direction and weightings. (Negative weightings will correspond to inhibitory connections.)

With the appropriate weightings between units, a neural net can map patterns of input activations on to patterns of output activations in sophisticated ways. Given appropriate interpretations of these input and output activations, nets can be seen to perform many useful and complex tasks, including tasks normally taken to require cognition when performed by humans.

An important feature of neural nets is that they can be 'taught' or trained to adjust their output to patterns of input. In training mode, it is possible to successively adjust the weights of the connections so that mismatches between the pattern of activations at the output layer and the correct pattern for an input are reduced. There are many ways this can be done.[11]

---

[11] An early influential example of a neural net was Sejnowski and Rosenberg's NETtalk — a simulated text to speech 'reader'. To allow for the irregularities of English orthography, the input to NETtalk was a seven letter window, giving three letters of context either side of a single letter. The network has 203 (= 7 x 29) input units, 80 hidden units and 26 output units, coding phonemes.

It is worth emphasising something that is often taken for granted. Typically, what makes an output correct or not is its interpretation in relation to the interpretation of its input nodes. To make this specific, consider a simplified net in which the input and output nodes have only two levels of activation, say 0 or 1. For a particular task — say, classifying an object on the basis of its properties — take each input node activation to represent which one of several properties an object has, and a single output node to represent whether or not it is an object of a specific kind. With this interpretation, the output will be correct if its activation level is 1 precisely when an object with the properties represented by active input nodes (activation level 1) and none of the properties represented by inactive input nodes (0) is an object of that specific kind. At one level, the neural net can be described as mapping patterns of input activation into patterns of output activation. When these levels of activation are interpreted in the way we have just suggested, it is seen to be classifying objects on the basis of their properties.

There are two general kinds of representation in connectionist systems — localist, like the example just given, and distributed. Where the representation is localist, levels of activation of individual units do the representing. In the example, levels of activation of individual input units represent the presence or absence of particular properties. In distributed representation, it is patterns of activation in groups of units (two or more) that representations are assigned to.

Neural nets have a number of important features. We identify just three here — learning, generalisation and graceful degradation. We have already discussed learning. After the weights have been automatically adjusted on a training set of input–output pairs, what is particularly impressive is how the weights of the resulting net can deliver the correct output patterns on new input patterns — ones they were not trained on. This ability is sometimes described as generalisation. Unfortunately, this does not always happen. It may require some experimental variation of the number of units — for example, hidden units. For example, if there are too many hidden units the net can adjust itself so that it can give the right answers for the training pairs of input and output without needing to compromise the weightings overall to get the best fit. If this happens, then the net may have in effect only learned the finite number of pairings it was trained on and will not generalise well.

Graceful degradation is contrasted with catastrophic failure. Simply put, a system has the property of graceful degradation if it fails gradually rather than abruptly. As conditions for the input or the system itself gradually change from being ones in which it works well, its performance deteriorates gradually. For example, the malfunction of only a small number of units in a neural net may lead to an indiscernible drop off in its performance. By contrast, in many classical systems, malfunctions in part of the system may knock out the whole system.

The capacity of neural nets to fit training sets of input–output pairs can be very useful where the theorist has limited information. For many domains, there is no known function connecting input to output — think of any of the abilities we have for which we have no account of a systematic connection. In this case, we do not have a specification of the ability. We can only manifest it. Suppose identifying adult faces as male or female is such an ability. A system, after training to match output to input over a finite number of cases, may generalise very well. If this happens, it can turn out that an examination of the system — the details of its weightings, and which units have high or low activation for particular inputs — may provide the researcher with clues to help formulate a theoretical account of how the task is done. For example, in the face–gender case, it could turn out that an examination of input and the structure of the neural net reveals that the systems is 'paying attention to' nose length. This may provide a clue for what properties to include in a theoretical account.

On the other hand, such an examination (even with the help of sophisticated mathematical techniques) may only reveal a bewildering array of weightings and activations which mysteriously seems to get the job done but is theoretically unhelpful. Yet, even in this case, there can be benefits. First, if your aims are practical and not theoretical, developing a system that works successfully on a task can in itself be quite an achievement. A reliable face–gender system could, for example, be a useful part of a face recognition system — reducing the number of possible candidates for classification by that system. Second, such a system may be useful retrospectively when a theory of how the task is done has been or is being developed. Guided by the theory, a re-examination of the system may reveal that this system, too, performs the task using features or features of features (and so on) that the theory identifies.

FUNCTIONAL EXPLANATIONS

Explanations in terms of functions are widespread in both technical contexts and less formal ones. Simply put, a **function** of something is what it is *for*, something it does, some role it plays in a system, or some effect it has or should have. Notice that not every effect something has is one of its functions. A function of the heart is to pump blood and this is one of its effects, but it also makes a noise, which is not, of course, 'what it is for'.

There are two fruitful ways of connecting functions to explanation. On one view, the function of something is the particular effect it has that explains *why it is there*. The noise hearts make does not explain why animals have them. But their blood pumping effects do. We will see more of this kind of function next when we discuss adaptations in evolutionary explanation by natural selection.

Another view of function is closely connected with componential explanations that we discuss above. On this view, the function of something that is part of a system (that is, a component) is the dispositions it has which contribute to the componential explanation of some capacity or characteristics of the containing system. As Godfrey-Smith says (1995, p 187), 'They explain *how something is done*, not why something is there' (italics added).

The former view, that the function of something is the particular effect it has that explains why it is there, is central in many evolutionary explanations, which are the topic of the last section of this chapter.

EVOLUTIONARY EXPLANATIONS

An increasingly influential kind of explanation in psychology not included in the above classification scheme, but importantly related to the genetic, functional and purposive explanations as well as Dennett's 'design stance', is **evolutionary explanation**. A recent body of work incorporating this kind of explanation has come to be called evolutionary psychology. We turn now to discuss some of the assumptions and limitations of this kind of explanatory scheme.

The central ideas of the theory of evolution seem remarkably simple and are widely known, as is the general structure of many evolutionary explanations. But it is surprising how easy it is to reason badly with some of these ideas, so we draw attention to some distinctions it is useful to keep in mind and to some of the pitfalls in assessing the adequacy of explanations like these, especially as they are applied to human behaviour and human capacities.[12]

Simply put, a characteristic in a particular biological species evolves if it changes through time. For example, at some time the members of that species lack that characteristic and at a later time they exhibit it. The question arises as to what causes this change. Of the many explanatory possibilities, the most frequently cited is likely to be 'natural selection'.

The fundamental idea of evolution by natural selection is roughly, but usefully, captured in the phrase 'survival of the fittest'. Individuals have come to have certain characteristics because the possession of these characteristics by their ancestors enabled them to survive and reproduce. An example familiar to many is the recent evolution of dark

---

[12] Many evolutionary explanations in psychology relate to social behaviour, such as territoriality or courtship rituals. But in this chapter we will continue to examine cognitive capacities as exemplars of evolutionary arguments. Chapters 5 and 6 include discussions of the most common pitfalls of evolutionary accounts of complex social behaviour in humans based on human–animal analogies.

colouration in the peppered moth in parts of the north of England where soot-covered trees made the lighter ones easier for predators to see (Sober 1984, p 204).

Three key components inform the general idea of evolution by natural selection.

1 There is a population of units which vary in having (or having various degrees of) or lacking a particular characteristic.

2 Variations in this characteristic are inherited,

3 The presence (of degrees of) or absence of this characteristic affects the (degrees of) ability of the units to survive and reproduce (that is fitness). (Sober and Wilson 1998)

Notice that the key notion of *fitness* is taken to be the ability of the units to survive and *reproduce in a particular environment*. An **adaptation** is a characteristic (or trait) that can be explained by natural selection, and can be contrasted with **adaptiveness**, which is a measure of a characteristic's current effect on a unit's reproductive fitness. It is important to notice that although frequently related, neither is necessary or sufficient for the other.

> The ability to read is adaptive without being an adaptation. Literacy is highly adaptive in most modern human societies, as the disadvantages suffered by most dyslexic people testify. But the ability to read is probably a side effect of other, more ancient cognitive abilities. (Sterelney and Griffiths 1999, p 218)

Since one of our major concerns in this section is the adequacy of explanations by natural selection, it is useful to have criteria for judging the force of such explanations. Ron Amundson provides the following conditions for an explanation by natural selection. He calls them 'central conditions':

1 *Richness of variation:* The domain (of behaviour or biological morphology) shows variation which is:

   a   spontaneous;

   b   persistent (that is, biologically heritable);

   c   abundant; and

   d   small and continuous (or nearly so) in its effects.

2 *Nondirectedness of variation:* The variation is nondirected (or, as we sometimes say, random) with respect to the environmental needs of the organism.

3   *Nonpurposive sorting mechanism:* There is an environmental sorting (or 'selecting') mechanism which results in the preferential
persistence of those variations which happen to be suited to the
environmental needs of the organism or species — and (most
importantly) this sorting mechanism is itself *nonpurposive.*
(Amundson 1989, p 417)

He notes that these conditions may be met to differing degrees and are
criteria for the force of a selectionist explanation of a trait or characteristic — 'the explanatory significance of selection as opposed to any
alternative mechanism with respect to the particular character being
explained' (p 416). His conditions provide a checklist of other possible
explanations for the existence of the trait. As a quick look at the list will
confirm, if any one of these is *not* met there will be an alternative possible explanation. If, for example, condition 1 is not met and there has
not been richness of variation, then, as Amundson says, '... one will
tend to say that it is the mechanism of variation (its restrictiveness) that
explains the evolved character state, simply because the environment
has very little variation from which to select' (p 418). The central conditions can contribute to evaluating how well supported the claim is
that a trait or characteristic is an adaptation.

Evolutionary psychology proposes evolutionary selectionist
explanations for psychological characteristics. It is a blend of evolutionary theory and cognitive psychology. As Griffiths (1999) says,
'Evolutionary psychology claims that the human mind is a bundle of
cognitive adaptations. It does not claim that these adaptations are currently adaptive.' The claim is that the mind was shaped by our ancestors' two million years as Pleistocene hunter-gatherers, not by recent
conditions' (Barkow et al 1992, p 5).

Determining whether or not a characteristic is, in fact, an adaptation is a central problem for evolutionary psychology. Evolutionary
biologists have had to confront the same problem and have proposed
a number of criteria. These include, most generally, evidence of *special
design*. More specifically, they include complexity, efficiency, reliability
and specialisation. The first of these is particularly important. Pinker
and Bloom (1992, pp 454–5) claim that natural selection is the only
scientific explanation of adaptive complexity in living organisms.
'"Adaptive complexity" describes any system composed of many interacting parts where the parts' structure and arrangement suggest design
to fulfil some function.'

The problem we used in Chapter 2 to illustrate difficulties that people have in reasoning well with conditionals will serve us here as the
foundation for an illustration of an evolutionary hypothesis to account

for a psychological characteristic. We noted there that people perform the following task badly:

When presented with the following four cards:

each of which has a number on one side and a letter on the other, and asked which card or cards (if any) they need to turn over to test the following statement:

> If a card has an even number on one side, then it has a vowel on the other

surprisingly, while most people do not get the right answer for this problem — viz. 4 and *K* — they do much better on the following formally analogous problem: You are a bouncer in a Boston bar and will lose your job unless you enforce the following law:

> If a person is drinking beer, then he must be over 20 years old.

There are four cards with information about what a person is drinking on one side and their age on the other:

| drinking beer | drinking Coke | 25 years old | 16 years old |

Indicate only those card(s) you definitely need to turn over to see if any of these people are breaking the law (Cosmides and Tooby 1992, p 182).

The problem is to explain why people (even the same people) do well at the second problem and so poorly at the first. The difference in performance on problems like this is called a *content effect* — since the two problems are formally analogous, the difference in performance is thought to be due to differences in content. Research on the selection task has shown a wide variety of content effects, and the more general problem is to explain these.

Cosmides and Tooby argue from these differences, and other evidence, that 'people have inference procedures specialised for detecting cheaters: individuals who have illicitly taken benefits' (p 199). The easy problems are ones, as with the Boston bar bouncer above, where the content involves checking for cheating.

So far, of course, this is not an evolutionary hypothesis. The claim they make is that humans have developed a specialised cognitive ability. The evolutionary hypothesis is the further claim that this ability is an adaptation. That is, it is an ability that in turn can be explained by a process of natural selection. Here, among other things, the argument involves showing the benefits in hunter-gatherer communities of cheater detection mechanisms.

Notice in the preceding paragraph we said that this specialised ability could be *explained* by a process of natural selection. It is worth remarking on what kind of explanation this is or would be if accepted as true. It is a genetic explanation — an account of a way that modern humans could have come to possess such an ability. Such an account, if successful, will at least show that the possession of this ability is consistent with our evolution. It is an ability we could have evolved to possess. This will be one way of integrating psychological knowledge with other aspects of our knowledge of the natural world. One way an evolutionary explanation might do significantly more than this is to show that the ability in question is *likely* to have evolved. But, of course, showing this is a much taller order.

Given the time-scale of individual evolutionary processes in humans and the lack of direct evidence in historical time — among other considerations, cognitive adaptations do not leave fossils — much of the theorising about the way present cognitive abilities may have evolved is very speculative. We have emphasised in parts of this book that an important feature of much scientific inference is that it is *inference to the best explanation*. So, an important part of justifying inferences to an explanation is by showing that it is better than alternative explanations, possibly by eliminating them. This is often not an easy task. Daniel Dennett (1995, p 487) writes:

> The very considerations that in other parts of the biosphere count *for* an explanation in terms of natural selection of an adaptation — manifest utility, obvious value, undeniable reasonableness of design — count against the need for any such explanation in the case of human behaviour. If a trick is that good then it will be routinely rediscovered by every culture without need for either genetic descent or cultural transmission of the particulars.

A little earlier, he wrote:

> Even in the case of non-human animals the inference from adaptation to genetic basis is risky when the adaptation in question is not an anatomical feature but a behavioral pattern which is an obviously Good Trick. For then there is another possible explanation: the general *non-stupidity* of the species. (p 485)

We might add that, even for anatomical features, one must be wary.

One difficulty, then, for evaluating evolutionary hypotheses is that in many circumstances it is not difficult to formulate other competing ones of roughly comparable plausibility — so called just-so stories. One source of the difficulty is that we do not know in sufficient detail what conditions were like during the proposed period of natural selection, what might be called the 'environment of adaptation'. So, we take a current characteristic of humans and reconstruct what conditions might have been like for it to have been advantageous. But we usually have little independent evidence for their existence.

One feature of our ignorance of the 'environment of adaptation' is an assumption of natural selection, which is not always made explicit, that the environment presents a *lasting* problem. The third of Amundson's central conditions for natural selection listed above was that 'There is an environmental sorting (or "selecting") mechanism which results in the preferential persistence of those variations which happen to be suited to the environmental needs of the organism or species ...' The 'preferential persistence' of variations will typically require *persistence* of their suitability 'to the environmental needs of the organism or species'. But when the environmental problem is social or cultural, the effect of variation can be to dramatically change these needs. As Sterelney and Griffiths (1999, p 331) put it:

> The problems that confronted our ancestors did not stay the same, and the regularities in the world on which their solution depended were apt to change. Traits are sometimes adaptations to an independent impervious environment. But when evolution is driven by features of the social structure of the evolving species, evolution transforms the environment of the evolving organism. The evolution of language, of tool use and of indirect reciprocity are not solutions to pre-existing problems posed to the organism. There are no stable problems in these domains to which natural selection can grind out a solution.[13]

As a case study, to illustrate some of these general problems we present some criticism of the research just mentioned — the role of evolutionary arguments in the case for cheater detectors as an explanation for one aspect of the content effect in the selection task. This research has recently been criticised by Elizabeth Lloyd (1999). Lloyd presents a number of criticisms of this work (done predominantly by Cosmides).[14]

---

[13] They mention, as an example, the 'Machiavellian intelligence hypothesis' of cognitive evolution. 'According to this hypothesis our mental capacities evolved in an arms race within human populations. Their evolution was driven, perhaps, by the hope of exploiting others but certainly by the need to avoid exploitation by them' (p 328).

[14] In passing, a criticism that is tangential to the role of evolutionary reasoning is that Lloyd argues that Cosmides illegitimately takes her experimental work as providing a crucial experiment distinguishing her proposed explanation of the content effect from its main rival — she claimed to be providing evidence that not only supported her hypothesis but refuted its rival.

The central question is whether or not a characteristic is an adaptation. The characteristic under consideration here is the possession of a cheater detection mechanism, something taken to be necessary for social cooperation. Lloyd observes that '... as evolutionary theorists, since Darwin, have recognised, evolution involves more than the process of natural selection. Other evolutionary processes — involving chance genetic sampling, various kinds of constraints on variation and development and phylogenetic history are ever present and may be even more powerful than natural selection in the production of a given evolutionary outcome of interest' (Lloyd 1999, p 223). But not 'every trait — or even most traits — are evolutionary adaptations' (p 223).

She raises the worry, noted above by Dennett, concerning the possibility of learning.

> The problem of whether a characteristic is or is not an evolutionary adaptation is even worse in cases of behavioural traits involving learning or higher level cognitive functions ... While it is clear that *capacities* for learning patterns of reasoning may have evolved under natural selection ... it is always difficult to disentangle how much of a given pattern of responses is a part of the biological capacity and how much is the result of the interaction of that capacity with the organism's environment during its growth and development. (p 224)

But she also raises the problem of the warrant for inferring an 'organ' or 'module' behind the pattern:

> ... it is not *scientifically acceptable* within evolutionary biology to conclude that because a given pattern of responses contributes to evolutionary success then there is some 'organ' (or part of the brain) producing such a pattern ... This is because the organ or module may not actually exist as a biologically real trait and even if it does its current function may not be the same as its past function. (p 224)

Here is the standard used by Cosmides and Tooby to evaluate whether a trait is an adaptation:

> To show that an aspect of the phenotype is an adaptation to perform a particular function one must show that it is particularly well designed for performing that function, and that it cannot be better explained as a by-product of some other adaptation or physical law. (1995, p 90)

And then Lloyd notes:

> But their experiments were not designed to answer evolutionary

questions at all: they did not examine whether the 'aspect of the phenotype' was in fact a well-defined biological trait; they did not examine whether variants of the phenotype were correlated with variants of fitness: and they did not demonstrate whether that aspect of the phenotype was better explained as an adaptation or otherwise. (1999, p 226)

This is effective criticism. Perhaps Cosmides would reply that there is generally evidence of special design — the central feature of adaptations in the thought of evolutionary psychologists. But Lloyd's point could be put by saying that evidence of special design is only prima facie evidence of an adaptation. There is much more work to be done.

As elsewhere in this chapter, bringing in other sources of information can help the research. Within evolutionary theory, comparative methods can be very informative. But as Sterelney (reported by Griffiths 1997, p 113) has pointed out, there are limitations on comparative evolutionary methods for studying human cognition because 'Human cognitive adaptations are supposed to have evolved after the separation of hominids from other primates. Homo sapiens is the only living representative of the lineage involved. It is therefore not possible [to] test hypotheses about these adaptations by looking at the distribution of homologous traits in related taxa.'[15]

Interestingly, Lloyd in her criticism of Cosmides and Tooby thinks this method *can* be used here. She argues that there is evidence of social exchange in our nearest living relatives — chimpanzees and bonobos — in their sophisticated social intelligence and she speculates that they, too, may have needed such specialised modules.

---

[15] Taxa are groups of organisms in biological classification. Homologous traits are ones that members of taxa have by inheritance from shared ancestors.

SUMMARY

In this chapter we have examined a number of special kinds of explanations.

Reductionist explanations attempt to use one science to provide explanations for another. We have warned against simply assuming this is possible, and we have distinguished reduction from supervenience.

Folk psychological explanations are the familiar belief/desire/intention explanations of daily life.

Informational explanations are usually based on computer models of cognitive processing.

Other types of explanations or putative explanations are considered, and it is emphasised that independent evidence for the explanans is necessary for explanatory adequacy.

In proposing to explain psychological phenomena, many philosophers of science have distinguished various 'levels' of analysis: Dennett, for instance, distinguishes the 'intentional', the 'design' and the 'physical' *stance*.

The postulation of unnecessary 'internal agents' (humunculi) as explanatory fictions is discussed, as is the problem of inferring adaptations in retrospective evolutionary explanations.

KEYWORDS

TYPES OF EXPLANATIONS: GENETIC, DISPOSITIONAL, FOLK PSYCHOLOGICAL AND FUNCTIONAL • REDUCTIONISM • SUPERVENIENCE • INTENTIONAL STANCE • DESIGN STANCE • PHYSICAL STANCE • COMPONENTIAL EXPLANATION • HOMUNCULUS FALLACY • CONNECTIONIST SYSTEMS, FUNCTION • EVOLUTIONARY EXPLANATION • ADAPTATION • ADAPTIVENESS

EXERCISES

1 (i) Unless, as scientists, we are to allow non-material 'substances' to intrude into the domain of psychology, we must use the word 'dreaming' to refer to certain patterns of electro-physiological activity in people's brains. Only then can scientists study the phenomenon without recourse to the mentalistic speculations of the Freudians and similar groups. Science, being concerned with what dreams *are* (not with what they *mean*) must accept this step if it is to explain dreaming in relation to other activities of the brain

   (ii) It would not matter whether dreaming occurred in one's 'brain' or one's toenail — if it is experienced as a series of images and sounds which make sense (to varying degrees), then it cannot be 'reduced' to non-mental phenomena. It is an essentially psychological event, although of course it does 'take place in the brain'. Psychological explanation is concerned with what dreams mean and why a particular person's dreams have a particular meaning. This cannot be established by looking at the electrophysiological activity of the brain.

a   What implicit definition of science is proposed in (i)?

What definition of psychology is assumed in (ii)?

b   Do these definitions, in effect, beg the question concerning the best (or only) 'scientific' way of studying dreaming?

c   Although (i) is a reductionist and (ii) an anti-reductionist argument, are they really contradictory, or could they be more accurately described as addressing different issues?

d   If the latter, can the two viewpoints be reconciled?

2   We are rapidly approaching the time when purely physical tests of intelligence will be possible. It is already known that the evoked (electrical) potentials ('brain waves' on the electroencephalograph) recorded after a sudden stimulus differ for 'bright' and 'dull' subjects: the brighter the subject, the 'quicker' the waves. Hence, conventional (so-called psychological) tests of intelligence, as brain function is measured directly; after all, what is intelligence if it is not brain function?

a   What reductionist claims are made in the passage? Is the supporting argument convincing?

b   Discuss the problems involved in *defining* intelligence in terms of brain function(s) alone.

3   Consider the following accounts of simple animal behaviour:

(i)   After three previously reinforced trials, the food-deprived rat ran up the main alley of the T-maze and turned right, entering the goal box 3.5 seconds after being placed in the start box.

(ii)   After three previously reinforced trials, the hungry rat ran up the alley of the T-maze to the choice point and turned right in order to acquire the food in the goal box. This took 3.5 seconds.

a   Does (ii) make assumptions not made in (i)? What are these?

b   How important might these be if we wished to explain why the animal behaved as reported?

c   If it were a human, not a rat, involved, would the second description be any more defensible? Why or why not?

4 (i)   The burglar's purpose in stealing the jewellery was to seek revenge on its owner. This was his real motive, not wealth, for he stole the jewels with the most sentimental value, not necessarily those of greatest monetary worth.

(ii)   The burglar's behaviour in stealing the sentimentally valuable jewels was the result of his neurotic fixation on jewels as symbolic of their owner, who had previously frustrated his sexual advances.

a   How are these two passages different from each other?

b   Are they incompatible in terms of the explanations they propose?

c   Is either of greater *explanatory value* than the other? Why or why not?

5   That human beings possess an instinct for survival cannot be doubted. Their behaviour inevitably leads to their survival — eating, breathing, copulating, and so on. All are directed towards the survival of the individual, and through it, the species.

Does postulating abstract 'instincts for survival' or 'life forces' help to explain any particular aspect of human behaviour? Why or why not? (That is, even allowing that eating, breathing and copulating are all necessary for survival, and that humans are biologically predisposed to these behaviours, what further information is provided by saying that these behaviours have a certain purpose?)

6   Using a variety of methods, Garcia let rats drink a novel-tasting liquid, and then made the rats sick over an hour later. The question was whether rats would learn to avoid the place they were sick, the unconditioned stimulus immediately connected with their sickness, or the solution they drank, although it was remote in time from the unconditioned response. The latter uniformly occurred. The usual laws of conditioning did not hold. Garcia argued that rats know instinctively that nausea must be due to something they ate, not stimuli present at the time of sickness. This makes good evolutionary sense, for sickness in the wild is more likely to be caused by drinking tainted water than by the bush under which the rat was sitting when it felt sick.

   Connecting taste with sickness is more biologically adaptive than connecting it with visual or auditory stimuli. It appears, therefore, that evolution constrains what stimuli may be associated with what responses. (Leahey 1991, p 319)

This passage falls into two parts. The first reports some experimental results and draws a conclusion about the laws of conditioning. What does the second part do, how well is its conclusion argued, and what bearing does it have on the first part?

Consider what roles the references to evolution and biological adaptiveness play in this passage. What is meant by the claim that rats know something instinctively?

7   (*Difficult*) According to Lloyd:

> ... Cosmides relates *perceived* benefits to *perceived* costs (1989: p 197). She argues that providing a benefit doesn't necessarily have a cost, and the benefit doesn't have to actually be a benefit, just 'something that he or she considers to be a benefit' (1989, pp 235–36).

Lloyd continues:

> Cosmides can't really mean this. In order for these social interactions to play the role she assigns them in evolutionary processes, the benefit needs to be a *real* benefit in terms of evolutionary fitness. In other words the benefit must actually contribute to the probability of the reproductive success of its owner. (Lloyd 1999, p 227)

Discuss this argument. According to folk psychology, we base our actions on our beliefs — on how we take the world to be, not how it is. Is this true and, if so, can this claim be used in Cosmides' defence?

chapter 8

Measurement and numerical reasoning

... unluckily our professors of psychology in general are not up to quantitative logic.

Edward L Thorndike

INTRODUCTION

This topic may seem rather advanced for an introduction to reasoning and arguing in psychology. However, as you will have discovered in your preliminary study of the field, psychologists prefer numerical forms of data and statistical methods of analysis, and these are generally thought to require measurement. So, in this chapter we discuss the nature of measurement in general, and then critically consider some of the widely accepted definitions of measurement in psychology. We do this by focusing on one of the controversial areas in which psychologists have claimed to be measuring, viz., the perennial problem of assessing and quantifying 'intelligence'. This is as contentious today as it has been for decades in **psychometrics**, so it is an illuminating and important problem which, we hope to show, makes clear the assumptions which experts and beginning students alike make in claiming to measure 'intelligence' (in particular, our example is 'general intelligence', known for decades as 'g').

You may be one of the many psychology students bewildered at finding numerical methods emphasised in a subject which, because it deals with the mind, you had hoped would be nearer the humanities than quantitative science. Yet, it is precisely here, where the subject matter of psychology meets the quantitative methods of 'hard' science, that understanding is needed, for here logical problems not only abound but, because they are neglected, fester. Standard textbooks in psychology lead directly into 'psychological measurement', as if 'to study variables, you must first observe them (detect their presence) and then measure them' (Whitley 1996, p 98). Are there not other ways to study *variables* (attributes that may vary from one instance to another) than *measuring* them? This is a question few ponder. Some psychologists (Merton et al 1984) endorse dictums like Lord Kelvin's that 'when you can measure what you are speaking about and express it in numbers you know something about it; but when you cannot measure it, ... you have scarcely, in your thoughts, advanced to the stage of *science*' (Thomson 1891, pp 80–81). They construct their scales for assessing attributes like general intelligence (or g), believing that such attributes can thereby 'be objectively defined and measured' (Jensen 1998, p 45). Others agree with Cliff's claim that 'it is hard to give more than ordinal justification for many of our variables across almost the whole spectrum of our field' (1996, p ix). Whether or not psychological attributes are measurable, merely orderable or something else is an issue fundamental to numerical reasoning in psychology. It is an issue more of a *logical* than *mathematical* character and, therefore, one presuming little mathematical expertise.

In this chapter, we explain what *numerical data* are; the issue of whether or not psychological data must be numerical will be discussed; and the ways in which psychologists obtain numerical data (*counting*, *measuring*, *estimating* and *coding*) are described. The greater part of the chapter, however, considers two major problems to do with numerical reasoning in psychology: the issue of whether or not psychological attributes are measurable; and the special problems that arise when non-quantitative data are coded numerically.

NUMERICAL DATA IN PSYCHOLOGY

WHAT ARE NUMERICAL DATA?

Psychologists prefer numerical data because it is thought that the analysis of non-numerical (or qualitative) data 'is necessarily subjective' (Whitley 1996, p 351). That is a matter we will return to, but first, what exactly are **numerical data**? They are data expressed using *numerals*. Numerals are *signs* for numbers. Thus, '3' and 'III' are different numerals, '3' is arabic and 'III' is roman, but both refer to the same number, viz., three. The *number* three, on the other hand, is a feature variously located in the natural world like, say, the colour red is also a natural feature. While we have little difficulty identifying this feature (say, *three books* on the desk, or *three participants* in the experiment), some have difficulty defining it. This is because it is a *relational feature* and such features may seem slippery. *Being three in number* is a feature of things only in relation to something else, *a unit*. The things on the table are three (books), 30 (chapters), 900 (pages), several million (molecules of carbon), and so on, a different relation holding between these things and each of various possible units. Just because numbers are relational features, it does not follow that numerical facts are only *relatively* true. They are as *absolute* as any facts. This can be seen by considering other relative features, such as spatial ones. For example, the fact that my book is on the table is as absolute as any, even though any situation in which one thing is upon another is always relational. So, whether I note three books or 30 chapters on my desk, in each case I note matters of fact, the facts involving relations between an aggregate (the things on my desk) and a unit (books or chapters). The number of Xs in some aggregate, Y, is a *relation* between Y and X.

Numerical data are of three kinds: descriptions of *frequencies*; descriptions of *magnitudes*; and descriptions using *numerical codes*. For example, the number of items that a person answers correctly on a psychological test of some kind is a frequency. The best way to assess frequencies is by counting them. The time it takes a person to respond to the presentation of a stimulus in an experiment is a magnitude of a quantitative attribute. The best way to assess magnitudes is to measure them relative to a unit (in this case, the attribute is temporal duration and the unit may be the duration known as a second). The responses of participants to an attitude statement relative to the response categories, *agree, neutral, disagree,* may be coded numerically, for convenience, as *+1, 0,* and *−1.* All numerical data in psychology are of one or more of these kinds.

There is a stereotype of numerical data: they are thought of as a collection of numbers. Kerlinger says that '"Data," as used in behavioral research, means research results ... usually numerical results, like scores of tests' (1986, p 125). However, data are never *just* numbers. When, for example, the number of correct answers in a test of word knowledge is 27, the datum is not the score, twenty-seven, and certainly not the numeral, '27'. It is a *proposition* of the form, *The number of items answered correctly by person X on test Y was 27.* In recording data, some elements of the description may be taken as understood and, so, only numbers appear on the data sheet. This list alone is never the data. The data are the propositions about the phenomena, understood as true.

MUST PSYCHOLOGICAL DATA BE NUMERICAL?

There is a common misconception that data can only be *truly* scientific if they are quantitative. The founding psychometrician, EL Thorndike's *credo,* that 'whatever exists at all exists in some amount. To know it thoroughly involves knowing its quantity' (1918, p 16), is still widely endorsed (for example, Eysenck 1973, p x). If all natural attributes were quantitative, then this *credo* would be true. However, structures of all kinds, quantitative and non-quantitative, are found in the world around us, and quantitative and non-quantitative structures alike can be studied scientifically. The character of data, whether they are **quantitative data** or not, depends upon the character of the *features* described. There are only two kinds of quantitative features — frequencies and magnitudes. Frequencies are the number of things of some kind in an aggregate (they answer the question, *how many?*); magnitudes are levels of a continuously quantitative attribute (they answer the question, *how much?*). Quantitative features are *intrinsically numerical.* They cannot be accurately described in any other than numerical terms. Non-quantitative features, on the other hand, can always be described non-numerically. However, it is sometimes convenient to code non-quantitative features numerically. Thus, not all scientific data are numerical and not all numerical data are quantitative.

If the facts observed are non-quantitative (what are sometimes called *qualitative*), then a non-numerical description will always be potentially less misleading than a numerical one. A psychologist describing the grammatical structure of children's utterances, for example, thereby collects non-numerical data (for example, instances of various kinds of grammatical structures) and, as a result, may arrive at scientific generalisations as significant as any dependent upon numerical data. Just because data and analyses are non-numerical, it does not follow that they are subjective. The objective/subjective and numerical/non-numerical distinctions are different. Understanding is not advanced by confusing them.

WAYS OF OBTAINING NUMERICAL DATA IN PSYCHOLOGY

There are four sources of numerical data in psychology: *counting* of frequencies; *measuring* magnitudes; *estimating* magnitudes; and *coding* non-quantitative attributes.

Counting

Counting is the easiest way to collect numerical data and it has been used in modern psychology since Fechner's (1860) research on psychophysics. Counting is always possible, because every situation studied in science involves some number of things of some kind.

In psychological research, the participants studied and/or their responses may always be classified into categories and the resulting frequencies counted. A common example is the assessment of human intellectual abilities, where the answers given to test items are classified as 'correct' or 'incorrect' and the number of correct answers counted for each person. This number is called the person's *observed score*. A detailed treatment of psychological test scores is given by Lord and Novick (1968). Participants falling into one or another category may be counted as well. For example, Milgram (1963), in his famous study of obedience, counted the number of people who continued to obey the experimenter's instructions to shock a third person as the voltage was increased.

Measuring

Because the participants studied in psychological research are biological entities, and because their responses always have physical effects, physical attributes can be measured in psychological research. The most commonly measured attribute is the time it takes a participant to respond following the presentation of a stimulus. This temporal duration is referred to as reaction time. Since every event that ever occurs has its temporal relations to its various causes, reaction times are always available for measurement. Luce's (1986) detailed study shows their significance in psychology.

Many psychologists, studying the emotional conditions of physical illness and health, use physiological measurements (which are really just physical measurements of physiological attributes). For example, in their famous study of Type A personalities, Friedman and Rosenman (1959) measured such physiological attributes as serum cholesterol level, blood coagulation (clotting) time and electrocardiographical parameters.

Estimating

Numerical data obtained by using the human participant as the 'measuring instrument' are of special interest to psychologists. In this procedure, popularised by SS Stevens (1956, 1975), a person is instructed to make direct numerical judgments of the intensity of a physical stimulus (say, a light of a specific level of brightness) relative to a nominated standard. This procedure, called *magnitude estimation*, is now widely used in psychophysics (see Bolanowski and Gescheider 1991). Stevens and others thought of it as a way of *measuring* the psychological attribute, sensation intensity. We will see that this invites all of the problems mentioned in the next section. However, it can be interpreted as an attempt by the participant to *estimate the magnitude* of a physical, quantitative attribute and, hence, as a rough and ready form of physical measurement, one of interest to psychologists studying the perceptual capacities of humans.

Coding

When the attributes that psychologists study are not quantitative, it is still always possible to obtain numerical data via numerical coding. The most common example is when data are simply ordinal. A set of objects are *ordered* when they fall along a line, each object before or after each other object such that if any object, X, comes before any other, Y, and Y comes before another, Z, then X must also come before Z. Since the numbers are also an ordered sequence in this sense, any order can always be coded numerically by assigning numerals to the objects so that the order of the numbers named by the numerals matches the order of the objects they are assigned to. However, the numerals used to code an order are never unique: a different set of ordered numerals could always have been used instead. Furthermore, order relations, considered on their own, are not intrinsically numerical and, so, can generally be adequately described without resorting to numerical coding.

The most common use of numerical coding in psychology is with rating scales. A rating scale consists of an ordered set of response categories. One category is selected by the rater as the most appropriate for the object rated. The idea of numerically coding rating categories was popularised in psychology by Likert (1932) and has since become ubiquitous (see Aiken 1996). When numerical ratings code ordinal information and nothing more, the practice of summing them (the method of *summated ratings*) is problematic, as discussed later in the chapter.

Reasoning with numerical data obtained by counting frequencies or measuring quantitative physical attributes, as such, involves no special problems beyond those that might be encountered in any quantitative science. Similarly, magnitude estimations, providing they are understood only as estimates of physical measures, involve no special problems. Problems unique to psychology emerge when attempts are made to measure *psychological attributes* (as distinct from physical attributes) and when numerical data produced by coding non-quantitative structures are treated as if genuinely quantitative.

IS THE MEASUREMENT OF PSYCHOLOGICAL ATTRIBUTES POSSIBLE?

Surely, another source of numerical data in psychology is the measurement of psychological attributes, such as general intellectual ability, extroversion, attitudes towards abortion, and so on? In the case of all psychological attributes, attempts to measure them always involve, in the first instance, the collection of numerical data by the methods mentioned above. For example, attempts to measure general intellectual ability involve, first, counting test scores and, second, an inference from such frequencies to the supposed measure of ability. Similarly, in attempting to measure extroversion, the number of responses thought to be indicative of extroversion on a personality questionnaire is counted, and then a putative measure obtained by inference. In the case of attitudes, ratings of a person's degree of agreement or disagreement with each of a range of attitude statements may be obtained. The rating categories used are coded numerically and, for each person tested, the numbers coding their ratings are summed and these sums (possibly transformed numerically) are thought to be measures of the relevant attitude.

THE SCIENTIFIC CONDITIONS NECESSARY FOR MEASUREMENT

Before knowing whether or not to measure an attribute, the scientist needs to know whether or not it is *quantitative*. There is no logical necessity that any attribute be quantitative. It is an empirical issue. The scientist needs to study the attribute's character, specifically, to discover whether it is quantitative or not. This requires knowing the marks of quantity.

Let us consider the case of length, because it is a familiar quantitative attribute. Then we will generalise. There are many different, specific lengths, such as the length of this page, the length (or distance) from London to New York, the length of your pen, the length (or distance) from the Sun to the Earth, and so on, indefinitely. Length is quantitative because of the way in which all of these specific lengths relate to one another: in short, each specific length is related *additively* to other specific lengths. If, for example, the length of this page is greater than the length of your pen, the latter length will equal that of a part of the page. The length of the remaining part plus the length of your pen equals the length of the page. It is in this kind of way that every length is *additively related* to other lengths. That is, for every pair of lengths, X and Y, where $X < Y$, there exists a length Z such that $Y = X + Z$.

The *character* of this additive relation between different lengths is crucial. First, if a length, X, is the sum of lengths Y and Z, in that order, then X is also the sum of these lengths in the opposite order (that is, for any lengths, Y and Z, $Y + Z = Z + Y$). Second, if a length is a sum of three other lengths, X, Y and Z, it is the same whether it is X plus the sum of Y and Z or Z plus the sum of X and Y (that is, for any lengths, X, Y and Z, $X + (Y + Z) = (X + Y) + Z$). Because all lengths are additively related to other lengths in this way, the attribute, length, is *additive*. In order to test that length is quantitative in character, we need to be able to identify different instances of length and test whether or not they conform to these conditions of additivity.

All measurable attributes are additive in structure. If measurable, then it is in principle possible to discover the magnitude of any particular level of the attribute (for example, any specific length) relative to a unit. The magnitude of one level, X, relative to another, Y, is just the number of Ys it takes to equal X (where, obviously, this *number* need not be a whole number). That is, if $X = r \times Y$, then r is the magnitude (or *measure*) of X relative to Y. This only makes sense if measurable attributes have additive structure.

Thus, the claim that any attribute is quantitative is not one that can be merely *assumed* true. What counts is appropriate evidence. In the case of length, for example, evidence for additive structure is fairly directly obtainable by simple manipulations upon, say, rigid straight rods of manageable lengths. For other attributes, such as density or temperature, evidence is less direct. This is not a problem. The truth of many scientific hypotheses is difficult to ascertain and often all that scientists can do, at least initially, is to approach matters indirectly. Details of the manner in which indirect evidence for the additive structure of attributes can be gained are beyond our scope. They are described in Michell (1990) and, much more technically, in Krantz et al (1971).

There is a view that because, in some instances, numerical data (say, test scores) correlate to a useful extent with some criterion (say, exam results) it follows that the numerical data are measurements. Psychometricians as varied as Jensen (1981), Lord and Novick (1968), McDonald (1985) and Thorndike (1982) all agree on this. However, given what we have said above about measurement, the existence of such useful correlations only *raises* a scientific issue, never *settles* one.

The scientific issue raised is this: *Why does this relationship occur?* For example, to take the case of test scores predicting exam results, the hypothesis that the test in question *measures* an ability, A, and that A partially causes performance on the exam, is a valid one, deserving investigation. However, before this hypothesis can be accepted, it must be shown that ability A possesses quantitative structure. Without that, the existence of a useful correlation does not warrant the claim that the test actually *measures A*.

PSYCHOLOGY AND MEASUREMENT

Surprisingly, very few people have ever investigated the issue of whether or not psychological attributes, such as the various intellectual abilities, personality traits and social attitudes, are actually quantitative. Most simply *postulate* that they are. As Bertrand Russell (1919, p 71) noted, '"postulating" what we want has many advantages; they are the same as the advantages of theft over honest toil'. Scrupulous researchers always say when their conclusions are tentative, not because there is anything wrong with speculation, but because we need to know when conclusions are on firm ground and when they are not. In attempting to sort out firm from flimsy conclusions in this area, you need to link the conclusions drawn to the data on which they are based. For example, when interpreting studies purporting to be about intellectual abilities, but in which the researcher has made use of test scores, you need to confine conclusions to propositions only about scores on the specific tests used, in the first instance. The conclusions that the psychologist comes to about postulated abilities will then be seen correctly as *speculations* about what *might be* the case *if* certain other propositions are also true, propositions the truth or falsity of which no one yet knows.

For example, consider the claims made by modern psychometricians (for example, Jensen 1981 and Carroll 1996) regarding g, the concept of general intellectual ability. This was a concept introduced into modern psychology by one of its founders, C Spearman (1904). Spearman invented the widely used analytical method of factor analysis (see McDonald 1985 for an introduction). Both Carroll and Jensen write as if the proposition that psychological tests enable the measurement of g is one securely based on scientific research. However, in the light of comments made in this chapter about measurement, this claim is clearly speculative. It is based upon test scores and their interrelationships. Hypotheses about g, on the other hand, are hypotheses about the *causes* of test scores. It is a well-established principle of scientific reasoning that there are no *logical* relationships between causes and effects. Hence, we can never reason from test scores and their interrelationships (effects) to g (a cause) without additional assumptions. What are

Carroll's and Jensen's assumptions? In using factor analysis to make inferences about *g*, they assume a package: first, that the causes of human intellectual performance are quantitative attributes; and second, that within each person these quantitative attributes (the various abilities, including *g*) add together to produce test scores. This package cannot be lightly dismissed, but neither is it the only theory available. The conclusions that Carroll and Jensen are able to draw from test scores alone go no further than test scores. Beyond that, they postulate. This, in itself, is no problem. It becomes one when postulation is disguised as unquestionable knowledge.

STEVENS' DEFINITION OF MEASUREMENT AND OPERATIONALISM

Operational definitions were considered in previous chapters. Similar considerations arise again in thinking about psychological measurement. In the following, we discuss a widespread misconception about what is meant by 'measuring' psychological attributes. This is an important issue for all students to be clear about, because it arises frequently in undergraduate study.

The American psychologist SS Stevens proposed that measurement is *'the assignment of numerals to objects or events according to rule'* (1946, p 667). This remains the definition of measurement used most frequently by psychologists (Michell 1997). Kerlinger says that it 'succinctly expresses the basic nature of measurement' (1986, p 391) and that it is 'an excellent example of a powerful definition' (1979, p 129). In fact, anyone accepting it would, thereby, disregard the need to test the hypothesis that attributes are quantitative. But this may be unjustified. It is true that because measurement involves numerical description, it involves the use of numerals, but to think that this defines measurement is to confuse one simple, ancillary feature with the concept in its entirety.

When measuring, numerals are never literally *assigned* to anything. They are used to *describe* numerical facts. This distinction is important because descriptions of facts are either *true* or *false*, but assignments are not. While assignments of numerals to things — to code features, for example — might be *useful* or *useless*, assignments are never true. It is only because descriptions can be true that they can count as data. In suggesting that measurement involves numerical assignments to *objects or events*, Stevens deflects attention from the fact that, strictly speaking, measurement is always of *attributes* of objects and events and, more narrowly still, only of attributes having what we called above *additive structure*.

In Chapter 4 of this book, we looked at operational definitions, as advocated by PW Bridgman. Bridgman's idea is still widely applied in attempts to measure psychological attributes. 'An operational definition defines a variable by the operations used to measure it' (Heiman

1995, p 37). Hypotheses about intellectual abilities might be said, for example, to be operationalised in terms of scores on cognitive tests. That is, the operational meaning of the theoretical concept of ability is said to be given by operations leading to test scores. This practice is 'a radically different way of thinking and operating, a way that has revolutionised behavioral research' (Kerlinger 1979, p 41). Combining Bridgman's operationism with Stevens' definition leads to the view that tests *measure* abilities. As a result, 'the success of behavioral scientists in measuring behavioral variables is remarkable', it has been claimed (Kerlinger 1979, p 142). But we will question this claim.

It is not difficult see what is really going on here. It is normal in science to hypothesise about how theoretical concepts, such as intellectual abilities, relate to observable concepts, such as test scores. However, hypotheses relating theoretical concepts, like *ability*, to observable concepts, like *test score*, cannot provide the *meaning* of the theoretical concepts because the two sets of concepts are held to be *causally* related. For example, intellectual abilities are hypothesised to be the main factor *causing* test performance. If the meaning of intellectual abilities was equated with test scores, then any attempt to use the former to explain the latter would be *circular* (recall our discussion in Chapter 5). So, their meanings must be quite distinct. Therefore, the hypothesis that test scores measure intellectual abilities is an independent scientific hypothesis, one in need of investigation in its own right. This hypothesis includes the further hypothesis that intellectual abilities are quantitative attributes. These hypotheses must be investigated scientifically. They cannot be defined away. (We discussed definitions that give the illusion of being explanatory in Chapter 4.)

The relationship between intellectual abilities and test scores may not be quantitative. If intellectual abilities are non-quantitative, then they cannot be quantitatively related to anything. Perhaps they are only ordinal structures. If so, then the sorts of methods of data analysis explored by Cliff (1996) would be better suited to this area of psychology than those conventionally employed. Perhaps they are not even ordinal. At present, we simply do not know. Science only makes progress when we distinguish what is known from what is not known and set about investigating the latter.

REASONING WITH NUMERICAL CODINGS

Special problems arise when numerical data are produced by coding non-quantitative information. As noted, psychologists often mistakenly treat data as simply a set of numbers, and there is a widely shared view that 'the numbers do not know where they came from' (for example, Gaito 1980, p 566). Believing this, there is a strong temptation to treat numerical codings arithmetically, just the same as genuinely quantitative data. This may lead unsuspecting researchers to draw conclusions from numerical codings that depend only upon arbitrary features of the code used, rather than upon features representing the empirical information coded. Stevens (1946) called this the *problem of permissible statistics.*

Suppose a social psychologist invites participants to indicate their degree of agreement or disagreement with an attitude statement, using the standard rating categories, *strongly agree, agree, neutral, disagree,* and *strongly disagree.* These categories may be coded numerically, as is typical, by the ordered set, +2, +1, 0, −1, and −2, the order of the numbers reflecting the order of the categories. In attitude research, if the attitudes of two or more groups were compared, then it would be standard practice to average these numerically coded ratings within groups of participants. Stevens (1946, 1951) regarded the computation of means (averages) as inappropriate when numerical data resulted from coding merely ordinal information.

Stevens' reasoning may be illustrated via a simple example. Suppose there are three participants, *A*, *B*, and *C*, who give ratings of *agree, neutral* and *disagree,* respectively, which are coded as +1, 0 and −1. Their average rating is $[(+1) + 0 + (−1)]/3 = 0$, which is the code for *neutral* and is, also, the numerical code of *B*'s rating. Now, if these numerals code merely ordinal information, then they can be changed in any way we like that preserves this information — that is, by a new set of numbers in the same order. For example, the five categories could be numerically coded by +5, +4, 0, −1, −2. Now, the numerically coded ratings given by *A*, *B*, and *C* become +4, 0 and −1, respectively, and the average becomes $[(+4) + 0 + (−1)]/3 = +1$, which does not mean *neutral* and no longer matches *B*'s rating. That is, although we have changed the numbers in a way that preserves the purely ordinal information present in the ratings (that is, we have applied what Stevens calls an *admissible transformation*), the location of the mean has changed relative to *B*'s rating and its meaning relative to the rating categories is not invariant. Hence, with numerically coded ordinal information, the location of the mean is not invariant under an admissible transformation. Therefore, concluded Stevens, means should not be computed with such data.

Now, compare what happens to the mean with numerical data of a different kind. Suppose we measure the maximum temperature over three days and find it to be *−15°, 0°* and *+15°* Celsius, respectively. The average maximum temperature over these three days is $((−15) + 0 + 15)/3 = 0$, the maximum temperature on day 2 and, as we all know, the freezing point of water. Now we know that temperature can also be measured in degrees Fahrenheit. Transforming these measures to Fahrenheit (using the linear transformation, $F = 32 + (9C/5)$) gives

6°, *32°*, and *59°*, respectively, for the three days. The average becomes *(6 + 32 + 59)/3 = 32*, still the maximum temperature on day 2 and still the freezing point of water. The Celsius and Fahrenheit scales capture more than ordinal information. They measure temperature *differences*. They do so, of course, relative to different units (while the difference between the boiling and freezing points of water is *100°* Celsius, it is *180°* Fahrenheit) and relative to different zero points. The important thing to note is that when measuring temperature (as opposed to coding an order), a change of unit does not alter the reference of the mean. Thus, Stevens says, means are appropriate statistics with measurements.

Clear as these numerical facts are, Stevens' views on permissible statistics remain highly controversial in psychology, because he never showed why the mean's lack of invariance given admissible transformations of numerical codings entails the inappropriateness of means for such data. The best way to understand Stevens' view is via the concept of *validity of inference* (see Michell 1986, 1990). Other analyses of this problem have been given (Suppes and Zinnes 1963; Adams et al 1965; Luce et al 1990). Psychologists (and other scientists) use arithmetic as a step in a chain of inference. A *valid inference* is one in which the truth of the conclusion is inescapable given the truth of the premisses. When inferences are drawn in science, the scrupulous scientist will report when they follow validly and when not.

Applying this distinction to Stevens' issue of permissible statistics, it can be seen in the attitude scaling example that when the first numerical coding of the different levels of agreement is used, the mean rating is *0* (equal to *neutral*) and when the second is used, *+1* (not equal to *neutral*). These conclusions all follow validly from the data. What does not follow validly from the data is the conclusion that:

The average level of agreement of *A*, *B*, and *C* is *neutral*.

This conclusion might seem to follow from the ratings when the first numerical code is used. However, this cannot be the case because if this conclusion follows validly from the data when the first numerical code is used, then the contradictory conclusion would follow by the same logic from the data when the second numerical code is used:

The average level of agreement of *A*, *B*, and *C* is not *neutral*.

Since a contradiction cannot validly follow from the same (consistent) set of data, neither follows validly. Note that the earlier conclusions, about the numerical values of the means, are about the numbers used, while these last two conclusions are about the levels of agreement involved. So, the problem that Stevens was attempting to identify is not that the mean is an inappropriate statistic with ordinal data, but rather that certain conclusions concerning average levels of the attribute coded *do not follow validly* from the numerical data.

A recent study by Rozin et al (1997) on attitudes relating to vegetarianism illustrates this problem. These researchers compared the tendency to feel disgust at the prospect of eating meat in a group of participants who gave exclusively moral reasons for becoming vegetarians, with another group who gave exclusively health reasons. They assessed the participants' tendency to feel such disgust by considering responses to three statements:

1   *The thought of eating 'meat' makes me nauseous.* (This statement was answered as either TRUE or FALSE, the former response being taken as indicative of a greater tendency to disgust than the latter and coded by 4, while the latter (false) was coded by 0.)

2   *Consider a soup that you like. Rate your liking for this soup if a tiny, untastable drop of 'meat' broth accidentally fell into it.* (The participants' rating was made on a scale ranging from 4.5 (*dislike extremely*) to 0.5 (*like extremely*), the increasing order of numerical values being taken as indicative of greater tendencies to disgust.)

3   *I resist (avoid) eating 'meat' because eating 'meat' is offensive, repulsive or disgusting.* (The participants rated the level of their agreement or disagreement with this statement on a scale ranging from 1 (*disagree strongly*) to 5 (*agree strongly*), the increasing order of numerical values again being taken as indicative of greater tendencies to disgust.)

For each participant, the numerical codings of their three responses were summed to obtain a 'disgust score' and after calculating the mean disgust scores for each group and performing a test of the significance of the difference between two means, the researchers concluded that 'Moral-origin vegetarians show significantly higher disgust scores than do health-origin vegetarians' (p 71). Assuming no arithmetic errors in the calculations, and interpreting their conclusion as applying to the means of the two groups, this conclusion follows deductively from the numerical codings of the participants and is, therefore true. However, this is a conclusion about *average disgust scores*, not about disgust itself. What can be concluded about the tendency of the two groups to feel disgust? Assuming that the participants' reports are completely honest, we could only conclude that, on average, the group of 'moral-origin vegetarians' have a greater tendency than the group of 'health-origin vegetarians' to feel disgust at the prospect of eating meat if the significant difference between the disgust scores found by these researchers remained under all admissible transformations (in this case, order preserving transformations) of the original codings. The researchers do not report that this is so, and without access to the original data we cannot tell. Hence, not knowing the extent to which the researchers' conclusion is dependent upon arbitrary features of the codings used, we can infer *no valid conclusions* on this question. However, had the responses of the two groups been compared directly, rather than indirectly via the numerical codes used, then perhaps some interesting conclusions could have been *validly* derived.

Where a conclusion based upon numerical data does not remain true when those data are transformed admissibly, then it is a sign the researcher is skating on thin ice. If, in such circumstances, a researcher wants to draw conclusions, not about the *numbers* used, but about the *attributes* coded, then before such conclusions may be treated as valid, the researcher needs to show that contradictory conclusions could not be drawn if the numerical data are transformed in admissible ways. Of course, passing this test does not ensure that the conclusion obtained follows validly from the data, but failing it does mean that the inference is invalid. It is a necessary, but not sufficient, condition for validity. In numerical coding, the facts represented are not intrinsically numerical and, so, coding them numerically can mislead. Not just psychologists, but many others who employ numbers in science, or in practical affairs, regularly draw conclusions which would fail the above test. One area where invalid conclusions are easily drawn in this kind of way is that of examination marks, a particularly important issue in relation to matriculation success, for example.

Exam answers are typically marked relative to an ordered set of categories (for example, *high distinction, distinction, credit, pass, fail*) and these may be coded numerically, say, as follows: *high distinction, 10; distinction, 9* or *8; credit, 7* or *6; pass, 5* or *4;* and *fail, 3, 2, 1* or *0*. A student's total mark for an exam is the sum of the marks assigned to components. No one has ever shown that exam marks carry more than ordinal information. Unfortunately, a sum of numerical codings suffers the same difficulty as does the mean, viz., conclusions derived from it are not always invariant under admissible scale transformations. For example, if on three essays student *A* gets *8, 5* and *3* and *B* gets *5, 5* and *7*, then *B*'s total exceeds *A*'s and an examiner might conclude that *B*'s overall performance is better than *A*'s. However, a different numerical coding of these ordered categories in which, say, *8* is replaced by *10, 7* by *8, 5* is left at *5*, and *3* is replaced by *4* results in *A*'s total (*10 + 5 + 4 = 19*) exceeding *B*'s (*5 + 5 + 8 = 18*). Now, it seems, we could conclude that A's overall performance is better than B's. These conclusions are both invalid and are artefacts of arbitrary features of the numerical codes used. So, when examiners sum marks on individual course components (as they sometimes do) and infer a rank ordering of the quality of students' performances from these sums, then they are drawing conclusions which may not follow from the information originally coded.

For example, in the university department in which one of us teaches, Honours Year students were assessed on each of three components (an Empirical Thesis, a Theoretical Thesis and a Coursework Examination) on a scale of 11 ordered categories (coded 0 to 10). A final rank ordering of students was obtained by summing scores on the three components to get a total mark for each student. By implication, a rank order of students orders each pair of them. Pairs of students can also be ordered directly in terms of their three original assessments: the overall performance of student X is better than that of Y if X does at least as well as Y on all three components and better on at least one. If X is better than Y in this sense, then no matter what numbers are used to code the original assessments, providing they capture the ordinal information, the sum of X's marks will be greater than the sum of Y's. However, for any such coding, the implication does not move in the opposite direction: the fact that X's total is greater than Y's does not entail that X's overall performance is better than Y's. A close analysis of the examination results for two consecutive years showed that only 51 per cent (in one year involving 42 students) and 56 per cent (the next, involving 42) of the orders between all pairs of students were of this kind, the remaining 49 per cent and 44 per cent of orders could only be derived via the total marks and, so, were artefacts of the particular numerical coding used. That is, for slightly less than half the pairs of students, the order between them entailed by their total marks did not follow validly from the information contained in their original assessments. Invalid inferences from numerical codings are not free of consequences.

FURTHER ISSUES IN NUMERICAL REASONING

The problems of numerical reasoning in psychology go well beyond the relatively basic issues addressed in this chapter into issues such as the *reliability* of numerical data and the problems of making *statistical inferences* from numerical data. These issues are too technical to take up here. The fact that they are technical and often require a level of mathematics beyond the competence of most psychology students tends to discourage even critical students from looking into them too closely. But you need to be confident that invariably with such issues, the mathematics is never in doubt and, so, is never the real problem. It is in the logical analysis that lies behind the application of the mathematics that the problems lie and if you look here, then deep problems requiring critical attention will always be found. The paper by Gigerenzer (1993) provides a good example of this in the area of statistical inference.

SUMMARY

Numerical data are data expressed using numerals. There are three kinds: descriptions of frequencies; descriptions of magnitudes; and descriptions employing numerical coding.

All data are descriptions. Not all data are numerical. Not all numerical data are quantitative.

Numerical data in psychology are obtained by counting, measuring, estimating and coding.All measurable attributes are quantitative (additive in structure). The distinction between quantitative and non-quantitative attributes is empirical.

No psychological attributes are known to be quantitative. Some psychologists claim to be able to measure psychological attributes. Such claims are, so far, no more than speculations.

Stevens' definition of measurement combined with operationalism is used to justify psychological measurement. It overlooks the empirical issues involved.

When non-quantitative data is coded numerically, conclusions drawn using standard arithmetic methods may not be validly entailed by the original non-quantitative data. Conclusions subject to contradiction under admissible transformations of the original code do not validly follow from the data.

KEYWORDS

PSYCHOMETRICS • NUMERICAL DATA • QUANTITATIVE DATA • ATTRIBUTE • COUNTING • MEASURING • OPERATIONAL • ESTIMATING • ADDITIVITY • CODING • PERMISSIBLE STATISTICS • ADMISSIBLE TRANSFORMATION • VALIDITY

EXERCISES

1   Aiken (1996, p 8) expresses a not atypical view of the role of measurement in science when he writes, 'The value of scientific data depends on the precision with which the variables under consideration are observed and measured. ... Historically, science and measurement go hand in hand: Progress in science leads to new measuring devices, and the new devices lead to further scientific progress.'

a   Define the concepts of *data* and *measurement*.

b   Is the value of scientific data necessarily linked to measurement? Give examples of psychological research that might not involve any measurement at all.

c   Under what conditions is progress in science linked to progress in measurement?

2 Jensen (1981, pp 72–73) asserts:

> The one thing that you can be virtually certain of when taking any kind of mental test (other than personality, attitude, preference, and interest inventories) is that the test measures *g*, whatever other abilities it may measure.

a What does Jensen presuppose about the character of *g*?

b Is this presupposition a logical necessity? (A logical necessity is a proposition that could not be false under any circumstances, no matter how different the world was.)

c Jensen refers to no empirical evidence supporting the proposition that *g* is a quantitative attribute, nor does he seem to be aware that there is an empirical issue here. What does this tell us about his understanding of measurement?

3 Kerlinger (1986, pp 28–29) says:

> An **operational definition** assigns meaning to a construct or a variable by specifying the activities or 'operations' necessary to measure it. ... A well-known, if extreme, example of an operational definition is: Intelligence is what X intelligence test measures. This definition tells us what to do to measure intelligence. ... an operational definition is an equation where we say, 'Let intelligence equal the scores on X test of intelligence'.

a If a researcher accepted what Kerlinger says in this quotation and also accepted Stevens' definition of *measurement*, how would they react to the claim that a test like the Wechsler Adult Intelligence Scale *measures* intelligence?

b If the scores on a test *define* a psychological concept, like general ability, what can be made of the hypothesis that a person's level of general ability *causes* (at least partially) their performance on this test?

c If measurement is the discovery or estimation of the magnitude of some quantitative attribute relative to a unit, and theoretical psychological attributes are hypothesised to be causes of test performance, what are we to make of Kerlinger's claims?

4 Make a list of psychological attributes that psychologists claim to be able to measure.

a Are any of the attributes on your list known to be quantitative?

b What does this imply about psychology as a quantitative science?

5   In a psychology course at a certain university, students are assessed on each of three course components using an ordered set of 11 categories, coded numerically from 0 to 10, the order of the numbers reflecting the order of students' quality. The marks and totals of 10 students are as follows:

	Component			
Student	1	2	3	Total
a	10	8	7	25
b	9	6	9	24
c	8	8	7	23
d	9	6	7	22
e	7	7	7	21
f	7	9	4	20
g	8	5	6	19
h	8	2	8	18
i	6	6	5	17
j	4	4	8	16

a   If the component marks simply code ordinal information, what admissible transformations may be carried out on them?

b   Explain why the totals are not permissible statistics in Stevens' view.

c   Student X performs better overall than student Y if and only if X does at least as well as Y on each component and better than Y on at least one component. Taking the students pair by pair, locate the pairs where one student performs better overall than another.

d   In what way is it misleading to base a rank ordering of the students upon totals?

chapter 9

Researching psychological projects

> *Knowledge is of two kinds. We know a subject ourselves or we know where we can find information upon it.*
>
> Samuel Johnson

Writing essays and reports means using the library. In this chapter, a general guide to the use of library resources and their function in essay and examination preparation will be provided. This is particularly necessary in psychology, as much of the relevant literature is classified under general headings more naturally associated with other disciplines, including medicine (for example, psychiatry), sociology, physiology, education or philosophy.

We outline how psychological information is organised in the two principal English-language library systems — the Dewey System and the Library of Congress System. Electronic (Internet) searches are also introduced.

Use of the library should be guided by the particular purpose you are seeking to achieve, such as writing an essay, preparing a report, or researching a topic for an exam. You should plan your visit to the library based on the issues, authors, topics or other key references you intend to research. Indeed, it is best to prepare a list of tasks before you begin to use the library's resources. To take the most typical task, essay writing, as our example, your library work should follow the steps that are involved in preparing the notes and collecting the resources (quotations, tables, and so on) to be used in your essay: These include: interpreting the question and arranging the literature to be studied according to particular sub-questions; using a card system (or equivalent on your computer) for notes; and arranging these in order to match your sub-questions. In doing this, we recommend that you try hard to avoid inappropriately heavy reliance on photocopying.

USING THE LIBRARY

As a psychology student, you will use library resources for two main purposes: (1) for researching essays; and (2) for study preparatory to examinations, usually concentrating on textbook information which supplements lecture material. In either case, psychological literature often appears either too specific (for example, journals are too advanced or esoteric), or too general (for example, introductory texts tend to summarise only rather superficial aspects of various well-defined content areas such as 'cognition', 'motivation' and 'individual differences'). Additionally, there is a wide range of 'survey' books, or collections of important papers, which focus on specific topics at the level of generality and technical detail more appropriate for an undergraduate essay. For example, there are books on the works of Piaget, Freud, cognition, theories of personality, social psychology, and so on. These do not suffer from the inevitable problems of all-purpose introductory texts. Detailed, sophisticated surveys of specific sub-fields of the ever-changing discipline are published as *Handbooks of...* (for example, Social Psychology). There are also journals which present research findings in relatively non-technical ways (such as *Psychology Today*), and which are appropriate as *preliminary* reading in undergraduate literature searches.

Literature searches generally begin with a list of references relevant to an essay topic or project specified by your tutor or lecturer. These references are essential reading for you to complete the assignment. In some cases, however, no such list is provided, the object being to encourage you, the student, to approach the topic in your own way, using the resources of the library on your own initiative. (In the case of more advanced thesis preparation, it is essential that the *student* initiate and execute a thorough library search.) Lecturers will usually arrange for the most relevant literature to be made available in a Reserve section of the university library. So, at least in the first years of study, searching through the library will be restricted to finding supplementary material to that nominated by the course teacher.

LIBRARY SYSTEMS OF CLASSIFICATION

University libraries most commonly employ the Dewey Decimal System of classification, although this is not the only system used. The United States Library of Congress (LC) System is being employed with increasing frequency. So, you must first establish which system operates in the libraries you will use. The Dewey System employs general headings and specific sub-classifications, but was initiated before psychology covered many of the fields which now give it its character, so large, important areas may be classified under what are today less important subjects or under rather archaic headings (such as 'mental hygiene').

The Library of Congress System is not based on a 'logical' set of branching sub-classifications of actual content. New areas of knowledge are added with a new number, under the alphabetical heading for the social or the behavioural sciences, for example, to yield a numerical listing under one or two letters. (The social sciences and humanities are listed under the letters B to P.)

Dewey library classification is from the general to the specific, beginning with headings as global as 'Intelligence', 'Social Psychology', and so on, and moving to more detailed sub-categories such as 'The Use of Psychological Tests' or 'Public Opinion'. However, these latter categories are still quite broad and are by themselves no guarantee that all and only the information relevant to a specific topic is contained therein. For this reason, there is little to be said for the practice of searching through such general classifications in the hope of discovering precisely relevant information. Even the more specific Dewey classifications are unlikely to guide you to literature that would not otherwise have been found through different methods (for example, the use of abstracts, below).

There are two general Dewey sections for psychology: 130–9 and 150–9.

130–9: Branches of psychology and pseudo-psychology
This includes:

130.1	Theories of Mind and Body (that is, philosophical aspects of psychology — 'mental' events, and so on)
131.3	Mental Hygiene (including Psychoanalysis, 131.34)
132.1	Mental Illness
133.4	Witchcraft
134.5	Hypnotic Phenomena
137.7	Graphology (the art of 'interpreting' handwriting)

You will have noticed that these subject headings are somewhat misleading and certainly do not reflect the relative importance of a subject area in contemporary psychology. For instance, given its historical importance, *Psychoanalysis* would seem worthy of classification either separately, or, at least, under 132, *Abnormal Psychology*, rather than as a subsection of the anachronistic *Mental Hygiene* area. *Mental Hygiene* is a category of 131, *Physiological Psychology*, which effectively classifies Freud's theories as outcomes of physiological investigation — the antithesis of their actual origin. Hence, the Dewey System can be quite misleading as to the type of material its classifications demarcate. The arbitrary nature of the classifications is evident in (1) above, where *Graphology* appears to be a more important topic of psychological research than *Psychoanalysis*. Examples such as these greatly reduce the value of searching through the library from the general to the particular if the categories you are exploring are specified solely by the Dewey classifications.

General psychology
This section includes:

151	Intelligence
152	Sensation and Perception
152.1	Visual Sensation and Perception
152.8	Psychophysics
153	Cognition
159	Volition and Motivation

The main limitations of this section are the omission of *Educational Psychology* (370.15), and of physiological aspects of psychology, some of which are included under 612, *Human Physiology*. *Social Psychology* (301.15) and aspects of *Criminology* and *Delinquency* (364.3, 364.2) are also excluded.

ELECTRONIC LIBRARY AND INTERNET RESOURCES

The Library of Congress System is not arranged around fixed general subject headings, and 'grows' horizontally to reflect changing foci of the discipline. In this way it is less 'logical', but more practically useful. Your university library will have an electronic version of this (or of the Dewey System). If you search via the **Internet**, you may begin by entering **'psychinfo'** and following increasingly specific subject names, branching to **'abstracts'** (brief summaries of current journal articles). Addresses which will help you to begin your search, if 'psychinfo' does not lead you to the relevant catalogues, include:

- http://www.library.yale.edu/scilib/help/psych.html
- http://www.apa.org/journals/alpha.html

Most university libraries allow searches to be conducted by means of author or title, although merely entering precise (the more specific the better) keywords (such as 'memory', 'cognition', 'schizophrenia') will lead to listings from which you may further select titles you wish to follow up. A typical library catalogue will display information as follows;

UNSW LIBRARY CATALOGUE - Brief listing

Author	Bell, Philip, 1947 –				
Title	Reasoning and argument in psychology/Philip Brian Bell, Phillip James Staines				
Edition	Bell, Philip, 1947 –		Format	Bell, Philip, 1947 –	
Place	Kensington, NSW: Norwalk, Conn.:		Publisher	UNSW Press; Books Australia,	Date 1979

Call number	Location	Loan Period
S153.42/32	Open Reserve	Three hours
RSC153.42/32A	Registrar: Stud. Counselg	Not for Loan
S153.42/32B	Level 3	Four weeks
S153.42/32C	Level 3	Four weeks
153.42/32D	Missing	Four weeks
S153.42/32E	Level 3	Four weeks

FULL RECORD

NEW SEARCH

or select back on your browser to return to the itm list

Library

last revised - 19th May 1997

Traditionally, the library catalogue is arranged under subjects or/and author–title entries.

The **subject catalogue** lists titles of books under headings that indicate the general topic to which the book is most closely related. Subjects may include persons. (For example, books about Freud, Piaget or their respective theories would be listed under headings such as 'Freud, S, books about'.) It is best to use this catalogue before consulting the author–title catalogue, because the information in the subject catalogue is general and somewhat arbitrarily classified. This means that your classification of the subject you are pursuing need not correspond closely to the library's classification, thus reducing the value of searching the subject catalogue if you pursue only books listed under a small number of topics, however relevant these topics may appear. Of course, the entries (which were once cards) do refer the user to related topics, but this process may be somewhat time-consuming, with no guarantee of exhausting the relevant material. It is much more efficient to search electronically, because links can be made across many keywords and because an author's works are listed completely once you have nominated them precisely by name (as in Eysenck, HJ, above).

The **author–title catalogue** is a list of all the monographs (books) and serials (journals, periodicals) held by the library. Monographs are entered under author or editor, and the entry lists details of the Dewey (or other) classifications. These include:

> Title; place of publication; publisher; date of publication; information about the number of copies held in the library (or in other university departmental libraries) and the number of pages in the book (if a monograph). This is the information on the electronic page, above.

Serials (journals, periodicals) are generally listed under the author–title catalogue[1] by their respective titles, or under the name of the organisation by which they are issued. Those which some libraries call 'distinctive' titles are listed by title: for example, *Journal of Clinical Psychology, Journal of the History of the Behavioral Sciences*. Those issued by a society or institution which include the name of that body as an important part of the title are listed under such names. These are often called serials with non-distinctive titles (for example, reports of the proceedings of various professional organisations). Catalogue entries for serials usually provide the following information:

---

[1] Libraries generally issue a special, regularly revised, computer listing of serials.

Title; place of publication; the dates (issues) held by the library —
for example, vol 1 (1945) +; the frequency of publication (for
example, annual, quarterly) whether additional copies of the journal are available in the library or associated libraries, and if so at
what call numbers.

It is not advisable merely to 'browse' through serials in the hope of
encountering relevant information for an essay or project. Journals
publish very specific papers which will look quite foreign to students
simply leafing through their pages. Journals are more fruitfully consulted by means of abstracts (see below).

**The principal journals which provide general or overview
papers on the discipline are:**

- *Psychological Bulletin* — a monthly publication which focuses on
  critical reviews of research in specific areas, rather than publishing
  original empirical research papers.
- *Psychological Review* — a bimonthly collection of theoretical articles of considerable sophistication.
- *Annual Review of Psychology*, vol I (1958) — This reviews literature in particular areas (for example, personality, maturation, statistics, abnormal psychology) in a most comprehensive manner.
  Experts in the particular field describe, interpret and evaluate the
  year's progress in that area. A cumulative author and subject
  index is included.

More specifically focused journals include:

- *Cognition*
- *Memory and Cognition*
- *Theory and Psychology*
- *Journal of Transpersonal Psychology*
- *Behaviour and Brain Sciences*
- *Journal of Mathematical Psychology*
- *Journal of Experimental Analysis of Behaviour*
- *Behavioural Neuroscience*
- *Journal of Applied Behaviour Analysis*
- *Philosophical Psychology*

These, and similar, journals should be consulted for specific papers,
rather than as potential sources of information on particular research
areas or project topics.

However, remember that there are serials concerned with every conceivable aspect of psychology, and that their titles are usually an accurate indication of their general content. Not all journals are American, of course. There are British journals of (general) psychology, educational psychology, and so on, as well as Canadian, Australian and other national series, usually published under the auspices of the professional Psychological Society of their respective country. Of the better known internationally read journals originating in the United States, many of those discussed above are listed on the World Wide Web. For instance, the American Psychological Association has a home page (http://www.apa.org/) which gives access to exhaustive information and includes instructions on the use of **Psychcrawler**, a search facility designed to access the psychological literature.

Resources of value to students and to other researchers are proliferating on the World Wide Web. Kardas (1999) catalogues these under 15 general headings, from 'Biological Bases of Behavior' to 'Research (methods) and Statistics', from 'Human Development' to 'Language and Cognition'. He lists not only organisational sites (such as the American Psychological Association's address, above) but also Index sites, Quizzes, On-line Periodicals, Software and On-line graphic resources of use in preparing psychological reports and essays. To cite some of the most potentially useful of these, we list the following examples:

- The American Psychological Society
  http://psych.hanover.edu/APS
- Psych Web
  http://www.psych-web.com
- Amoeba Web: Psychology Web Resources
  http://www.sccu.edu/programs/academic/psych/
  amoebaweb.html
- Psychsite
  http://stange.simplenet.com/psychsit

Kardas also lists specific sites such as one on Kohlberg's stages of moral development, Vygotsky on language, and the Minnesota Twin Family Study.

PSYCHOLOGICAL ABSTRACTS

Perhaps the most important and useful sources of information for psychology students are the editions of psychological abstracts. These abstracts consist of short (100–150 words) summaries of original material published in all major (and very many minor) journals throughout the world. Each month, a publication of up-to-date research abstracts appears, and author and subject indexes are added every six months. Major sections covered include books, articles, films, psychological tests and unpublished doctoral theses. Libraries will have on-line access to these abstracts or will have regularly up-dated CD-Roms.

It is usual for students undertaking theses, extensive literature searches, or searching for, say, all the works of a particular author, to consult the psychological abstracts as the first stage of their enquiry. Undoubtedly, all students wishing to pursue advanced study of psychology would be well advised to familiarise themselves with the use of these sources of information in their university library.

DICTIONARIES

Dictionaries of psychological terms and concepts can be of value in researching an essay or report. They may be consulted to indicate the descriptive definition of a term (see Chapter 1) and thereby to suggest related concepts and theories to pursue in the preparation of an essay. For example:

- Reber, AS (1985) *The Penguin Dictionary of Psychology*, Harmondsworth: Penguin.
- Chaplin, JP (1968) *Dictionary of Psychology*, New York: Dell Publishing Co.

A more advanced, technical source, providing detailed explanation of many terms is:

- English, HB and English AC (1958) *A Comprehensive Dictionary of Psychological and Psychoanalytical Terms*, New York: Longmans.

The terminology of psychoanalysis has been judged sufficiently complex to warrant its own dictionary:

- Laplanche, J and Pontalis, J-B (1973) *The Language of Psychoanalysis*, London: Hogarth.

STUDYING THE RELEVANT LITERATURE

Given that you are confidently familiar with the use of the library, how should you go about reading the literature that is set for a particular project? To provide some reasonably specific guidelines for this important task, let us restrict discussion to cases where you are required to research an essay topic for which a reading list has been provided. The hypothetical essay is to be about 2000 words long.

Just as there are strategies and techniques for writing psychological essays (see next chapter), so there are some general strategies for reading and preparing to write them. First, it is virtually useless to read psychological literature as you might browse through, say, a news magazine. Unlike reading for personal pleasure or searching for interesting information on a number of topics, reading in preparation for writing an essay or academic paper must involve deliberate, strategic attempts to gain specific information. The difference might be stated thus: you do not read an essay reference with the aim of merely understanding what it says, but more with the goal of answering specific questions, or of *testing certain statements against the author's point of view or research finding*.

As we put it in Chapter 2, you should read for *conceptual understanding*, not merely for *linguistic understanding*. Let us try to explain this by means of a hypothetical case.

Consider an essay of 2000 words to be written on the topic, 'In what sense might the process of stereotyping shape intellectual identity and performance? (We have chosen this question, as an essay by Claude M Steele addressing this issue can be found in *American Psychologist*, June 1997, no 6, pp 613–29, and it could be read to see how diverse is the literature relevant to this topic, and how a cogent essay can integrate and synthesise such a wide range of material.)

If the recommended reading list for the essay is adequate it should include some references which cover the following two aspects of the topic:

1   They provide definition(s) or at least some analysis of the terms 'stereotype' and 'intellectual identity'. 'Performance' requires little theory-related definition.

2   They provide evidence, or analyse examples, of the process and significance of stereotyping, by which that process can be causally related to intellectual identity.

Hence, before reading any of the literature, you must *understand the question*. That is, you must interpret the question and decide (even write down) what an adequate answer would need to cover. When this is done, you should focus your proposed reading on these specific aspects and select the references to this end. To do this, the title alone may suffice; if not, the abstract (if one is available) is usually an adequate basis for determining if a paper is relevant. In some cases, a preliminary reading may be required.

So, the second step in researching the essay is to order (prioritise) the references according to your interpretation of the question.

Although, in practice, it is sometimes difficult to decide in advance in what order the references should be studied, it is a good idea to rank them whenever possible. This should at least reduce the amount of re-reading that would otherwise be necessary.

Given a tentative, logical ordering of the references, the next step is to *study*, not merely *read*, each paper and book. Study involves reading and thinking, taking descriptive or summary notes, making written critical comments arguing for or against the paper, and, most importantly, relating the paper to the topic being researched (that is, to the topic as interpreted). In the present example, you should try to analyse the argument and summarise the evidence presented concerning the two aspects of the question which have been previously distinguished. Your notes should analyse and summarise evidence of differences between groups of people subjected to positive or negative stereotyping, for example. You might also note down different explicit or implied definitions and the authors of each. This can be very useful later in helping to define clearly your approach to the essay question.

The notes that summarise and criticise any paper you are studying should include a paraphrase of its major conclusion (or conclusions), plus a brief description of the evidence provided in its support. Should particular quotations be reported verbatim, they should be completely documented and marked so that they are not confused with your own notes when it comes to writing the essay. A third section of the notes might be headed 'Comments' or 'Criticisms' or 'Discussion'. This section should note inadequacies, inconsistencies or peculiar interpretations made by the paper which differ from those of comparable papers, as well as your judgment of the relevance of the paper to the topic as interpreted.

To facilitate writing the essay, we recommend that you use either large (150mm x 125mm) filing cards or loose-leafed paper or the electronic equivalent, if you can type (or dictate). In both cases, these can subsequently be reordered as the structure of your proposed essay requires. A typical card or page of preparatory notes should include (perhaps at the top, or in a margin) the author's name, title of paper and library location. A margin, in which page references of important quotations or paraphrases are recorded, is essential. All too frequently you may wish to quote an author's words in an essay, only to find that you have to retrace their exact page of origin by rereading the paper. This can be avoided by the consistent application of a clerical procedure such as the one recommended here.

Therefore, when you prepare an essay, you should produce a series of documented notes on interchangeable cards (or, of course, an electronic version of such a system) which summarises the thesis and supporting evidence from each relevant paper, and includes quotations and critical commentary. This greatly simplifies the organisational and clerical work involved when you have to actually write the essay. For instance, one of its advantages is that the essay's bibliography can be listed simply by sorting the cards into alphabetical order (by author) and copying down the respective titles, after the essay has been written. On the word processor, of course, this stage only involves copying from your preparatory notes.

A NOTE ON PHOTOCOPYING: THE SEDUCTION OF REPRODUCTION

Easy access to inexpensive photocopying machines has greatly affected methods of research for undergraduate essays. It is at least possible to copy all references and use the copies as your sources of information. You can underline and annotate the copies of papers and (it might be hoped) avoid some, at least, of the study processes that have been briefly outlined in this chapter.

However, it is generally *not* a good idea to rely on photocopying to reduce study time if this means that you avoid writing summaries or critical commentaries. First, this reliance will lead to a very uneconomical source of information from which to write an essay or report. As we have emphasised in preceding chapters, being able to translate others' ideas into your own words and to draw implications from these ideas are essential aspects of understanding. If no notes are taken, you may read, but not necessarily understand, an article or monograph. Second, photocopying carries the temptation to avoid reading altogether while collecting ever-increasing stocks of unpleasant-smelling paper. There is a curious tendency to believe that merely photocopying an article is tantamount to committing it to memory. This is obviously a dangerous (but quite common) misconception. So it is probably a good rule not to photocopy material until *after* you have read it. Certainly, it is advisable not to photocopy more than can be properly studied before you have further access to the tempting machine. It is pointless to amass piles of unstudied texts that are merely left to gather dust — the unfortunate fate of much psychological literature.

Increasingly, papers you may have photocopied are becoming available on-line — for example, in electronic journals or at the author's web site. Many of the same morals apply. Having a paper in your computer's memory is no substitute for reading it critically and understanding it. In this form, it is easy to let the computer search articles for words or phrases that might express concepts or ideas you are pursuing, and if you choose to quote from the article you should be able to circumvent clerical errors.

chapter 10

Writing psychological essays

My words fly up, my thoughts remain below:
Words without thoughts never to heaven go.

William Shakespeare

Essays demand clear analytical and critical writing based on research and planning. An essay must show your understanding of the topic under discussion, but it must, more importantly, answer the question asked. An essay needs to do more than simply discuss the topic. This involves presenting clear definitions and a precise interpretation of the question and its assumptions. Relevant evidence must be evaluated critically and comparatively to allow you to draw subtle conclusions.

This chapter analyses examples of student (undergraduate) essays to show how to structure your psychological arguments. It outlines conventions relating to style, the citation of sources and referencing. Plagiarism must be avoided in all written work. Methods for avoiding this problem, which reflects an inadequate understanding of the literature, are presented.

INTRODUCTION

Writing essays is the bane of the student's academic life. Yet essays present a unique opportunity to learn and to communicate your learning. But, writing essays about psychology is no simple matter. In addition to the formal aspects of definition and argument which we have discussed in the first sections of this book, and the detailed research of the relevant literature which is necessary preparation, there is the problem of actually formulating your ideas in coherent, precise and informative English.

Ideally, an essay should contribute new knowledge to the area that it discusses. At the minimum it should show that the authors know what they are talking about — that they understand the subject. Assessors may hope to learn something about their field of expertise from a student's essay, but failing this, they will be looking at least for evidence of your grasp of the topic. They will be looking for evidence of breadth of information, depth of understanding and level of critical skill (your ability to evaluate the literature and to direct your research to the question). It is important not only that the essay-writer have such information, understanding and critical skills, but that, especially in writing essays, they demonstrate them. The essay must show unequivocal evidence of these abilities.

In the preceding chapters, we were concerned with evaluating the written work of others. But in essay writing the tables are turned: instead of being the audience trying to evaluate critically the material received, the student has to produce material which will stand up to critical scrutiny. Nevertheless, the advice given earlier is still highly germane. All essayists, in the selection of their material, must be their own critics. They must produce ideas and arguments that can not only be clearly understood, but that will also stand up to critical evaluation.

Essays should, at least, show that their authors *understand* the topic

— that is, that they have critically evaluated relevant information. Since understanding is so important, it is worth recalling (and rereading) a number of distinctions made in Chapter 1. There we distinguised two levels of understanding — the linguistic level and the conceptual level. The former concerns understanding material to the point of being able to express it in your own words; the latter involved seeing both the implications of statements and the questions they answer. Both these levels were seen to be essential for the evaluation of statements and arguments, and their importance will be apparent throughout this chapter, for an essay is an attempt to show these levels of understanding.

An essay is an **expository** work. Exposition is the art of demonstrating, expounding or setting forth information, and therefore argument. In classical rhetoric (the art of verbal persuasion), exposition involves showing, telling and convincing one's listener/reader of the truth of one's conclusion. Expository speech presents evidence, examples, analysis (including definition) and so seeks to persuade the listener/reader of the truth of what is presented. So, essays require the presentation of arguments and therefore should exhibit the conceptual distinctions and methodological principles which have been presented (exposited) in the preceding chapters of this book.

To show how to write essays, we will consider particular examples. The hypothetical questions that we analyse in this chapter are sufficiently non-technical to illustrate some important features of essay writing without requiring the reader to possess any specialist knowledge of their respective contents. Although the person assessing the essays would be familiar with the relevant literature, it is nevertheless instructive to read the examples without the benefit of similar background information. The following general features should be noted, for these are clearly important to the assessor of essays, regardless of the topic under discussion.

1   *The coherence and soundness of the arguments* presented are largely due to the way in which the author organises his or her ideas. There are at least three levels at which such organisation can be analysed:

a   *Within sentences*: Are the ideas (propositions or statements) expressed by the one sentence closely related, or would they be more appropriately separated into individual sentences? Does the structure of the sentence reflect the relative importance of its component statements?

b   *Within paragraphs*: How do the statements included within each paragraph contribute to the one central idea? What is this major idea which the **topic sentence** of the paragraph embodies? (This assumes that it is possible to isolate such a 'topic sentence'. In an extended argument, this should usually be identifiable as an intermediate conclusion to the major point at issue.) Are the paragraph boundaries appropriate? Are the lengths of the sentences within the paragraph varied in a manner appropriate to their content?

c *Overall structure*: How do the various sub-arguments embodied in various paragraphs develop or reinforce the major argument(s) being advanced in the essay? Is the direction and structure of the essay clearly indicated by means of the sequence and prominence of the paragraphs, or is the order somewhat random?

2 *Vocabulary and style:* Psychological essays are not assessed by purely 'literary' criteria. Still, the communication of ideas demands lucid, economical prose. Choice of the appropriate word, varied and interesting sentence structure, unpretentious expression with minimal jargon — all contribute to the success of your essay.

3 *Conventions:* Failure to follow certain organisational and linguistic conventions can lead to uneconomical essays. Precise rules concerning the **documentation of sources** also need to be followed if the suspicion of **plagiarism** is to be avoided.

ESSAY STRUCTURE

The example below pays attention to each of the practices we have listed above.

It addresses the question:

'Discuss the differences and possible connections between gender identity and sexual object choice.'

We have edited this example to show clearly how it is structured as an argument involving: definition, analysis, the presentation of evidence, interim conclusions and a qualified general conclusion. It also addresses potential criticisms of its argument and consequently presents a redefinition of the principal terms of the question posed.

1 Interpretation of the question, assumptions in the question analysed

It has traditionally been assumed that gender identity and sexual object choice are related in a highly consistent manner. A female is expected to be predominantly feminine in terms of gender identity and to orientate her sexual object choice towards males. Such a connection therefore predicts that a male with a feminine gender identity will also select a male as his sexual object choice.

The purpose of this paper is to question the validity of this assumption, based on information gathered from a number of research papers.

2 Definition of principal terms: gender identity; sexual object choice

Gender identity can be formally defined as '... the internal subjective concept of one's individuality as male or female' (Ruber 1985, p 295). The acquisition of gender identity is viewed as a developmental process, initially characterized by an awareness of belonging to either the male or the female sex ...

Sexual object choice can be described as the sex of the individual towards which sexual actions are directed. However, the term should not be considered synonymous with sexual preference.

3 Criticism of assumed male–female dichotomy found in the literature (that is, conceptual clarification)

Much of the research which addresses the relationship between gender identity and sexual object choice (Freund et al 1974; Oldham et al 1982; Storms 1980) does so on the basis of an assessment or measurement of the extent to which an individual's responses are more characteristic of one sex than the other. While this approach to measurement may be criticized on the ground that masculinity and femininity are culture-bound constructs, such a criticism should in fact be directed towards the concept of gender identity itself. Anthropologists (eg Mead 1950) have highlighted the cultural variations in what characterizes masculinity and femininity.

4 Evidence cited: relevance to question, introduction of other evidence claimed to be relevant (that is, transexualism)

However the demands of empiricism have directed research towards what appears to be the clearest expression of a connection between gender identity and sexual object choice — that of transsexualism. The firm conviction that, most commonly, a female identity is trapped inside an unsuitable male body invariably manifests in a homosexual object choice, that is homosexual based on the criteria of the original chromosomal and gonadal sex (Money 1974).

Transsexualism has been described as the most complete and chronic form of transposed gender identity (Money 1974). This view is supported by Freund (1974) who reported 33 transsexual males as scoring significantly higher on a feminine gender identity scale than most of the 147 homosexual male subjects. However, the few existing cases in which transsexualism is associated with heterosexual preference (that is, a male transsexual chooses a female partner) appear to lend support to the argument that gender identity and sexual object choice are to some degree independent. That is, feminine gender identity in a male transsexual does not necessarily predict a masculine object choice.

5   Redefinition of key terms in light of above

If transexualism is generally to be interpreted in terms of a chronic form of transposed gender identity, then Money suggests that homosexuality can subsequently be viewed ' ... with a less pervasive transposition of gender role ... his or her role reversal does not show in everyday occupational behaviour, but only in erotic life and the sex of the partner of choice' (Money 1974, p 69).

Indeed, Bieber et al (1962) found only 2 per cent of 106 male homosexuals to be 'markedly effeminate'. What is not clear in this study, however, is the degree to which Bieber et al's use of the expression 'markedly effeminate' refers to the subject's gender role as opposed to gender identity. It can perhaps be suggested that Bieber et al's (1962) description alludes to the overt expression of behaviours which indicate the degree of affiliation to femaleness. It cannot be assumed that gender behaviour necessarily correlates with gender identity, as in the case of transsexuals.

6   Criticism of evidence, leading to (7)

In addition, it is questionable whether Bieber et al's (1962) sample of male homosexuals seeking analysis has wider generaliseability to those who do not seek therapy.

It is interesting to note however, that when Evans (1969) replicated Bieber et al's (1962) study, it was found that 93 per cent of male homosexuals did consider themselves to be moderately or strongly masculine. Evans' (1969) study, therefore, is able to provide a clearer case for the independence of gender identity and sexual object choice because subjects (rather than therapeutic assessment) reported their own feelings about their masculinity.

7   Generalisation and interim conclusion

On the basis of these findings, therefore, it can be concluded that erotic fantasies are a potentially more reliable indicator of sexual object choice than is gender identity.

8   Further criticism of the possibility of a generalised answer to the question as asked

A recurring theme in the literature concerns the inconsistent nature of the evidence. This can perhaps be attributed to the wide range of scales used to measure gender identity and it is questionable as to whether or not these different scales do in fact 'tap' the same phenomena. Furthermore, the subjective nature of gender identity does not easily lend itself to quantitative assessment.

An additional criticism of the research concerns the fact that the samples used are not seen to be representative of the majority of homosexuals.

9 Conclusion, qualifications, and suggestions for further research

In conclusion, the usefulness of concepts such as gender identity and sexual object choice must be questioned, both as separate entities and when considered in the context of cultural and traditional influences. Finally, it is clear that inconsistencies in the research, coupled with the vagueness of definition, do not allow definitive conclusions to be drawn with regard to the differences and associations between gender identity and sexual object choice. A relationship between the two concepts can perhaps be assumed in transsexuals where evidence for a transposed gender identity is readily validated by the desire to change biological sex. Such a relationship, however, is questionable among homosexuals, although some homosexual women appear to possess a number of masculine traits. Until a more sensitive measure of gender identity can be developed, the debate will continue. However, the recent evidence suggesting that erotic imagery may be useful as a predictor of sexual preference allows for interesting speculation.

You will notice that this essay is theoretical and definitional (what we call 'analytical'), as well as summarising empirical (experimental or other observational) evidence. That is, it does more than merely present evidence relating the particular relationship between the variables or concepts in the question asked. It relates the evidence to a reconceptualisation of the terms that are at stake in the question. This makes it quite a sophisticated example of psychological argument and of conceptual analysis. Yet the essay is frequently unnecessarily abstract and 'passive'. So, it can be criticised as rather vague in its introduction and conclusion (see under 'Style', below).

The next example is less sophisticated than the last. On the credit side, it attempts to describe properly documented, relevant evidence and to develop general themes, if not detailed arguments. It lacks really detailed analysis of the key concepts. We will discuss its demerits after presenting four of the most important paragraphs verbatim.

The question:

'It has often been suggested that watching violent films and reading about violent acts encourages aggressive and violent behaviour. Critically discuss this claim.'

Para. 1 Violence has increased at a rapid rate in western societies such as the USA since the turn of the twentieth century. During this time there has also been an enormous increase in strength and power of the media (ie newspapers, TV, motion pictures). These are dominated by tales of violence depicted in various ways. It is doubtful if the above is just coincidence.

Para. 2 Aggression may be defined as 'behaviour intentionally causing physical harm to another person'. Violence and aggression may expend a great amount of energy but in this modern age they may also be carried out in a cool, calm and impersonal manner. Many theories have been expounded on the causes of aggression in the human race. Ardrey (1967) and Storr (1968) view aggression as innate in man. However, contrary evidence is available. Studies of two primitive tribes indicate that aggression is learned during childhood. In child-rearing, the Arapesh tribe sows seeds of passiveness. They treat the child as a soft vulnerable thing which they protect continuously and feed often. The Mundugumore, on the other hand, are vicious and quarrelsome head-hunters, who rapidly instil such characteristics in their offspring.

Bonta (1997) summarises the anthropological evidence for the argument that child-rearing practices reproduce non-violent and affiliative attitudes in societies which are cooperative and peaceful:

> *The most striking conclusion is that, for many of these societies, the central, defining elements in their beliefs are strong opposition to competition and support for cooperation. (p 312)*

The essay then summarises other evidence for the statement that aggression is 'learned' — mentioning child-rearing studies, imitation of aggressive models in films and surveys of the amount of violence in TV programs. Next it treats the issue of whether viewed violence can have a cathartic (emotionally releasing) effect. Typical of these paragraphs is the following:

Para. 3 Experiments by Bandura support Berkowitz's beliefs (concerning imitation of violence). His experiments involved children viewing an adult engaged in violence on TV, film, cartoon, and in real life. The child was then mildly annoyed and his free-play observed. As well as finding 'twice as much aggressiveness', Bandura observed that the children were 'not too inclined to give precise imitations (of cartoon characters) but many behaved like carbon copies of real-life and filmed models'. The National Television Violence Study found that: '... viewing violence in the mass media can lead to aggressive behaviour'; '... prolonged viewing of media violence can lead to emotional desensitisation'; and '... viewing violence can increase the fear of becoming a victim of violence' (1996, exec. summary, p 4).

The concluding paragraph follows immediately:

Para. 4 This reinforces the view that aggression and violence under certain conditions are learned and later adopted by people. If the violence and aggression viewed are appealing, and in carrying out that violence one feels morally justified, one's inhibitions to violence are decreased. The portrayal of violence on TV and film does tend to lead people astray.

This example is sufficiently well organised to allow us to discuss it in three general sections.

1 Introductory paragraphs 1 and 2: defining the problem or question

The first paragraph is quite typical of those found in mediocre undergraduate essays: it is rhetorical and vague, containing assertions for which no documentation or evidence are deemed necessary. With its occasional redundancy ('strength and power') and patent generalisations, the paragraph is quite innocuous. However, given the question being answered, it could be claimed that the entire paragraph is really unnecessary, for it avoids, rather than confronts, the question.

The second paragraph is considerably better, although that is not to say that it is ideal. The writer does attempt to define aggression, however cursorily. Second, he cites two proponents of an important point of view concerning the origins of human aggression and indicates the relevance of empirical methods to settling the issue raised. On the other hand, in doing this, the author does set up quite rigid dichotomies ('instinct' or 'learning') and offers no detailed justification for selecting either the authors or ideas he introduces. Moreover, the definition of aggression which he offers is very specific, and could easily be confused with a definition of 'violence' (the two are not usually taken to be synonymous). He mentions impersonal violence but does not relate this point to his general discussion. More importantly, there is no analysis of the concept of instinct, not even an outline of Storr's or of the National Television Violence Study's definitions. Had this concept been examined in detail, the rigid dichotomisation of the 'nature–nurture' issue in the essay might have been qualified or replaced by more workable categories. Were this done, the very relevant anthropological evidence mentioned could have formed a separate, quite extensive section of the essay in its own right.

2   Discussion of evidence

Paragraph 3 of our example attempts to summarise one study (by Bandura), with only limited success. Although the general findings of the study are reported, a more lucid summary could have been given. Generally, however, this paragraph is typical of those found in students' essays. It does confirm and extend the writer's argument quite well. In conjunction with other evidence (which we have not quoted) the 'body' of this essay is relevant to the question under discussion and is adequately documented.

3   Conclusion

The concluding paragraph 4 is not very satisfactory. Instead of drawing together the major themes of the evidence reviewed and showing how these relate to the question, the writer is content merely to repeat the results of one series of studies and attach a generalisation with which to end the essay. However, an *ending* is not necessarily a *conclusion*. Although not entirely irrelevant, the last paragraph could be more precise and its conclusions qualified to explicitly answer the question. The final statement is essentially moralistic ('… lead people astray') and much too vague to answer the question adequately.

Keeping in mind the examples we have quoted, let us approach the task of writing essays in a more positive way, beginning where you, the student, begins — confronted by a question (which you may or may not understand).

THE QUESTION

It is surprising how many students write essays on topics that bear only indirect or tangential relevance to the question assigned. Leaving aside those students who fail completely to understand the question, many others tend to write vaguely about issues related, but not central to, the question. But there is a distinction between 'topic' and 'question': the 'topic' is the more general concept or subject area about which particular questions can be asked. So, begin by analysing the question as it is asked. Consider the following:

1   What does the question mean? In the second example, above, you would have to ask what the words 'violent' and 'aggressive' mean. This is not as simple as it at first appears. The terms may not be synonymous, and they would require careful definition.

2   Can the question be analysed (broken down) into implied or subsidiary questions (For example, about violent behaviour as separate from aggressive behaviour more generally)? Then ask: How are the component questions to be answered in relation to each other? This involves deciding which (if either) is the major question and how much importance should be given to it and the subsidiary issues. It is not sufficient to write an essay about one aspect of the total question and simply append a cursory sentence or two that pays lip service to the minor issues.

A second issue arises in direct relation to the way the question is phrased. An essay question almost invariably requires elementary logical analysis before it can be properly answered, that is, the logical structure of the question needs to be elucidated. For example, consider the essay question, *"Stereotypes are necessary for prejudice." Discuss.'* First, it is important to notice what the question does not say. It does not merely say 'Discuss the relationship between stereotypes and prejudice', or 'Stereotypes may lead to prejudice' (or vice versa).

Therefore, without knowing too much about either 'stereotypes' or 'prejudice', you can analyse the logical structure of the question in this negative way. What is more, this analysis can be very revealing. In the present case, it demonstrates that you would have to answer the original question negatively (that is, disagree with the quoted statement) unless you could show that prejudice *always* involved stereotypes. It would not be sufficient to demonstrate that stereotypes sometimes or frequently lead to prejudiced attitudes. It would have to be shown that prejudice could not occur without stereotypes. One of the authors has actually marked essays on this topic and found that very few students are aware of the *logic* of the question that they discuss. So, you are strongly advised to analyse the logical status of each question you consider and to ask what (possible) evidence would provide arguments for or against the question *before* reading the relevant literature. Otherwise, you will have no way of knowing which literature actually is relevant to the question. At the risk of repeating our earlier recommendation, it is not just what the question asks, but what it does *not* ask, that must be understood before you search for answers.

Once the logic of the question is clear, the next step is to analyse the major concepts involved. In Chapter 4 we noted the importance of clarifying and defining terms whenever there is some possibility of misunderstanding between writers and readers. In essay work, the writer is the student and the reader (assessor) is likely to have been their teacher, which may seem to reduce the need for clarification and definition of terms. However, the processes are still important, owing to the double purpose of essay writing. You not only have to write competently on a particular topic, but also show as unequivocally as you can that you understand what you, yourself, have written. This often requires that you define and clarify some of the more important terms being used — particularly new terms and those that are used in a technical sense which differs from their everyday usage.

We have seen that many psychological concepts are open to a variety of interpretations and can be defined by a variety of procedures. In the second example (above), the writer defined 'aggression' as 'behaviour intentionally causing physical harm to another person'. But aggression could be defined more broadly than this. For instance, it could include 'psychological' assaults such as insults and other interpersonal 'attacks'. Second, the writer of that essay offered no definition of violence as distinct from (or as one aspect of) aggression. Yet, the essay question implied that aggression and violence were not synonymous.

Other essay topics may involve even less precise terms than these. For example, the following: *'"The behavioural control techniques in current use dehumanise man." Evaluate this claim discussing specific examples.'* The word 'dehumanise' is very difficult to define. Consequently, many students who wrote on this topic during a course on the principles of behaviour control were content to assume that no definition was necessary. As a result, they usually failed to relate the techniques of control to any relevant evaluative concept. They may have shown, for example, that such practices raised a number of ethical problems, involved practical difficulties, caused pain or eliminated 'human responsibility', but failed to argue how any of these should necessarily be regarded as 'dehumanising'.

This example raises another problem involved in the interpretation of essay topics. Although the above question does not explicitly require it, it seems to ask implicitly for some kind of **comparison**. It is certainly possible to interpret the question as requiring a comparison of current behaviour control techniques with other forms of psychological intervention in people's lives. It would be of limited interest to show that the behavioural techniques were 'dehumanising' if it could also be claimed that *all* forms of psychotherapeutic intervention were equally likely to restrict individual freedom and dignity (one possible interpretation of dehumanisation).

Consequently, you need to look beyond the explicit question to see if comparisons and contrasts are called for, and ask how relevant these are to the answer you propose. This is a very important point and arises in relation to many psychological questions. Recall the discussion of the comparative nature of evidence (Chapter 5) where the *relative* effects of variables were stressed. The present points are an extension of the argument advanced there.

EVIDENCE

The importance of thinking carefully about the meaning and internal logic of an essay question can be seen when you attempt to research the topic. Without such an analysis, you cannot read the literature with specific questions in mind. You will scarcely comprehend, let alone remember, technical arguments from the literature unless they can be related to issues about which you have formulated precise questions. The general strategy you adopt, given a coherent interpretation of the major questions at issue, should focus on the following: *What evidence would refute possible answers to the question?* (This is not a question of what the evidence is, but of what it *could* be.) As a corollary, you should ask: *What evidence would confirm (support) possible answers to the topic question?*

In keeping with the (admittedly oversimplified) version of the logic of scientific argument outlined in Chapter 2, it is suggested that these questions are of crucial importance. Although the first appears rather negative, its practical value is considerable. In particular, it is important to formulate, *in advance* of reading specific studies, the evidence that could be relevant to both positive and negative conclusions regarding the question being discussed. To do this, the points considered in Chapter 5 should be studied carefully — especially the distinction between correlation and cause, and the need for appropriate comparison conditions.

THE CONCLUSION

Most students' essays *end* rather than *conclude* (that is, reach a conclusion). However, there is a great potential difference between merely ending a discussion and concluding an argument. Trivially, this difference is shown by the fact that the conclusion of an essay-form argument need not be presented in the final sections of the essay. A conclusion may be presented prior to the supporting argument and evidence, although this is not generally the case. But, regardless of where it occurs, some conclusion is essential to any written essay-style argument.

In its most mundane form, a conclusion may simply consist of a paraphrase of the question, preceded by an appropriate word or phrase like 'thus', 'therefore', or 'it can be seen that …'. However, this is seldom ideal. Usually, the conclusion of an essay involves a number of careful qualifications. For example, the concluding paragraph in example (2) (above) attempts to specify the precise conditions under which aggressive behaviour may be encouraged by the media. Although that example is rather vague and brief, the attempt is preferable to asserting dogmatically that 'the media cause aggression', for instance. Such glib generalisations are unlikely to reflect the complexity of the psychological literature relevant to an undergraduate essay. It is much more likely that conclusions will be of the form 'certain people, under certain conditions, for certain duration (perhaps at certain ages) will be influenced in particular ways …'. It must be admitted that the formulation of essay questions may predispose students to look for crude general solutions to issues, for the questions themselves usually involve brief, unqualified phrases. It is part of the skill of essay writing to be able to avoid merely reproducing the oversimplified categories assumed in many questions.

Finally, let us emphasise that the conclusion of an essay does not need to pretend to be the ultimate statement on the topic. Highly qualified and conditional conclusions are preferable to the dramatic overstated assertions that are often found in students' work. Essays are not dramatic literary exercises: they need no emotional climax or rousing final scene. Assessors do not need to be told that 'the issue of racial prejudice is the most important problem facing the world and must be solved for fear of World War III', nor that 'Behavioural Control Techniques are the realisation of society's gravest fear of a Brave New World, where its every detail is controlled'. The soundness of a conclusion is not necessarily proportional to its rhetorical vigour.

STYLE

In discussing the verbal style of psychological essays, we do not wish to propose unduly restrictive guidelines, for there is no particular style that is obligatory in such cases. However, there appear to be several common stylistic weaknesses in undergraduate essays that are relatively easily rectified. These involve:

1 topic sentences and themes
2 passive voice
3 personal informality
4 pseudo-scientific jargon
5 inappropriate choice of words.

TOPIC SENTENCES AND 'THEMES'

We have emphasised the need to *answer the question*, not merely to *write on the topic* in psychological (indeed, in all academic) essays. The precise formation of topic sentences in each paragraph is the most important task in achieving this goal. Topic sentences are the backbone of their respective paragraphs.

Each paragraph should be structured as expressions of a precise topic sentence, which is its theme or subject. This need not begin the paragraph, but it should be clearly the point or the proposition that encapsulates the meaning of the paragraph.

The paragraph is the larger unit of meaning which usually *illustrates* (by citing examples), *demonstrates* (by presenting evidence from research), or *analyses* (by discussing concepts and definitions) the proposition expressed in the topic sentence.

A paragraph, then, is a **cohesive unit** (a linked set of sentences about the topic sentence) which is one component of the argument of the essay. By 'cohesive' it is meant that each sentence should use or refer to concepts or grammatical subjects introduced in the paragraph itself. Cohesion is most easily maintained if topic sentences express one proposition in a simple, rather than compound, sentence. A compound sentence is one in which two independent clauses are linked by means of a conjunction. Obviously, such a sentence may multiply the topics of a paragraph by proposing two or more subjects to be expanded in the remainder of the paragraph. For instance: '*The evidence from cross-cultural studies shows that child-rearing practices are crucial in determining academic success and in influencing children's self- esteem.*'

By separating this sentence into two topic sentences in two distinct (but linked) paragraphs, cohesive discussion of each subject (academic success and self-esteem) would be facilitated.

THE PASSIVE VOICE AND MODALITY

Consider the sentence: '*The individual is a set of potentialities which are actualised (in temporal sequence) by operating in a social dialectic.*'

This passive sentence employs nouns such as 'potentialities', '(temporal) sequence' and 'dialectic' which abstract the processes referred to. These words make the processes vague and non-specific. The passive voice ('… are actualised by operating …') and the relational verb ('is') could be replaced by more active locutions and by active 'doing' verbs. The vague nouns could also be altered to yield a sentence which proposes a particular proposition about what makes one an individual (if that is the point) or about what affects or realises people's potentials.

Such a passive structure would be a difficult topic sentence around which to build a paragraph. If it were to be so used, it would need very concrete and descriptive expatiation. Unfortunately, the example quoted actually continues thus:

> The individual is a set of potentialities which are actualised (in temporal sequence) by operating in the social dialectic. He is born into a particular social situation inhabited by significant others who mediate those aspects of the objective world according to their socio-economic location, and as ongoingly experiential selves with idiosyncratic and peculiar biographies.

So the passage would need to be rewritten completely to be made more precise, active and meaningful. Perhaps it could read:

> An individual's potentials develop in a social context. His (sic) experiences are mediated by others according to their different social and economic positions. They represent unique influences.

Not that this is a very informative paragraph even as it is rewritten. However, it is less tautological and vague because the reader can determine who (or what) is claimed to do what to whom, at least.

Student essays are often written in the passive voice and use many vague or abstract words as a sign of formality and objectivity. In linguistics, the formal use of words in passive or otherwise tentative assertions is termed 'low-modality' writing. **Modality** refers to the writer's confidence in the truth of his or her statements. It has become a convention of academic essays to use low modality. Hence, they sound undogmatic and less conclusive, more open to argument than, say, journalistic commentary. However, essay writers should not adopt such a style merely to sound 'expert' if the price paid is to sound merely tentative, vague or equivocal without good reason.

PERSONAL INFORMALITY

Whenever writers adopt the first person singular ('I') or, worse, the first person plural ('we'), there is a tendency to intrude unnecessarily into the text. Typical phrases that signify this type of intrusion are:

> *'I think that ...'*
> *'It is my opinion that ...'*

or, worse,

> *'It is my considered opinion that ...'*
> *'It is my firm belief that ...'*

Sometimes the first person locution may be used to argue more 'authoritatively':

> *'When I was in Alabama, I saw ...'*

or

> *'Having been to New Guinea, I know what village conditions are like ...'*

or

> *'Having studied genetics, I can vouch for the validity of X's arguments.'*

Such appeals to personal authority and experience should be avoided whenever possible, for the reasons outlined in Chapter 6.

The first person plural ('we') is often used by individual authors as a device for taking the reader into their confidence. For instance, the writer of a textbook might proceed:

> *'If we now study the evidence from Freud, then we can see clearly that ...'*

or

> *'We have seen that ...'*

This is sometimes unpretentious and appropriate, although it is difficult to justify the intimate (and condescending) tone in essays. When 'we' is in what amounts to the 'royal plural', it is quite unnecessary.

JARGON

All disciplines have their own specialised vocabulary, and psychology is no exception. Students are expected to acquire knowledge of a technical vocabulary as they study this subject. You will talk about 'ego strength', 'reafference', 'operant conditioning', and so on. Some technical terminology is necessary and, in most cases, efficient for communication.

But unnecessary **jargon** (what is sometimes called '**cant**') may be used to obscure and inflate, rather than to clarify and explain, one's ideas. Students are given plenty of examples of the use of pseudo-scientific vocabulary by their mentors. Psychologists seem to be capable of manufacturing a new word for any phenomenon they study. The danger is that the technical vocabulary may be redundant, obscure or both. A recent symposium on computer technology included references to a 'voice-oriented, point-to-point channel switched network' (a telephone system) and 'the informationarisation' of society, and referred to computer-controlled cities as 'computopolises'. One speaker (we hope facetiously) referred to a 'computer peace corps' that included an 'uneducated people eradication team'.

Psychological jargon, we hope, has not reached that stage, but many examples of cant may be found. The reader might attempt to paraphrase the following:

1 The input to the child's neural structures.

2 Developing competence for coping with negative emotions.

3 The study of environmental processes from the point of view of a particular participant creates a situation dichotomised into

participant on the one hand, and all other environmental components on the other. (Proshansky et al 1970, p 35)

4   In other words, when we speak of design, the real object of discussion is ... the ensemble comprising the form and its context ...

5   There is a wide variety of ensembles ... The biological ensemble made up of a natural organism and its physical environment is the most familiar; in this case we are used to defining the fit between the two as well-adaptedness. (Proshansky et al 1970, p 43)

These examples are replete with rather inflated, 'scientific' words and phrases. Some may well have more precise meanings than less formal expressions which would be more readily comprehended by non-specialists. But other expressions seem to be unnecessarily technical (for example, 'neural structures'; 'negative emotions'; 'biological ensemble', 'well-adaptedness'). It is not merely the choice of such words, but the very passive grammatical structure which each author adopts that makes the passages very 'dense' (for example, 'process creates a situation dichotomised ...'). Jargon is even more noticeable when it is interspersed with non-technical language in students' essays, especially if there is the suggestion that the student is not totally familiar with the meaning of the jargon they employ. Unfortunately, the specialist also sometimes falls between the excesses of glib jargon and more prosaic expression, as the following examples indicate:

> Of particular interest were territoriality patterns with respect to beds, chairs and parts of the room and social distances maintained by teammates in free-time activities. It was anticipated that isolated and non-isolated groups, and groups formed according to different personality compositions would differ in spatial behaviour. Prior research had shown that incompatibility and compatibility of dyad members on need affiliation, need achievement and dogmatism affected performance stress and interpersonal exchange in isolation. (Altman and Haythorn, in Proshansky et al 1970, p 227)

The density with which technical expressions are packed into this passage concerning the way sailors use the space and furniture in their living quarters renders it almost incomprehensible on first reading, even to someone familiar with the area of research. It is amusing to compare the passage above with part of a satirical paper titled 'An Ethological Analysis of Reproductive Behaviour' (Germana 1971). Under the heading 'The male–female sexuality as a mechanism of social organisation', Germana writes:

> Whenever a group of animals is first brought together, they demonstrate little or no social organisation. Such social structure is

> produced through the establishment of dominance-submission relationships; only in terms of this social hierarchy can an individual demonstrate an appropriate differentiation of behaviour. This behaviour differentiation permits the survival of the individual within the group — that is, it is the 'primary behaviour adaptation' to which all other behaviours interrelate. (p 55)

This passage sounds informative; it seems to be quite impressively so. Notice, however, that this style results from the passivised formality and the cliches borrowed from, or invented to imitate, conventional jargon (especially 'primary behaviour adaptation'). Unfortunately, students' essays are sometimes unintentionally parodic in a rather similar way, as the following quotation attests:

> When faced with a problem, an organism will respond in a certain way. His decision or reaction will be a variable, dependent on many different variables …

It is hard to imagine a less informative statement, despite the words 'organism', 'decision', 'reaction' and 'variable'.

Another example of jargon is the use of 'systems' and computer language in psychology. In some cases this has been of great benefit in formulating old problems in new ways (for example, in the psychology of language acquisition and cognition generally). Too often, however, students have adopted the jargon in a glib, pretentious manner. Humans are now 'encoders of input', which may result in various 'output' or 'throughput'. (Presumably, potential input that is ignored or rejected is 'backput'!)

An allied trend is the proliferation of hyphenated combinations of older words or prefixes and words. Hence, we hear of 'socio-political factors', 'intra-dyadic communication', 'sociograms', 'sociofugal spatial arrangements', 'neuropharmacological studies', and so on. Again, without wishing to proscribe the use of all such terms, it is probably fair to argue that these should be used sparingly, and not at all if not properly understood by the writer of an essay or report.

CHOOSING THE RIGHT WORD

Much of the difficulty that students find in writing psychological essays is that they do not really understand the meanings of many of the words they have read in the literature. It is only when you are required to express ideas precisely and unambiguously that this becomes apparent. The result may be that you choose slightly inappropriate words, which, in a technical essay or report, can seriously mislead the reader (or irritate the marker). The following is a very simple example of slightly inappropriate words in a technical context:

1   The participants in the study were all white teenage boys.
2   Subjects in the experiment were all Caucasian males aged between 13 and 19.

These two sentences are very similar, and either might be acceptable in most contexts. Yet, the words chosen in (2) are more appropriate to formal psychological literature than the alternatives in (1). This is because each word in (2) is more precise, and its meaning is more limited and unambiguous than its counterpart in (1). Without being too pedantic, the following comments might be made: 'participants' is vague enough to include the experimenter as well as the subjects; 'study' might refer to things other than experiments (such as field research); and 'white' suggests racial classification solely on the basis of skin colour (which in some contexts may be difficult, if not impossible, to use).

   Recall that when we discussed the assumptions inherent in various definitions, it was emphasised that the choice of particular words could have a crucial bearing on the theoretical orientation of an argument. The point being emphasised in this section relates to the precision and scope of the meaning of words, regardless of their more theoretical functions. But it is still an important practical aspect of the language of psychology that each word needs to be carefully chosen and its precise meaning fully comprehended. Words that appear to have identical meanings may be different in subtle ways that greatly affect the force of particular arguments. Consider the italicised words in the following brief discussion of group differences in intelligence:

> The Irish race has been shown to score below the English in tests of *intellectual ability*. Such differences in *intelligence* are probably inborn because the educational systems of both countries are *comparable*. This proves that the difference is instinctive rather than learned.

This might be compared with:

> The Irish *population* has been shown to score below the English population in tests of IQ. Such a difference in IQ is probably *innately determined* because the educational systems of both countries are *similar*. This suggests that the difference is *not due to environmental influences*.

   The most appropriate way to emphasise the importance of precision in your written work is to participate actively in constructing sentences which reflect the differences between the meanings of pairs of words which are frequently confused. The following list offers some typical examples. Try to construct pairs of sentences using one of each illustrative pair of words in as precise and appropriate a manner as possible.

instinctive	genetic
effect	affect
deviant	sick
intelligence	IQ
abnormal	perverted
motive	cause
diagnosis	classification
gender	sex
behaviour	actions
language	speech
prejudiced	ethnocentric
innate	inborn
supports	proves
disconfirms	disproves
race	ethnic group
imitation	identification

Notice that it cannot be assumed that these words have exactly the meaning assigned to them in common speech; however, even there, the differences between members of the pairs are generally quite important.

If further evidence of this is required, you might re-examine the examples with which this chapter began. Apparently very simple differences (for example, between 'aggression' and 'violence') were seen to have critical consequences for the meaning of an argument. It cannot be emphasised too strongly that your ideas are capable of being judged only through the medium of words, the choice of which requires the most careful consideration.

CONVENTIONS

Like most technical disciplines, psychology has evolved a set of widely accepted conventions with which students need to be familiar. These conventions relate to bibliographies, the acknowledgment of sources of information, certain stylistic practices, and, although less well-defined, the general format of empirical reports. Being aware of these conventions greatly facilitates the research for an essay, as well as its actual organisation and presentation.

In itemising and illustrating the major conventions to be found in the literature, we do not wish to imply that these are completely unchangeable Minor variations will often be found if one covers a wide range of material. However, such variations need not cause any real confusion in students' written work. By definition, conventions are somewhat arbitrary. Their justification is that they are both economical and unambiguous, if adopted generally.

IDENTIFICATION OF BOOKS AND JOURNAL ARTICLES

Books are usually identified by the following means (acceptable punctuation is indicated): Author's name, Initials (year of publication) *Title of Book*, Place of publication: Publisher. Examples follow.

- Bandura, A (1973) *Aggression: A Social Learning Analysis*, Englewood Cliffs, NJ: Prentice-Hall.

Where there is more than one author:

- Redl, F and Wineman, D (1951) *Children Who Hate: The Disorganization and Breakdown of Behavior Controls*, Glencoe, Ill: The Free Press.

If there are *editors* rather than authors, the format is:

- Maple, T and Matheson, DW (eds) (1973) *Aggression, Hostility and Violence: Nature or Nurture?* New York: Holt, Rinehart & Winston.

Journal articles are identified thus (punctuation again being indicated): Author's name, Initials (Year) Title of paper, *Title of Journal*, vol, page numbers.

- Friedman, A, Todd, J and Kariuki, PW (1995) 'Cooperative and competitive behavior of urban and rural children in Kenya', *Journal of Cross-Cultural Psychology*, vol 26, pp 374–83.

In cases where the conventions do not literally apply, it is advisable to give too much, rather than too little, information while remaining within the broad framework of the above. For instance:

- Mann, J, Sidman, J and Starr, S (1971) 'Effects of erotic films on the sexual behavior of married couples', in *Technical Report of the Commission on Obscenity and Pornography, vol 8: Erotica and Social Behavior*, Washington, DC: US Government Printing Office.

The rule to observe in all cases is to provide sufficient information for the reader to locate the source to which the author refers. The conventions are not merely pedantic rituals but are very functional. This is often overlooked by students who hastily list references by title and author only.

It should be noted that the manner of identification of books and journal articles varies according to the 'house style' of the publishing house concerned.

Whenever written work is submitted as part of an academic course, all the books and journal articles to which reference is made should be listed in alphabetical order in accordance with these conventions. In the text of your essay, then, all you need to do to avoid plagiarism is to cite the author's name (or names) and the date and page(s) of the publication from which you are quoting or which you are paraphrasing.

PLAGIARISM AND THE USE OF SOURCES

Plagiarism is the cardinal academic sin. Yet, it is committed by a very large number of students whenever they are required to submit essays and reports. This may be due to ignorance rather than deliberate intent, so let us examine the practice in some detail.

A typical dictionary definition of 'plagiarism' might read 'to steal another's thoughts and pass off as one's own; to publish ideas or writings of another under one's own name'.

In a world where university teaching staff must frequently take the role of academic Robin Hoods, stealing from the intellectually rich to give to the educationally poor, the dividing line between plagiarism and teaching may be difficult to draw. Similarly, a student cannot always recall the origin of every idea proposed in the course of a lengthy essay. Nevertheless, both teacher and student are responsible for acknowledging sources whenever possible. This is so for quotations and paraphrases, as well as for summaries of other authors' ideas.

Failure to acknowledge direct quotations must be considered deliberate plagiarism. If a student copies large segments of text or reference books and passes these off as their own work, then the assessor will have no option but to call for a resubmission of the essay, or award zero credit for the work. (Sometimes even more serious consequences follow!) Strictly speaking, any phrase or sentence that is quoted without being acknowledged as deriving from another source is an example of plagiarism, although this would seldom be penalised if only an isolated instance. However, it is not uncommon to find extensive sections of essays stolen from books which the student apparently hopes will not be familiar to the marker. There are also instances of students jointly writing essays and submitting the same work as their respective individual efforts. This practice will also be regarded as plagiarist.

In addition to the obvious moral reasons against all forms of plagiarism, there are also excellent practical, educational reasons. Recall that one of the qualities an assessor is looking for in an essay is some evidence of a student's understanding of the topic. If the essayist simply 'borrows' an author's exact words, they will not show that they understand those words even in the limited sense of being able to paraphrase them. To repeat another's words (parrot fashion) is not to *show* that you understand their ideas (even if it is true that you do!).

Consequently, if the aim of writing an essay is to display your understanding of authors' works, it is best not to rely solely on direct quotations, even if these are acknowledged.

Similarly, a simple grammatical paraphrase does not demonstrate understanding. Anyone who speaks English can turn 'Differential reinforcement inhibits generalisation' into 'Generalisation is inhibited by differential reinforcement' without understanding any learning theory. It shows at most that the grammar of the sentence has been understood. Such turns of phrase are also best avoided, if you wish to give unequivocal evidence of understanding. Specifically, in this case, it is wisest to give evidence that you understand the technical terms the sentence uses.

Paraphrases of books and papers are much more common than direct quotations. Students frequently argue that unless they paraphrase other sources, they could not compose an essay at all! They point out that virtually every idea they originate will inevitably be found somewhere in the extensive literature on a given topic. Although this is true to some extent, it does not really justify plagiarism. On the contrary, it is a simple matter to indicate when your original ideas coincide with some published argument without simply 'borrowing' that argument and paraphrasing it without acknowledgment. Moreover, if you have to express these ideas in an original manner rather than by merely altering a similar presentation in superficial respects, you become aware of important subtleties that may pass unnoticed if you merely paraphrase. Hence, it is best to formulate your thoughts *in your own words* and acknowledge their relation to other authors' arguments where necessary, rather than merely to present a series of paraphrases of other sources.

There are simple conventions regarding the acknowledgment of sources in psychological literature. These both avoid plagiarism and provide consistent, thorough documentation of all sources relevant to a particular piece of work.

Two classes of sources may be distinguished — primary and secondary. A *primary source* is any book, report or journal article *actually consulted* during the preparation of an essay. A *secondary source* is any book or article that furnishes information about another article, report or book, the latter not being consulted itself. For example, summaries and critical discussions in textbooks of original research published elsewhere are secondary sources of information about that research.

The most generally accepted conventions are:

1   *Direct quotations (all sources):* Place the entire quoted passage in quotation marks; cite the author's name and the date of the publication to which reference is made, together with the page(s) from which the quotation is taken. These particulars are placed in

parentheses. If only one phrase or sentence is quoted, these details can precede or follow the quotation, depending on context. For example:

(a)   Brown (1998, p 167) argues: 'There is considerable consensus concerning the origins of juvenile delinquency.'

or

(b)   'There is considerable consensus concerning the origins of juvenile delinquency', argues Brown (1998, p l67).

Such short quotations would normally be integrated into a paragraph without any other emphasis. Longer passages, such as complete paragraphs, are frequently accentuated by means of indentation and/or different spacing. Usually they are indented and single-spaced if the rest of the essay is double-spaced. Otherwise their acknowledgment is as above.

Should more than one publication by a particular author during one year be referred to in an essay, then each title may be distinguished thus: Brown (1998a); Brown (1998b), and so on.

Where a figure (for example, a graph) or table of data is to be reproduced from a primary or secondary source, it also needs to be acknowledged by reference to the author, publication date and page number.

Notice that these conventions obviate the use of any footnotes. The reference list at the end of the essay adequately identifies the source of the quotation.

Direct quotations from a secondary source are also possible. For instance, if Smith (1998) in a textbook on, say, aggression, quotes a passage from a journal article or book by Jones (1994), then the passage may be used in your essay, provided that it is acknowledged appropriately. Because you have not read the primary source, you must indicate this when quoting. For example:

(c)   Jones argues that 'aggression is a bio-social phenomenon in all primates' (Smith 1998, p 200).

The convention is important for distinguishing primary from secondary sources. It would be necessary to record only the secondary source in your references in the above example.

2   *Paraphrases and summaries:* When material from either primary or secondary sources is summarised or paraphrased, conventions apply which are similar to those employed when making direct quotations. For instance:

(a) Brown (1994, p 167) considers that there is general agree-
    ment about the causes of delinquency (cf example 1).

Or, for secondary sources,

(b) Jones (Smith 1998, p 200) sees aggression as a bio-social
    phenomenon.

(Note: Brown and Jones are not real names.)

When longer arguments or research projects are summarised, similar acknowledgments are quite adequate. Of course, many stylistic
variations are possible which provide subtle differences of emphasis,
but these will develop as your reading of the psychological literature
progresses.

SUMMARY

Essays demand clear analytical and critical writing based on research and planning. An essay must show your understanding of the topic under discussion, but it must, more importantly, answer the question asked. An essay therefore needs to do more than simply discuss the topic. It involves presenting clear definitions and a precise interpretation of the question and its assumptions. Relevant evidence must be evaluated critically and comparatively to allow subtle conclusions to be drawn.

This chapter has outlined how expository writing needs to be coherent, emphasising the importance of topic sentences, cohesion and structure. Essays should avoid vagueness, passivisation and unnecessary jargon. Modality should be high, and personalised informality should be avoided.

Conventions for citing sources, and thereby avoiding plagiarism, have been outlined. Plagiarism reflects an inadequate understanding of the literature and is severely judged in all academic writing.

KEYWORDS

COHERENCE • EXPOSITION • TOPIC SENTENCE • THEME • MODALITY • PASSIVE/ACTIVE VOICE • FORMALITY/INFORMALITY • JARGON (CANT) • REFERENCING SOURCES, PRIMARY/SECONDARY SOURCES • PLAGIARISM

EXERCISES

1   Consider the following hypothetical essay topics, assuming that you are to write 2000 words on each question. In each case,

   a   Specify which terms require interpretation and/or definition.

   b   Explicate the logical nature of the question (that is, spell out what is the *precise* relationship between the variables in the question, as was done for the example discussed in Chapter 9 under the heading 'Studying the relevant literature').

   (i)   'The theory of the Authoritarian Personality is relevant to, though not sufficient to explain all, racial prejudice.' Discuss.

   (ii)   'Language acquisition is a function of complex maturational variables with which environmental factors interact. It is not simply a matter of "learning" in the sense of imitation.' Discuss.

   (iii)   'Perceptual illusions are the necessary consequence of perceptual constancies. There cannot be the latter without the former.' Discuss.

2   Throughout this book we have cited numerous examples of good
      and bad arguments, careful and careless definitions, and so on,
      concerned with the issue of human aggression. The following pas-
      sages are taken from students' essays on a question about the ori-
      gins of human aggression. Each involves errors, omissions, verbal
      imprecisions, conceptual and stylistic confusions, or poor organi-
      sation. Putting yourself in the position of a marker, consider how
      well each of the quoted passages *introduces* an essay on the topic:

*'Although humans are claimed to be the most aggressive creatures on
earth, this alone does not mean that humans possess instincts which
cause them to engage in acts of war.' Discuss.*

Of each passage, ask the following specific questions.

a   What, if any, interpretation is given of the logic or meaning
      of the question as a whole and of its major terms?

b   Does the passage *assume*, rather than argue, an answer to the
      question, at least implicitly? Where?

c   Although introductory paragraphs do not usually cite evi-
      dence, they may anticipate the type of evidence to be consid-
      ered in the body of the essay. Does the passage do this?
      Where? With what success?

d   Are there any generalisations which lack empirical support in
      the passage?

e   Does the passage require reorganisation, either within or
      between sentences, or between paragraphs? Suggest changes.

f   More theoretically, does the passage assume purposivism or
      reductionism (or their opposites)?

g   Is the style anthropomorphic?

h   Is there unnecessary jargon?

i   Is the passage properly documented?

(i) The fact that man has an instinct of aggression seems to be
      supported by arguments of many people such as Freud, but
      the way in which this aggression is directed or the reason
      why it exists has been expressed in many different ways.
      Freud argues that aggression is a death instinct in that the
      aggressor is trying to bring living matter back into an inac-
      tive condition. On the other hand social psychologists fre-
      quently see aggression as an attempt by a person to find their
      own identity by asserting themselves as individuals. The fact
      that humans have an instinct of aggression seems to be quite
      well founded because when a person is cornered or attacked

they will fight to free themselves and they seem to meet aggression with aggression. That is, a person will seek revenge for a wrong done to them ... But is man the 'most aggressive creature on earth?

(ii) The history of human civilisation is the history of aggression, a history of conflict between nations, of conquest, of subjugation or rebellion. What makes humans unique in the animal kingdom in that they are the only species which commits acts of mass murder against other members of the species. The reason often given is that humans are naturally aggressive. *Although man is often claimed to be the most aggressive creature on earth, this alone does not mean that humans possess instincts which cause them to engage in acts of war.* The answer lies in man's innate aggressive nature, his territorial behavioural pattern, and as a result of his cultural evolution.

Before any discussion of this broad statement (bold above) can take place one must clearly define the meaning of the principal terms. What is aggression? Does its field of definition cover all forms of aggressive behaviour — the 'pushy' salesman trying to make a sale, the strong competitor striving to reach the summit of his field, the keen executive trying to reach the top position in his company. All these people exhibit aggressive behaviour, but not behaviour that could be termed hostile or physically injurious to other persons. Because the latter part of the statement refers to 'war', this essay shall regard the terms 'aggressive' and 'hostile' as synonymous, and denote any behaviour described by these terms as that which is aimed at the injury of other persons. Following on from this, 'war' is defined as an armed contest between two independent groups by means of organised military force, in the pursuit of a tribal or national policy. The term 'instinct' must also be clearly defined. An instinct is an inherited tendency to action of a specific kind, usually set off by a limited range of stimuli, and having definite survival or biological value in the struggle for existence.'

Having provided a basis for discussion of this statement, one is now confronted with a series of questions which must be answered. Do humans possess an aggressive nature? If so, is this aggressive nature instinctive or is it 'learned'? Given that they do possess this aggression, what set of circumstances lead them into acts of war?

[This is a paraphrase of: O Klineberg (1964) *The Human Dimension in International Relations*, New York Holt, Rinehart & Winston, p 10.]

3   The following are two concluding paragraphs from student essays on the topic considered in (2). Compare these, asking the following questions:

a   How successful is each in formulating a concluding statement about the question asked?

b   What rhetorical and moralistic comment does each contain? Is this relevant to the question asked?

c   What stylistic faults and organisational or conceptual confusions need to be rectified in each?

(i)   In the main, man's aggression is more than an instinctive response to frustration — it is an attempt to assert himself as an individual, to separate himself from the herd, to find his identity. This aggression only becomes dangerous when it is suppressed or disowned. The man who is able to assert himself is seldom vicious, it is the weak who revert to aggression. It is impossible to believe that all aggressive potential springs from frustration.

It seems probable that the denial or repression of our aggression is liable to cause disharmony within ourselves. We are constantly seeking opportunities for the vicarious expression of aggressive drives, such as sports, alcoholism and suicide. In war these impulses used to find an acceptable channel for discharge. Abolition of war would only cause an increase in civilian aggression which is already occurring.

(ii)   In conclusion we can say that there is no clear cut answer to the question of whether humans possess instincts which cause them to engage in acts such as war. We have seen that definitions of the three terms 'aggressive', 'instinct' and 'war' are so vague or broad that this adds extra complexities to an already complex area. All that can be concluded is that among psychologists, there appears to be a weakening of the idea that aggression is an instinct which makes war inevitable, and a strengthening of the idea that aggression is both biologically and socially determined and therefore that war is not inevitable.

4 (i)   Poor and under-achievers exhibit *inappropriate affect*, restricted ego development, a certain tendency to self-consciousness in *dyadic interpersonal communication* situations and poor *super-ego functioning*. They are also *disproportionately representative of family systems* with a *less-than-adequate monetary income* and certain disadvantages on other *socio-economic indices*.

   (ii) Language acquisition is thus a linear process starting from a primitive form of *behavioural control*, which involves some kind of *tangible reinforcement* through a succession of approximations, involving shifts in *response typography*, the *antecedent controlling stimuli* to the *point in time* where the *verbal behaviour* typifies the form and *emission pattern* of adult verbal behaviour.

   a   Attempt to paraphrase these passages.

   b   What stylistic improvements are required to render them more intelligible?

   c   Are the words in italics essential to the meaning of the passage, or could they be replaced by less 'technical' expressions?

chapter 11

Reporting observational studies

When, as becomes a man who would prepare
For such an arduous work, I through myself
Make rigorous inquisition, the report is often cheering.

William Wordsworth

Psychology students may write several empirical reports in each year of study. These describe simple projects such as demonstrations of perceptual illusions, naturalistic observations of animal behaviour, elementary learning experiments, or small-sample attitude surveys. In their final year of study, students may describe an original, technically sophisticated experiment, similar in form to those reported in technical journals. In both the elementary and more sophisticated projects, there is a set of widely accepted conventions that govern the form which such reports follow. Therefore, in this chapter, techniques and conventions of writing empirical reports are outlined, and particular attention is paid to the economical verbal style that reports demand.

Let us first clarify a possible ambiguity: the word 'experiment' is sometimes restricted to observational studies in which there is deliberate manipulation of the conditions in which subjects are treated. But it might be used more generally to cover any empirical study, including field studies, attitude surveys, evaluations of methods of therapy, and so on. In this chapter the word will be employed in the latter, more general (if somewhat ambiguous) sense. This is because in all cases, methodology and findings need to be presented economically, yet with sufficient detail to allow the study to be either replicated or amended by other researchers. When replication is not possible (for example, psychiatric case studies could not be replicated in further research), the methodology must be explicit enough for comparisons to be made with similar studies or cases. This means that many technical details (such as specification of sample size, equipment and materials used, and statistical methodology) have to be included. However, these should not be allowed to obscure the major theoretical arguments which give rise to the hypothesis being tested. To achieve this balance, the empirical report needs to be organised around a set of unambiguous headings such as one finds in technical journals. Typically, these include:

1 *Introduction* (sometimes untitled)
2 *Method* — Subjects
           — Materials
           — Procedure
3 *Results*
4 *Discussion*
5 *References* (discussed in Chapter 10)

THE INTRODUCTION TO A REPORT

The major aim of this section of an observational report is to present the theoretical argument and summarise the empirical literature relevant to the hypothesis evaluated in the subsequent experiment. This should be done briefly, yet with sufficient documentation of sources to allow readers to research the literature relevant to the report.

For example, Walker et al (in the journal, *Applied Cognitive Psychology*, vol 11, 1997, pp 399–413) describe two experiments which observed the effects of retention intervals on the recollection of the (positive or negative, pleasant or unpleasant) content of events. Theirs is a relatively non-technical and conventional report which we will use to illustrate typical features of reporting experiments. We will only quote from the first of their two studies. Their introduction began:

> Our experience tells us that emotions fade over time. Most adults have had at least one extremely unpleasant experience, such as the death of a loved one or the failure of an important personal relationship. The emotion produced by such events is intense, painful and long lasting. However, as months and years pass by, the unpleasantness associated with the event memory gradually loses intensity. Of course, the phenomenon of fading occurs for pleasant events as well. The focus of this study is on how the pleasantness compared to the unpleasantness associated with autobiographical memories fade over time.
>
> There has been much research on the effects of pleasantness on memory. Many empirical studies have focused on the relationship between the affective component of the event and the ability to recall the event (eg see Banaji and Hardin, 1994; Holmes, 1990).
>
> One overall trend in the research is that pleasant events are recalled slightly better than unpleasant events (Bower and Gilligan, 1979; Brewer, 1988; Holmes, 1970; Linton, 1975; Matlin and Stang, 1978; Robinson, 1980; Thompson, Skowronski, Larsen and Betz, 1996; Wagenaar, 1986). However, there have been several exceptions to the general rule (Banaji, 1986; Kreitler and Kreitler, 1968; Skowronski and Carlston, 1987). Several researchers have suggested that these contradictory results are due to the relationship between the emotional intensity at the time the event was encoded and the emotional intensity at the time the event was retrieved (eg Bower, Monteiro and Gilligan, 1978; Holmes, 1970). The argument is based on the differential fading of emotions first described by Cason (1932).

Further description of comparable studies followed, and the reasons for conducting their reported experiment were advanced:

> Based on the findings of Cason, Holmes (1970) suggested that negative affect would drop more than positive affect over time. He

also hypothesised that more emotionally intense events were more likely to be recalled than less emotionally intense events [...]

Holmes' (1970) data showed that unpleasant events faded in emotional intensity more quickly than pleasant events. However, although participants recalled more events that were initially pleasant than events that were initially unpleasant, the difference was not statistically reliable.

Holmes (1970) offered several possible explanations for why unpleasant events decreased in affective intensity more rapidly than pleasant events. He suggested that, after a period of time, the event did not produce the negative consequences that were anticipated. Also, a person could take action to remedy the situation thus changing the feeling associated with the event. Holmes stated that 'during the retention interval something occurred or was done so that the tension or intensity was reduced'.

While the data collected by Cason (1932) and Holmes (1970) are intriguing and seem intuitively correct, there are problems with both studies.

So, in a typical 'Introduction' section, the relevant literature is reviewed and the reasons for conducting the reported study are advanced, briefly and precisely. This leads to a statement of the hypotheses (expectations or precise predictions) of the study:

The present study was conducted to replicate and extend the findings from both the Cason (1932) and Holmes (1970) studies. Several retention intervals were used to determine whether changes in emotional intensity could be attributed to regression towards the mean. Alternatively, we suggest that if the emotion connected to memories fades over time, the emotional intensity should drop systematically as retention interval increases. Similarly, if there is differential fading of pleasant and unpleasant emotions, that difference should increase with increasing retention intervals [...]

Following Holmes (1970), we hypothesized that the emotional intensity of unpleasant events would fade faster than the emotional intensity of pleasant events. We also hypothesized that initially pleasant events would be recalled better than initially unpleasant events. Finally, we hypothesized that the emotional state at the time of test was more important for predicting recall than the emotional state at the time of the event.

The terse prose of this example is not unnecessarily compressed or jargonised. It is clearly written but not bland. Although some typically 'academic', and some technical, expressions (such as 'regression to the mean') are used, the report is introduced in a way which allows both the specialist and the non-specialist (including the student) reader to see why the experiment was conducted.

Notice that there are few passive sentences. When writing introductions it is tempting to put the description into the passive voice in the (mistaken) belief that this is a more 'objective', scientific style. Undergraduate reports abound in phrases such as 'In an experiment by Brown (1998) it was found that ...' and 'It has been demonstrated by Brown that ...' However, these stylistic variations are less economical and add no information to the active voice: 'Brown (1998) showed that ...' It is advisable to avoid the passive altogether rather than risk its over-use, especially in empirical reports.

The quoted study is typical of most papers in its use of the past tense, both for describing past research and for proposing the hypotheses ('Thus, one purpose of the present study was to determine ...'). Unless there are some special reasons for not doing so, all empirical reports employ the past tense.

Given these general points, the introduction to an empirical report should:

a   outline the aims (including hypotheses) of the study;

b   describe research relevant to these hypotheses (experiments should be summarised very briefly, with one or two sentences usually being sufficient for each);

c   present methodological or theoretical criticisms of these studies insofar as such criticisms relate to the hypotheses being investigated; and

d   if necessary, define the terms of major importance, perhaps mentioning the relationship between the proposed definitions and operational criteria adopted in the experiment.

METHOD

It is conventional to report experimental method under at least three sub-headings: *Subjects* (or *Participants*); *Materials* (and/or *Apparatus*); and *Procedure*. This classification will be followed in our discussion, although the convention is not rigid.

SUBJECTS (PARTICIPANTS)

Participants (or 'subjects') should be described in relevant detail to allow replication. For example:

> Twenty male and 20 female undergraduate psychology students, 19–22 years of age, served as subjects. All were of European descent and attended the University of X. All spoke English as their first language and none had a history of auditory or visual defects of any kind. WAIS IQs ranged between 110 and 123 (median 117).

In this example, background factors such as age, social class, ethnic group, potentially relevant medical information, IQ and/or school grade are reported. These factors may be quite important to readers wishing to compare the reported study with others investigating similar phenomena. For instance, the socioeconomic background of children in two otherwise comparable studies may be slightly different. This may affect the results of the studies quite significantly. So, although background information may often appear to be pedantic or unnecessary, it can be most important.

Should animals be the subjects in an experiment, information about age, breeding strain, body weight and even cage history may be relevant. When you are in doubt as to the necessary detail, it is best to consult literature on comparable research as a guide, for there can be no general rules to cover all possibilities.

MATERIALS/APPARATUS

As for the previous section, the general principle to follow when reporting the materials and/or apparatus used in your research is to err on the side of too much, rather than too little, detail. Particulars concerning all materials (TAT cards; ability tests; verbal stories, and so on) should be presented in replicable detail. 'Apparatus' covers technical details of equipment such as display panels, timing mechanisms, Skinner box dimensions, response-recording devices, EEG machines, and so on.

Such details may be very important: For instance, Milgram (1965) reports a series of experiments in which a facsimile of a 'shock generator' was employed on which subjects ostensibly administered electric shocks to other subjects. This study could not be replicated unless details of the shock generator were copied very closely, for it is crucial that subjects accept the authenticity of the apparatus. Hence, Milgram describes it very precisely, even mentioning the engraving of the fictitious manufacturer's plaque.

Similar, if more mundane, detail is provided in a typical report by Daehler and Bukatko (1974). Under the heading 'Apparatus and Stimuli', they include:

> The apparatus, located on a child-size table, consisted of an upright masonite panel 33 x 33 cm in size. The panel contained (1) a hook in each upper corner on which stimulus cards could be hung; (2) a delivery chute protruding from the centre and through which bead reinforcers could be delivered, and (3) a 10 x 15 cm opening at the bottom into which the positive stimulus could be placed.
>
> Stimuli consisted of cards 9 1/2 x 10 cm in size which depicted common objects in stylized coloured drawings. The cards were part of a pegboard series produced by the Ideal School Supply Company. When placed on the panel, the two stimuli for each problem were 10 cm apart.

> An assistant out of sight behind the panel operated a hand puppet at the top of the panel. The puppet was used to encourage responding and to provide social reinforcement for correct responses. (p 379)

Notice that much of this detail might have been judged as incidental rather than essential (for example, the size of the stimulus cards). In the interests of **potential replication**, however, it is described quite completely.

PROCEDURE

The choice of sub-headings in the section of a report describing method is determined by the information the writer wishes to report, not by prescribed rules. Walker et al (above) use appropriately specific sub-headings to describe their procedures. Their example shows how details of what was done in the experiment are included. Such details could be relevant should another researcher wish to replicate the study. Hence, even apparently inconsequential information such as the brand name of toys used, or the size of tables at which participants sat, might be reported in a study of child development. Let us illustrate the detail and style typical of this section of a report (again using our Walker et al example):

> Each of the participants recorded events for approximately 14 weeks. During the 15th week the participants were individually tested over the content of their diaries.
>
> *Prerating*
> At the time the event was recorded, the participants rated several aspects of the event. Only the unpleasantness of the event using a 7-point scale ranging from very pleasant (+3) to very unpleasant (−3) with a rating of 0 indicating neutral.
>
> *Testing*
> While testing, the events were read to the participants using a random order of presentation. In responding to each event, the participants provided several pieces of information for each event. Only the memory ratings and pleasant ratings will be considered.
>
> The participants first determined whether the event was unique. This procedure was used because it would not be possible for a participant to provide specific information for events that occurred more than once during the semester. If an event was not unique, it was deleted, and the participant went on the next event.
>
> Following the memory rating, the participants provided a pleasantness rating for the event at the time of test (ie how did the participants currently feel about the event?) The participants used the same 7-point scale that they had used at the time the event was recorded.

RESULTS (INCLUDING STATISTICAL ANALYSIS)

Conventionally, this section reports the data yielded by the experiment, but does not discuss their theoretical significance. It presents both the methods of statistical analysis and the decisions that these tests allow concerning the hypothesised outcomes of the experiment. In a typical analysis involving parametric inferential statistics (t-, F-tests), these decisions and the data on which they are based are presented in tabular form. The summary of the means and standard deviations (or variances) for the respective experimental (comparison) conditions provides a comprehensive, yet not a confusing, picture of the major trends in the data. These trends may be highlighted and clarified by means of graphs, which should be presented in the simplest possible way and which should be closely related to the relevant verbal description of results.

It is sometimes argued that all empirical reports should present the 'raw data' on which the statistical decisions are based, not merely the summary details (means, variances) suggested above. The justification for this viewpoint is that only then can the data be reanalysed by another researcher should they consider that the original analysis was either inappropriate or insufficient for the conclusions drawn. In most cases, however, reporting this much detail would be impractical, given the volume of data resulting from many studies. Nevertheless, when theses are submitted, it is usual to meet this condition by including raw data in an appendix — a practice worth following in shorter reports should the method of data analysis employed require any unusual justification or atypical assumptions. When this is so, the likelihood of reanalysis by another researcher is greater and the justification for complete data presentation correspondingly stronger.

Let us return to more typical cases. In a conventional learning experiment involving, say, four conditions, the data might be summarised in a series of tables, each accompanied by relevant verbal description. Typical tables might include:

TABLE 1

MEAN ERRORS ON ALL 20 TRIALS FOR ALL FOUR TRAINING
CONDITIONS

Training conditions	Mean errors	Standard deviation
1	6.8	1.9
2	3.5	0.9
3	2.9	1.7
4	4.1	1.4

TABLE 2

MEAN RESPONSE LATENCIES ON CORRECT TRIALS FOR ALL FOUR
TRAINING CONDITIONS

Training conditions	Mean response latency	Standard deviation
1	0.356 sec.	0.090 sec.
2	0.290 sec.	0.131 sec.
3	0.3S9 sec.	0.122 sec.
4	0.412 sec.	0.087 sec.

Notice that tables are generally headed in this manner and numbered with arabic rather than roman numerals. Graphs would be similarly labelled Figure 1 ... n, and integrated appropriately into the text. Statistical analyses are best presented in a manner which reflects the hypotheses being investigated: details of statistical methods (for example, F-, t-tests, planned contrasts, x^2-tests) may be presented in tabular form (for example, analysis of variance tables as presented in conventional statistics texts), and/or verbally described in relation to relevant hypotheses. Significance levels and degrees of freedom are always reported. It is best to report *all* statistical decisions relevant to your hypotheses, not only those that are consistent with predictions made at the outset. This is because unconfirmed hypotheses may provide as much information as those that are confirmed. (Recall our discussion of falsifiability in Chapter 3.)

Typical reporting of statistical results may read as follows (continuing our running example):

Change in pleasantness

Paired t-test were used to compare the initial and final pleasantness ratings for both pleasant and unpleasant events. Events that were initially rated as neutral (i.e. a rating of 0) were not included in these analyses. Neutral events accounted for approximately 4% of the data. The initially neutral events were excluded on the basis that systematic change was noted for initially neutral events at the time of the test. When the initial and final pleasantness ratings were compared, the analyses showed that final ratings were less extreme for both pleasant, $t(1567) = 2.30$, $P>0.05$, and unpleasant events, $t(682) = 5.28$, $P>0.01$. A significant effect of pleasantness was noted such that the change on pleasantness ratings was larger for unpleasant events than for pleasant events, $t(2249)$ 29.44, $P>0.001$.

(Numbers in brackets after 't' are the degrees of freedom appropriate to the 't' value. They are usually reprinted as subscripts.)

DISCUSSION

The discussion should be limited to the theoretical argument and the resulting hypotheses adumbrated in the introduction. This ensures strict relevance. To this end, it is advisable to refer frequently to the introduction when planning and writing the discussion. You should also concentrate on extending the Results section, placing the reported statistical decisions in theoretical context. The principal difference between the results and discussion is that the latter draws together the information yielded by the experiment in the light of the explicit aims of the study. That is, it considers results (data and statistically based decisions) in relation to theory by way of the hypotheses tested.

Insofar as we can specify a general format for the organisation of the discussion, it is of the following type: you usually begin by reporting the general support for, or refutation of, your hypotheses. The initial paragraph in the discussion section of Walker et al, as an example, reads:

> The data supported our hypotheses concerning three effects of retention interval on memory for pleasant and unpleasant events. First, both pleasant and unpleasant affects fade with time. However, the emotional intensity for unpleasant events fades faster over time than does the emotional intensity for pleasant events. Second, emotional intensity at time of test was the best predictor of an event's memorability. Third, events that are pleasant are slightly more memorable than events that are unpleasant.

The discussion section usually expands and qualifies the description of the findings. This serves to place the reported findings in the necessary context and leads naturally to the discussion of possible avenues of future research. Usually, suggestions for further research follow additional theoretical discussions which arise from the results. These may be quite technical. For example, Walker et al link their findings to theoretical issues in the following way:

> ... [W]e have chosen to examine the psychoanalytic concept of regression (Freud, 1900/1965) and Taylor's (1991) mobilization–minimization hypothesis. Both theories make speculations about how people cope with pleasant and unpleasant memories.
> Freud (1900/1965) proposed that unpleasant events might be forgotten through the mechanism of unconscious repression. According to Freud's theory of repression, the memories of unpleasant events are repressed into the unconscious while the emotions associated with those memories remain intact to bother the conscious mind. Put more simply, unpleasant memories are forgotten but unpleasant emotions are not. The data from the present studies suggest just the opposite. While it is true that memory ratings for

pleasant events were slightly higher than for unpleasant events, this effect was very small. Unpleasant emotions, however, did fade substantially more than pleasant emotions across all three retention intervals.

These data may also be described in term of the short-term mobilization and long-term minimization hypothesis proposed by Taylor (1991) [...]

Later, they compare laboratory and naturalistic studies of memory as these relate to their findings. Then they conclude:

The data presented in this paper represents the effects of a mechanism that apparently allows people to effectively minimize the impact of unpleasant events. The emotion associated with unpleasant events fades faster than the emotion associated with pleasant events. Further, these data are consistent with the previous work of Cason (1932) and Holmes (1970). Taylor's (1991) mobilization–minimization hypothesis is also completely consistent with these findings.

This quite typical, yet relatively non-technical example illustrates that the discussion section of an empirical report must be carefully organised and expressed in order to draw out the (justified) implications of the reported findings and to place these briefly in a theoretical context.

As with other aspects of report writing, there are no simple rules that can be slavishly followed, but there are guidelines. Careful organisation under appropriate sub-headings, concise, unpretentious language, and attention to detail will allow you to present lucid (even interesting) reports. It is advisable to consult publications in the area of psychology studied and to compare them with your own draft report prior to its submission. Second, because the most interpretive sections of a report are the introduction and discussion, and because these need to be clearly integrated, it is also advisable to compare these with each other before writing the final draft. At all times, remember that a very strict criterion of relevance applies to empirical reports, and this alone necessitates such a comparison.

SUMMARY

Observational reports, including reports of experiments, field studies and questionnaire surveys, should follow the form outlined in this chapter. Of course, some adjustments may be necessary to convey all the information that may be relevant for the study in question to be replicated by another researcher.

Conventionally, the following sections are distinguished in a report of a psychological experiment or other observational study:

- The **introduction** critically reviews the literature and formulates the hypotheses to be addressed in the study.

- Under the **method** section, several descriptive sub-sections outline what was done in the study, what materials or apparatus were used, and who participated as subjects.

- **Results** are presented in detail in a separate section and their statistical analysis and significance summarised.

- The **discussion** section shows how (or whether) the results support or contradict the hypotheses outlined in the introductory section, and evaluates the success of the study, suggesting possible further research on the topic at issue. The discussion should return to the theoretical implications of the observational study by being closely integrated with the introductory analysis or argument.

References

Adams, EW, Fagot, RF and Robinson, RE (1965) 'A Theory of Appropriate Statistics', *Psychometrika*, vol 30, pp 99–127.

Adorno, TW, Frenkel-Brunswik, E, Levinson, DJ and Sanford, RN (1950) *The Authoritarian Personality*, New York: Harper and Row.

Aiken, LR (1996) *Rating Scales and Checklists*, New York: Wiley.

Altman, I and Haythorn, WW (1970) 'The Ecology of Isolated Groups', in H Proshansky et al., *Environmental Psychology*, New York: Holt, Rinehart & Winston.

Amundson, R (1989) 'The Trials and Tribulations of Selectionist Explanations', in K Hahlweg and C Hooker, *Issues in Evolutionary Psychology*, Albany, NY: SUNY Press.

Ardrey, R (1969), *The Territorial Imperative*, London: Fontana.

Ashmore, RD (1990) 'Sex, Gender and the Individual', in LA Pervin, *Handbook of Personality: Theory and Research*, New York: Guildford Press.

Barkow, JH, Cosmides, L and Tooby, J (eds) (1992) *The Adapted Mind*, Oxford: Oxford University Press.

Blackburn, S (1994) *The Oxford Dictionary of Philosophy*, Oxford: Oxford University Press.

Bolanowski, SJ and Gescheider, GA (1991) *Ratio Scaling of Psychological Magnitude: In Honor of the Memory of SS Stevens*, Hillsdale, NJ: Erlbaum.

Bonta, BD (1997) 'Cooperation and Competition in Peaceful Societies', *Psychological Bulletin*, vol 121, no 2, pp 299–320.

Bowlby, J (1969) *Attachment*, London: Hogarth.

—— (1973) *Separation: Anxiety and Anger*, London: Hogarth.

Bridgman, PW (1927) *The Logic of Modern Physics*, New York: Macmillan.

Carroll, JB (1996) 'A Three-stratum Theory of Intelligence: Spearman's Contribution', in I Dennis and P Tapsfield (eds), *Human Abilities: Their Nature and Measurement*, Mahwah, NJ: Erlbaum.

Cattell, RB (1965) 'Factor Theory Psychology: A Statistical Approach to Personality', in WS Sahakian (ed), *Psychology of Personality: Readings in Theory*, Chicago: Rand McNally.

Chaplin, JP (1968) *Dictionary of Psychology*, New York: Dell Publishing Co.

Churchland, PM (1988) *Matter and Consciousness: A Contemporary Introduction to the Philosophy of Mind*, revised edition, Cambridge, MA: Bradford.

Clark, A (1997) *Being There: Putting Brain, Body and World Together Again*, Cambridge, MA: MIT Press.

Cliff, N (1996) *Ordinal Methods for Behavioral Data Analysis*, Mahwah, NJ: Erlbaum.

Cosmides, L and Tooby, J (1992), 'Cognitive Adaptations for Social Change', in JH Barkow, L Cosmides and J Tooby (eds), *The Adapted Mind*, Oxford: Oxford University Press.

—— (1995) 'Beyond Intuition and Instinct Blindness: Toward an Evolutionary Rigorous Cognitive Science', in J Mehler and S Franck (eds), *Cognition on Cognition*, Cambridge, MA: MIT Press.

Cummins, R (1983), *The Nature of Psychological Explanation*, Cambridge, MA: MIT Press.

Daehler, MW and Bukatko, D (1974) 'Discrimination Learning in Two-year-olds', *Child Development*, vol 45, no 2, pp 378–82.

Dennett, D (1995) *Darwin's Dangerous Idea*, London: Allen Lane, The Penguin Press.

—— (1998) *Brainchildren*, Harmondsworth: Penguin.

Dubos, R (1970) 'The Social Environment', in H Proshansky et al., *Environmental Psychology*, New York: Holt, Rinehart & Winston.

Elms, AC (1972) *Social Psychology and Social Relevance*, Boston: Little Brown and Co.

Evans, J St B, Newstead, S and Byrne, R (1993) *Human Reasoning: The Psychology of Deduction*, Hove: Lawrence Erlbaum.

Eysenck, HJ (1971) *Race, Intelligence and Education*, Melbourne: Sun Books.

—— (1973) *The Measurement of Intelligence*, Lancaster: Medical & Technical.

—— (1983) 'Personality, Conditioning and Antisocial Behavior', in WS Laaufer and JM Day (eds), *Personality Theory, Moral Development and Criminal Behavior*, Lexington, MA: Lexington Books.

Fechner, GT (1860), *Elemente der Psychophysik*, Leipzig: Breitkopf and Hartel (English translation by HE Adler, 1996, *Elements of Psychophysics*, vol 1, DH Howes and EG Boring (eds), New York: Rinehart & Winston).

Freud, S (1962) *Three Essays on the Theory of Sexuality*, New York: Avon.

Friedman, M and Rosenman, RH (1959) 'Association of Specific Overt Behavior Pattern With Blood Cardiovascular Findings', *Journal of American Medical Association*, vol 169, pp 1286–96.

Gaito, J (1980) 'Measurement Scales and Statistics: Resurgence of an Old Misconception', *Psychological Bulletin*, vol 87, pp 564–7.

Gardner, H (1998) 'Do Parents Count?', *New York Review of Books*, vol XIV, no 17, pp 19–22.

Germana, J (1971) *Contemporary Experimental Psychology: In Flagrante Delicto*, Monterey, CA: Brooks-Cole.

Gigerenzer, G (1993) 'The Superego, the Ego, and the Id in Statistical Reasoning', in G Keren and C Lewis (eds), *A Handbook for Data Analysis in the Behavioral Sciences: Methodological Issues*, Hillsdale, NJ: Erlbaum.

Glymour, C (1988a) 'What Went Wrong? Reflections on Science by Observation and the Bell Curve', *Philosophy of Science*, vol 65, pp 1–32.

—— (1988b) 'Learning Causes: Psychological Explanations of Causal Explanation', in *Minds and Machines*, vol 8, pp 39–60.

Godfrey-Smith, P (1995) 'Function', in J Kim and E Sosa (eds), *A Companion to Metaphysics*, Cambridge, MA: Blackwell.

Goldsmith, MH (1996) *Political Correctness*, Sydney: Hodder and Stoughton.

Greenspoon, J (1955) 'The Reinforcing Effect of Two Spoken Sounds on the Frequencies of Two Responses', *American Journal of Psychology*, vol 68, pp 409–16.

Gregory, I (1961) *Psychiatry: Biological and Social*, London: Saunders.

Gregory, RL (1966a) 'Visual Illusions', in BM Foss (ed), *New Horizons in Psychology*, Harmondsworth: Penguin.

—— (1966b), *Eye and Brain: The Psychology of Seeing*, London: Weidenfeld & Nicolson.

Griffiths, P (1997) *What Emotions Really Are: The Problem of Psychological Categories*, Chicago: University of Chicago Press.

—— (forthcoming), 'From Adaptive Heuristic to Phylogenetic Perspective: Some Lessons from the Evolutionary Psychology of Emotion', in PS Davies, *The Evolution of Minds: Psychological and Philosophical Perspectives*, Dordrecht: Kluwer.

Harlow, HF (1962), 'Love in Infant Monkeys', *Scientific American*, June.

—— (1971) *Learning to Love*, San Francisco: Albion.

Harlow, HF and Harlow, MK (1962) 'Social Deprivation in Monkeys', *Scientific American*, November.

Harris, JR (1998), *The Nature Assumption: Why Children Turn out the Way They Do*, New York: Simon & Schuster.

Heiman, GW (1995) *Research Methods in Psychology*, Boston: Houghton Mifflin.

Hempel, CG (1965) *Aspects of Scientific Explanation and Other Essays in the Philosophy of Science*, New York: Free Press.

—— (1966) *Philosophy of Natural Science*, Englewood Cliffs, NJ: Prentice-Hall.

Hunt, JMV (1969) 'Has Compensatory Education Failed? Has It Been Attempted?', in *Environment, Heredity and Intelligence: Harvard Education Review*, pp 130–52.

Jensen, AR (1981) *Straight Talk about Mental Tests*, London: Methuen.

—— (1986) 'Intelligence: "Definition", Measurement and Future Research', in RJ Sternberg and DK Detterman (eds), *What is Intelligence? Contemporary Viewpoints on its Nature and Definition*, New Jersey: Ablex.

—— (1998), *The g Factor: The Science of Mental Ability*, London: Praeger.

Kardas, EP (1999), *Psychology Resources on the World Wide Web*, Pacific Grove, CA: Brooks-Cole Publishing Company.

Kenrick, DT (1987) 'Gender, Genes and Social Environment: A Biosocial Interactionist Perspective', in P Shaver and C Hendrick (eds), *Sex and Gender*, San Francisco, CA: Sage.

Kerlinger, FN (1979) *Behavioral Research: A Conceptual Approach*, New York: Holt, Rinehart & Winston.

—— (1986) *Foundations of Behavioral Research*, New York: Holt, Rinehart & Winston.

Klineberg, O (1964) *The Human Dimension in International Relationships*, New York: Holt, Rinehart & Winston.

Krantz, DH, Luce, RD, Suppes, P and Tversky, A (1971) *Foundations of Measurement*, vol 1, New York: Academic Press.

Krech, D (1971) 'Psychoneurobiochemeducation', in IJ Gordon (ed), *Readings in Development Psychology*, Glenview, Ill: Scott, Foresman & Co.

Laing, RD and Esterson, A (1970) *Sanity, Madness and the Family*, Harmondsworth: Penguin.

Leahey, TH (1991) *A History of Modern Psychology*, Englewood Cliffs, NJ: Prentice-Hall.

Lehrer, K (1996), 'Skepticism, Lucid Content and the Metamental Loop', in A Clark, J Esquerro and JM Larrazabal (eds), *Philosophy and Cognitive Science: Categories, Consciousness and Reasoning*, Dortrecht: Kluwer.

Lewis, D (1986) 'Causal Explanation', in *Philosophical Papers*, vol 11, New York: Oxford University Press.

Likert, R (1932) 'A Technique for the Measurement of Attitudes', *Archives of Psychology*, vol 22, pp 44–53.

Lipton, P (1991) *Inference to the Best Explanation*, London: Routledge.

Lloyd, E (1999) 'Evolutionary Psychology: The Burdens of Proof', *Biology and Philosophy*, vol 14, pp 211–33.

Lord, FM and Novick, MR (1968) *Statistical Theories of Mental Test Scores*, Reading, MA: Addison-Wesley.

Lovell, K (1968) *An Introduction to Human Development*, London: Macmillan & Co.

Luce, RD (1986) *Response Times: Their Role in Inferring Elementary Mental Organization*, New York: Oxford University Press.

Luce, RD, Krantz, DH, Suppes, P and Tversky, A (1990) *Foundations of Measurement*, vol 3, San Diego, CA: Academic Press.

Maas, JB (ed) (1974) *Readings in Psychology Today*, third edition, Del Mar, CA: CRM.

Machamer, P (1993) 'Philosophy of Psychology', in M Salmon et al., *Introduction to the Philosophy of Science*, Englewood Cliffs, NJ: Prentice-Hall.

Mandler, G and Kessen, W (1959) *The Language of Psychology*, New York: Wiley.

Maple, T and Matheson, DW (eds) (1973) *Aggression, Hostility and Violence*, New York: Holt, Rinehart & Winston.

Marr, D (1982) *Vision*, New York: WH Freeman.

McClelland, D (1961) 'Some Social Consequences of Achievement Motivation', in RA King (ed), *Readings for an Introduction to Psychology*, New York: McGraw-Hill.

McDonald, RP (1985) *Factor Analysis and Related Methods*, Hillsdale, NJ: Erlbaum.

Merton, RK, Sills, DL and Stigler, SM (1984) 'The Kelvin Dictum and Social Science: An Excursion into the History of an Idea', *Journal of the History of Behavioral Sciences*, vol 20, pp 319–31.

Michell, J (1986) 'Measurement Scales and Statistics: A Clash of Paradigms', *Psychological Bulletin*, vol 100, pp 398–407.

—— (1990) *An Introduction to the Logic of Psychological Measurement*, Hillsdale, NJ: Erlbaum.

—— (1997) 'Quantitative Science and the Definition of Measurement in Psychology', *British Journal of Psychology*, vol 88, pp 355–83.

Milgram, S (1963) 'Behavioral Study of Obedience', *Journal of Abnormal and Social Psychology*, vol 67, pp 371–8.

—— (1965) 'Liberating Effects of Group Pressure', *Journal of Personality and Social Psychology*, vol 1, pp 127–34.

Milton, T (1990), 'The Disorders of Personality' in LA Pervin (ed), *Handbook of Personality: Theory and Research*, New York: Guildford Press.

Mitchell, J (1974) *Psychoanalysis and Feminism*, Harmondsworth: Penguin.

Mittler, P (1971) *The Study of Twins*, Harmondsworth: Penguin.

Money, J and Ehrhardt, AE (1972) *Man and Women; Boy and Girl*, Baltimore, MD: Johns Hopkins University Press.

Montagu, A (ed) (1968) *Man and Aggression*, London: Oxford University Press.

Moss, CS (1965) *Hypnosis in Perspective*, New York: Macmillan & Co.

Nagel, E (1961) *The Structure of Science: Problems in the Logic of Scientific Discovery*, London: Routledge and Kegan Paul.

Neisser, U (1997) 'The Future of Cognitive Science: An Ecological Analysis', in E Johnson and C Enerling (eds), *The Future of the Cognitive Revolution*, Oxford: Oxford University Press.

Newell, A, Rosenbloom, P and Laird, J (1989) 'Symbolic Architectures for Cognition', in MI Posner (ed), *Foundations of Cognitive Science*, Cambridge, MA: MIT Press.

Newell, A, Shaw, JC and Simon, HA (1960) 'Report on a General Problem Solving Program', in *Proc. Int. Conf. on Information Processing*, Paris: UNESCO.

Papineau, D (1978) *For Science in the Social Sciences*, London: Macmillan.

Pervin, LA (1993) *Personality: Theory and Research*, New York: John Wiley and Sons.

Pinker, S and Bloom, P (1992), 'Natural Language and Natural Selection', in JH Barkow, L Cosmides and J Tooby (eds), *The Adapted Mind*, Oxford, Oxford University Press.

Polkinghorne, DE (1992) 'Postmodern Epistemology of Practice', in S Kvale (ed), *Psychology and Postmodernism*, London: Sage.

Prentice, WCH (1959), 'The Systematic Psychology of Wolfgang Kohler', in S Koch (ed), *Psychology: A Study of a Science*, vol 1, New York: McGraw-Hill.

Proshansky, H et al. (1970), *Environmental Psychology*, New York: Holt, Rinehart & Winston.

Pylyshyn, Z (1984) *Computation and Cognition*, Cambridge, MA: Bradford.

—— (1989) 'Computing in Cognitive Science', in MI Posner (ed), *Foundations of Cognitive Science*, Cambridge, MA: MIT Press.

Quine, WV and Ullian, JS (1970) *The Web of Belief*, New York: Random House.

Rachman, S (1973) 'Schizophrenia: A Look at Laing's Views', *New Society*, vol 26, April, pp 184–6.

Rapley, M (1998) 'Just an ordinary Australian: Self-categorisation and the Discursive Construction of ... Facticity in "New Racist" Political Discourse', *British J. Social Psychology*, no 37, pp 325–44.

Roethlisberger, FJ and Dickson, WJ (1939) *Management and the Worker*, Cambridge, MA: Harvard University Press.

Rosenberg, J (1997) 'Connectionism and Cognition', in J Haugeland (ed), *Mind Design 11*, Cambridge, MA: MIT Press.

Rosenthal, R (1964) 'Experimenter Outcome-orientation and the Results of the Psychological Experiment', *Psychological Bulletin*, vol 61, pp 405–12.

—— (1966) *Experimenter Effects in Behavioral Research*, New York: Appleton-Century-Crofts.

Rosenthal, R and Jacobson, L (1968) *Pygmalion in the Classroom: Teacher Expectation and Pupils' Intellectual Development*, New York: Holt, Rinehart & Winston.

Rosnow, RL and Rosenthal, R (1997), *People Studying People: Artifacts and Ethics in Behavioral Research*, New York: WH Freeman & Co.

Rozin, P, Markwith, M and Stoess, C (1997) 'Moralization and Becoming a Vegetarian: The Transformation of Preferences into Values and the Recruitment of Disgust', *Psychological Science*, vol 8, pp 67–73.

Russell, B (1919) *Introduction to Mathematical Philosophy*, London: Routledge.

Rutter, M (1972) *Maternal Deprivation Reassessed*, Harmondsworth: Penguin.

Sampson, EE (1971) *Social Psychology and Contemporary Society*, New York: Wiley.

Seigler, M, Osmond, H and Mann, H (1972) 'Laing's Model of Madness', in R Boyers and R Orrill (eds), *Laing and Anti-Psychiatry*, Harmondsworth: Penguin.

Shanks, DR (1995) 'Is Human Learning Rational?', *Quarterly Journal of Experimental Psychology*, vol 48A, pp 257–79.

Shirato, T and Yell, S (1996), *Communication and Cultural Literacy: An Introduction*, Sydney: Allen & Unwin.

Skinner, BF (1973) *Beyond Freedom and Dignity*, Harmondsworth: Penguin.

Smith, BC (forthcoming) *The Age of Significance*, Cambridge, MA: MIT Press.

Smullyan, R (1978) *What is the Name of this Book?*, New York: Simon and Schuster.

Sober, E (1984) *The Nature of Selection: Evolutionary Theory in Philosophical Focus*, Cambridge, MA: MIT Press.

—— (1998) 'Black Box Inference: When Should Explanation by Intervening Variables Be Postulated?', *British Journal for the Philosophy of Science*, vol 49, pp 469–98.

Sober, E and Wilson, DS (1998) *Unto Others: The Evolution and Psychology of Unselfish Behavior*, Cambridge, MA: Harvard University Press.

Spearman, C (1904), 'General Intelligence, Objectively Determined and Measured', *American Journal of Psychology*, vol 15, pp 201–93.

Spirtes, P, Glymour, C and Scheines, R (1997) 'Reply to Humphrey and Freedman's Review of *Causation, Prediction and Search*', *British Journal of the Philosophy of Science*, vol 48, pp 555–68.

Staines, PJ (1996) 'Invalidity and the Massey Mistake', in P Hagar and J Roe (eds),

Out on a Lemma, Proceedings of the Fourth National Conference on Reasoning, Sydney: UTS.

Sterelney, K and Griffiths, P (1999) *Sex and Death*, Chicago: University of Chicago Press.

Stevens, SS (1946) 'On the Theory of Scales of Measurement', *Science*, vol 103, pp 667–80.

—— (1951) 'Mathematics, Measurement and Psychophysics', in SS Stevens (ed), *Handbook of Experimental Psychology*, New York: Wiley.

—— (1956) 'The Direct Estimation of Sensory Magnitude: Loudness', *American Journal of Psychology*, vol 69, pp 1–25.

—— (1975) *Psychophysics: Introduction to its Perceptual, Neural, and Social Prospects*, New York: Wiley.

Storr, A (1968) *Human Aggression*, Harmondsworth: Penguin.

Suppes, P and Zinnes, J (1963) 'Basic Measurement Theory', in RD Luce, RR Bush and E Galanter (eds), *Handbook of Mathematical Psychology*, vol 1, New York: Wiley.

Thomson, W (1891) *Popular Lectures and Addresses*, vol 1, London: Macmillan.

Thorndike, EL (1904) Letter to James McKeen Cattell, EL Thorndike Archive, Library of Congress, Washington, DC.

—— (1918) 'The Nature, Purposes, and General Methods of Measurements of Educational Products', in GM Whipple (ed), *Seventeenth Yearbook of the National Society for the Study of Education*, vol 2, Bloomington, Ill: Public School Publishing.

Thorndike, RL (1982) *Applied Psychometrics*, Boston: Houghton Mifflin.

von Eckardt, B (1997) 'The Empirical Naivete of the Current Philosophical Conception of Folk Psychology', in M Carrier and PK Machamer (eds), *Mindscapes: Philosophy, Science, and the Mind*, Pittsburgh, PA: University of Pittsburgh Press.

Walker, RW, Vogl, RJ and Thompson, CP (1997) 'Autobiographical Memory: Unpleasantness Fades Faster Than Pleasantness Over Time', *Applied Cognitive Psychology*, vol 11, pp 399–413.

Weisstein, N (1973) 'Psychology Constructs the Female', in P Brown (ed), *Radical Psychology*, London: Tavistock.

Whitley, BE (1996) *Principles of Research in Behavioral Science*, Mountain View, CA: Mayfield.

Wrangham, RW and Peterson, D (1997) *Demonic Males: Apes and the Origins of Human Violence*, Boston: Houghton Mifflin.

Name Index

Subject Index